The subject of our discussion
circle for the year 1962 - 1963
With my dear friends Sylvan
& Helen Tapentum.

Rabbi Joshua Stampfer

The Story of
JEWISH PHILOSOPHY

Books by Joseph L. Blau

THE CHRISTIAN INTERPRETATION OF THE CABALA

MEN AND MOVEMENTS IN AMERICAN PHILOSOPHY

CORNERSTONES OF RELIGIOUS FREEDOM IN AMERICA

THE STORY OF JEWISH PHILOSOPHY

THE STORY OF
JEWISH
PHILOSOPHY

by

JOSEPH L. BLAU

Random House, New York

First Printing

© Copyright, 1962, by Joseph L. Blau

All rights reserved under International and Pan-American Copyright
Conventions. Published in New York by Random House, Inc., and
simultaneously in Toronto, Canada, by Random House of Canada, Limited.

Library of Congress Catalog Card Number: 62-8451

Manufactured in the United States of America by Vail-Ballou Press, Inc.

NOTES indicated in the text by the superior letter n will be found at the end
of the volume.

FOR ELEANOR

POP II MAJOR

Preface

THIS BOOK is not written for philosophers or for scholars in the Jewish field, though I hope that even these may find in it something to arouse or to hold their interest. It is written as part of a larger program, spurred by the Jewish Heritage Foundation, to make the age-old tradition of the Jewish people available to modern men and women in a language that they can understand and an idiom that is not strange or obscure. As far as I know, it is the only book of its kind in any language written for the non-specialist and attempting to see the continuities and changes that have taken place in Jewish philosophic thought from the Bible to the twentieth century. Whenever I have felt it necessary to do so, I have tried to make clear the environmental forces that have led the Jews to certain types of reflective thinking about their religion.

I have written for the non-specialist, but I am aware that philosophic ideas are often presented on a level of abstraction that is hard to follow. Therefore, I have tried, wherever possible, to simplify the statement of the philosophers' views; there is a point beyond which simplification would be distortion. There may be times, in reading this book, when you will have to struggle with the ideas that are sketched here. To this degree, you will become philosophers in the reading.

The encouragement of Joseph Gaer has meant much to me; without his stimulation I doubt whether this long-dreamed-of book would have become a reality. My wife has, as she always does, borne the full brunt of the fleeting moods of authorship and served as

my first critic and chief assistant. Finally, this book could never
have been written but for the dedicated scholars who have toiled
selflessly in the study of Jewish philosophy; I have profited from
their work at every stage of mine.

COLUMBIA UNIVERSITY   *Joseph L. Blau*
NEW YORK CITY
JUNE 1961

Contents

ix

The Story of
JEWISH PHILOSOPHY

CHAPTER ONE

Philosophy and the Bible

THE BIBLE, in the Jewish tradition, means the Old Testament. Though we often speak of the Bible as if it were one book, it is actually a collection of thirty-nine shorter works. Even this number is too small to be truly exact, for several of the "books" of the Bible have been shown by scholars to be combinations of still shorter works, or of fragments of works written at different times, by different authors. The Bible is a selection from the literature of the Hebrew people. The writings contained within it span a period of at least a thousand years. During this long period, great changes took place in the political, social, and religious life of the Hebrews. Reflections of these changes are to be found throughout the Bible, and they help students to assign approximate dates to the various sections of the Bible. Changes of language are also valuable in dating parts of the Bible, for the Hebrew language was a living tongue, into which new forms of expression were introduced in the course of daily use.

The editors whose labors shaped the Bible as we have it out of the mass of Hebrew literature must surely be considered among the most influential men of all times. Their effective work provided a source of inspiration and religious direction that moves us today as it did the Hebrew people and others of a far earlier time. What they did has been used as a foundation on which other, later thinkers have built imposing religious and literary

3

structures, but it has not been superseded or destroyed. The influence of these editors has gone far beyond the merely religious. They gave form to the biographies of many men who have become heroic models for imitation over a large part of the world. How ironic it is, then, that we know nothing of their own lives—neither who they were nor, in most cases, their very names.

The one thing that we can do is to read back from their work some of the principles according to which they selected the writings to be included in the Bible. For surely there must have been many other books in Hebrew that were rejected. We cannot imagine that the handful of exceptional productions that have been preserved in the Bible made up the whole body of Hebrew literature over a thousand years of history. There were other songs and stories, myths and legends, that must have been popular and often repeated. There was more history recorded than those fragments that we have, perhaps even other laws and codes of law than those which the Bible preserves. How can we possibly believe that the heights of literary expression and the depths of spiritual profundity reached in the fifteen books of prophecy in the Bible rested on no inferior prophetic writings? We must ask, then, why the editors selected precisely those parts of just those books that were chosen.

When we ask this question, two principles immediately come to mind. First, those works were selected that best expressed the growth and development of religious belief and practice among the Hebrews. The Bible is, first and foremost, a religious anthology. Second, the works that were included were such as to generate in their readers a sense of national unity and a national ideal. The second most noticeable characteristic of the Bible is that it is an anthology of Hebrew nationalism. These two principles are closely related to each other. The God whose mighty works are celebrated throughout the Bible is the very same God with whom the Hebrew people entered into a sacred covenant at the foot of Mount Sinai. The Hebrew people of a later era are members of

4

a nation bound strictly to God by the covenant of Sinai. The continuity of the nation justifies the special demands imposed upon later generations. Like their forefathers, the Hebrews of Palestine are to be "a kingdom of priests and a holy nation."

The special brand of nationalism to which the Bible points is most unusual and surely could not have been the most typical form of historical recording. It was not national pride or national glory, but, for the most part, national humiliation and national degradation that best suited the religious aims of the editors. One of the longest and most glorious reigns in the history of the Northern Kingdom of Israel was that of Jeroboam, the son of Joash, who held the throne for forty-one years and "restored the coast of Israel from the entering of Hamath unto the sea of the plain." Yet this Jeroboam is dismissed quickly in the historical narrative of the Second Book of Kings, for "he did that which was evil in the sight of the Lord."

WHAT IS PHILOSOPHY?

In its original sense, the word "philosophy" means "love of wisdom." As the word has come to be used, however, it may refer to a number of different approaches to the love of wisdom. There is, for example, a common use of the word "philosophic" to describe a person who bears all the afflictions that are the common lot of men in the world with a spirit of fortitude. The "philosophic" person does not weep and wail and bemoan his fate, but bears all calmly. He may not be able to express in any general sentiment the principle of his life; yet his attitude might be summed up in such a principle as, "The wise man faces all the chances of life with indifference."

There is another way in which the word "philosophy" is in general use, and in this sense practically every human being is entitled to be called a philosopher. Thus: to have a philosophy

5

means to refer all one's particular beliefs or actions to some more general ideas or principles. It is not necessary for the general ideas to be related to each other; they need not form any kind of system. In fact, many of the principles employed as justifications for particular acts may contradict each other. The English writer Sir Francis Bacon once drew up a long list of general ideas in proverbial form, placing them in parallel columns. In every case, the proverbial principle in the second column contradicted that in the first. Yet, in popular parlance, a person who based his actions explicitly on the folk wisdom embodied in proverbial expressions would be called a philosopher.

Still a third meaning for the term would be suggested by the person who tries to use his own reason to resolve the contradictions of traditional wisdom. Such a person seeks for the residue of secure and accurate knowledge, expressed in firm and unyielding principles, that would remain after reason has eliminated much, perhaps most, of popular wisdom. For this sort of wisdom-lover, ultimate truth may prove to be very limited in quantity, but it is always self-consistent. In the end, he may find but one general principle to which he can give unqualified acceptance; with respect to all others, he will have the attitude of a skeptic. If this is his case, he must then find a reason for attaching every action of his life, every belief in his mind, to the one general principle that he finds acceptable, or else convict himself of the very inconsistency that he so deplores.

In addition to these popular meanings given to the word "philosophy" and its derivatives in ordinary language, there are meanings of a more technical sort. For example, philosophy may be defined as the attempt to discover the most general principles underlying all human knowledge. Alternatively, we may say that philosophy is a special method for analyzing the statements in which men flesh out their claim to knowledge. Still another such definition might be found in terms of the kinds of questions that are asked by philosophy's practitioners rather than the kinds of

6

answers that they give. Indeed, no two schools of technical philosophy would give an identical answer to the question "What is philosophy?" For this reason it has been said that the distinction between philosophy and other human enterprises is that self-definition is a part of the practice of philosophy. The question "What is psychology?" is not a psychological question; nor is the question "What is chemistry?" a chemical question; but the question "What is philosophy?" is itself a philosophic question, and will be differently answered according to what philosophy one holds.

Whatever definition we may accept for the technical discipline of philosophy, it is worth our while to note that the goal of the philosopher is to take nothing for granted. This ultimate ideal of readiness to call everything into question is not easily or often achieved. Far too frequently there are beliefs so deeply ingrained in the philosopher and in the society to which he belongs that he does not realize that these, too, are presuppositions that influence his thinking. A philosopher is, however, obligated by his profession to a far greater sensitivity to unexamined ideas than is any nonphilosopher. He is obligated to a perpetual questioning, a perpetual probing, a perpetual sifting and analyzing.

For this reason, philosophers are often awkward people to have in a society. The more they question, the less comfortable others around them may be. Socrates, the great Athenian philosopher, called himself a gadfly because his role in Athenian life was to sting his fellow citizens out of complacency into doubt. Ultimately, a jury of Athenians condemned Socrates to death, because, by his endless questioning of the eternal truths of Athenian belief, he seemed to them to be a corrupter of the minds and morals of Athenian youth.

For the moment we need not concern ourselves here with the more technical meanings of the term philosophy. Later, in our quick survey of many years of Jewish intellectual endeavor in many countries and under a wide variety of influences, we shall

7

have to consider some technical philosophic works. As we begin our story, we shall mean by "philosophy" the system of the most general ideas concerning God and man and their relations that we can find in the Bible.

IDEAS OF GOD IN THE BIBLE

The Bible, then, is a selected and edited group of Hebrew literary works, an anthology of eternal truths of religion and nationalism. Philosophy in a technical sense is an incessant and persistent questioning of precisely such claims to knowledge and truth as are included in the Bible. The conclusion inevitably follows that there is no technical philosophy in the Bible. The Bible is a testament of faith, not one of doubt. There may have been philosophers among the Hebrew people. If there were, no records of their thought have survived.

In spite of the absence of technical philosophy, the Bible is a work of philosophic interest in a more general sense. It is an interpretation of the meaning of life as this meaning was understood by the children of Israel. The Bible contains, in the form of legends, explanations of how the universe and all that is in it, including man himself, came to be. A number of legal codes, dating from various periods in the history of the Hebrew people, give expression to the moral ideas that were current and reflect the social ideals of those who made the laws. The works of the prophetic writers give evidence of a changing understanding of the meaning of history. Folk wisdom, in all its inconsistency, is exhibited in the book of Proverbs. In addition, the Bible approaches the border of technical philosophy, speculation grounded in doubt rather than in faith, in two books, Ecclesiastes and Job.

There seems to be some warrant for suggesting that the earliest ideas of God among the Hebrew people were like those of the surrounding peoples rather than like those of the later, more fully

8

developed belief of the time of Moses. Although the text with which we work has been overlaid with interpretations that tie the earlier legends to later beliefs, we can still surmise that the earliest Hebrew religion worshiped a number of deities. These were spirits associated with various natural objects, and in particular with trees, water, stones, and high places. These many minor spiritual beings may have been subordinate to a great God; if so, the analogy of other early groups suggests that it was the lesser gods to whom worship was given, because of their closeness and because of the immediate relation of those aspects of nature over which they ruled to the life of the people. There is an interesting passage (Genesis xxxv, 4) which hints at a change of belief. God has appeared to Jacob, and as a consequence of this manifestation, Jacob has accepted God as his Lord. Thereupon, Jacob buries the "strange gods" and some jewelry belonging to his followers beneath the sacred evergreen tree at Shechem. Thus it seems that Jacob is repudiating the "strange gods," but still believes in their power. In order to protect himself from their ill-will, therefore, he buries them under a tree sacred to his new God, a stronger God, one who could keep them under control.

Another interesting story that suggests a change of belief occurs in the book of Joshua (Joshua iv, 1–14). Here we are told that when the Holy Ark of the Covenant was carried across the River Jordan, twelve stones from the middle of the river were piled up on the bank as a sign and a memorial. One of the verses indicates that these were not just a haphazard lot of stones, but that they had previously formed a cairn in mid-river. Such a mid-river cairn would, in all probability, have been set up in honor of a river god. Moving the cairn to the bank of the river was literally a changing of gods in mid-stream. These same stones, we are told in verse 20, were later carried away to become part of a shrine at Gilgal, a further indication that these stones had a sacred character.

As time passed, and certainly by the time of Moses (about 1250 B.C.), the leading figures of the Hebrew group had come to believe in the one God whose name is given as YHVH. It is doubtful whether even at this time God was regarded as the *only* God. Stories from the still later age of King David suggest that the God of the Hebrews was one of a number of powerful divinities, each of whom was the protector of one of the peoples living in the ancient Near East. War between two of these peoples was regarded as a test of the strength of their different Gods. When the Israelites fought the Philistines, it was YHVH against Dagon, and YHVH was not inevitably the winner. Even during the reign of King Solomon, the exclusiveness of the Israelite God had not been firmly established; in the very Temple dedicated to the cult of YHVH, there were images of the various gods worshiped by the ladies of the king's harem. Not until the time of the great prophets, in the eighth century B.C. and after, had the idea of one universal God, divine ruler not only of the Hebrew people but of all men, developed.

All that had previously been assigned to other gods as their special province or responsibility now fell necessarily under the power of the One God. He is now the deity who created the world. Originally the story of the creation may have paralleled closely the Babylonian creation myth; for in that Near Eastern story, creation is the result of the mixing of two kinds of water, sweet water and salt water, river water and sea water, and in the Hebrew story in the Bible, the centrality of water is still kept. As we have the Biblical creation story, however, all is the work of God. This God is very much like man; in the book of Genesis, He is unabashedly spoken of in human terms. He walks in the Garden of Eden in the cool of the day; He personally supervises Adam and Eve; He visits with Abraham, sitting outside the tent of the Patriarch. With Moses, again, we come to a more refined view of the Divine nature. No man, not even Moses himself, is permitted to look upon the Lord and live. The idea of God still has its crudities; in the journey through the wilderness, God goes before the Israelites as a cloud by day and as a pillar of fire by night. There is even a hint that the Israelites believed that it was God Himself who was enclosed in the Holy Ark of the Covenant. But in general the book of Exodus reports a more advanced idea of God than does the book of Genesis.

Once more, the full refinement of the idea of God does not come until the prophetic writings. Here it is that the absolutely spiritual character of God is first consistently maintained. Perhaps there is some relation between this insistence on God's transcendence and the prophetic belief in the universality of God. For if God is One, He cannot be in any way limited in place or time. His qualities cannot be compared with those of men, because to make such a comparison would be to introduce a limitation into the idea of God. To describe His appearance or His actions in human terms (anthropomorphically) might be allowable either as a figure of speech or as a way of impressing simple people with God's majesty. But, in truth, God is incomparable because He is unique; only that can be compared which has another like itself. There is none like God. Prophetic monotheism so refined the idea of God that it left later religion a problem. If God were, indeed, as exalted as He was in the prophetic view, how could mere man, with all his human weaknesses and limitations, come into any relation with this Eminent Being? The answer that the prophets gave to this question emphasized another aspect of God, His righteousness. Man's way to make contact with God is by the leading of an ethical life.

BIBLICAL ETHICS AND LAW

In the Sumerian story which is the precursor of the Biblical legend of Cain and Abel, two gods, a shepherd god and an agricultural god, hold a good-natured debate about the relative merits of herding and farming as ways of life. Each is a suitor for the hand of a lovely goddess. Their descriptions of their respective ways of life are designed to induce the goddess to select one of them as a mate. The goddess chooses the farmer god. The shepherd god is at first somewhat upset but is finally reconciled, and they all part friends. There is, obviously, a comparison of two occupations, and a selection of the later-developed occupation of agriculture as better and more satisfactory than the earlier occupation of herding. In the Biblical story, too, herding and farming are compared. Abel is a shepherd; Cain is a farmer. Each offers of his produce to God. God looks with favor upon Abel's offering and rejects that of Cain. Thus far, the story shows that the Hebrew ethos retained a preference for the earlier activity of the remote nomadic past, herding, over the more recently developed economic activity of farming. Socially, it seems, the Hebrew people yearned for the retention of the simpler, nomadic life, reversing the Sumerian pattern. Characteristically, however, the Biblical story does not stop with this statement of preference; Cain and Abel are not reconciled, as in the Sumerian story. Instead, Cain loses his temper and slays his brother. Thus a moral twist is given to the economic preference; the sin of murder—the murder of a brother—is introduced into the world by the farmer. Now the impact of the story is that by moving into the occupation that is less satisfactory to God, one loses not only the favor of God but also his own moral restraints.

The form in which this ethical concept appears in the Bible is that of a story. Other ethical ideas also are presented in story form, rather than as systematically argued conclusions from theoretical principles. Thus the importance of the ethical obligation of marrying the widow of a brother (or, by extension, any close relative) who has died childless is illustrated in the story of Judah and Tamar in the book of Genesis. Later, as the moral ideal of the Hebrew people became less narrowly ethnic and nationalistic, although there was still a party opposed to marriage of Hebrews with the "heathen" women of the surrounding country, the beautiful idyl of the book of Ruth was written to suggest the acceptability of such intermarriages. The principle of the leviratical marriage was introduced into this tale as a universally understood and accepted moral obligation. The German poet Goethe called the book of Ruth "the loveliest little whole that has been preserved to us among the epics and idylls." The story tells of the loyalty of Ruth, a Moabitish woman, the daughter-in-law of Naomi. Ruth, the alien, the foreigner, is pictured as a person of prudence and diligence who deserves and gains great rewards. In the end, Boaz, a kinsman, fulfills the obligation by marrying Ruth, and some generations later their union led to the birth of King David. Thus a foreign wife, a Moabitish woman who by the law could never become a Jewess, indeed a woman from a most hated enemy of the Hebrew people, became the great-grandmother of one of the outstanding individuals in Hebrew history. Obviously, although the author of the book of Ruth was too fine an artist to belabor the moral, God does not look with indiscriminate disfavor on all mixed marriages, as He blessed the marriage of Boaz and Ruth in this remarkable fashion.

In addition to the inculcation of moral principles and ideals through tales and legends, a great many of the moral ideals set forth in the Bible are asserted in legal form. That is to say, these principles are given as rules without any argumentation to justify their statement. Because they appear in this form, they make up a series of ethical codes rather than an ethical philosophy. These codes date from different times. It is possible to see changes from one code to another, although in the present state of our knowledge we cannot date these codes so precisely as to discover a single line of development, an evolution of moral ideas. It is particularly interesting to trace the idea of justice through the Biblical codes. Early tales show that justice was of a rough-and-ready variety. An affront to one member of a family is wiped out by a blood bath, or a continuing blood feud begins. Later, "cities of refuge" are established by law. An unintentionally offending individual can escape the more serious consequences of his act by fleeing to one of these cities of refuge. Here he will be safe, but, in effect, imprisoned.

The most often discussed feature of Biblical ideas of justice is the law of retaliation (*lex talionis*). The formula of the classic Biblical text (see Exodus xxi, 18–25) is "Life for life, eye for eye, tooth for tooth, hand for hand, foot for foot, burning for burning, wound for wound, stripe for stripe." We must be very careful of the perspective in which we view this law of Like for Like. If we think of it from the perspective of modern conceptions of justice, it is clearly still primitive. If, however, we can cast it into the approximate period of its formulation, the impression it creates is quite different. For we may understand it as placing a limit on the penalty to be exacted. No longer, this law asserts, may the punishment *exceed* the crime. No longer shall a small offense be repaid a thousandfold. True, if a murder is committed, the death penalty remains; so it does today in many parts of the United States. But the death penalty may not be assessed for a lesser offense. Destruction of a tooth shall be punishable by *no more than* destruction of a tooth.

The law of retaliation is, then, an intermediate stage; society intervenes to place limits on the revenge that a family may exact for a crime. Two steps of importance are still to be taken: one, the acceptance of a substitute, such as money payment, for a lesser offense, appears in the Bible early, in the institution of "ransom" (*kofer*); the other, the more important step, is to transfer the right to punish from the individual or the family to society, and ultimately to permit the social instruments of justice to accept a law of equivalence for a law of likeness, a system of compensation (fines, imprisonment, etc.) for a system of physical mutilation in all except capital crimes. Before this can take place, society itself must be stable and well organized. This, in its turn, requires a settled state. During the nomadic period in the life of the Hebrew people, social organization was familial or, at the

14

most, tribal. Only after the settlement in the Promised Land did the conditions for a truly social system of law and justice appear.

THE ORIGIN OF LAW

In many ways the greatest contribution the Bible assigns to Moses is his welding together of the tribes of Israel into a nation, fused by a common relation to God. Whether or not this is historically accurate is of far less significance than an earlier generation thought. What is of significance is that the unification of the Hebrew people was a prerequisite for the establishment of a legal system, with strong religious sanctions. We may guess, perhaps, that a leader like Moses might have been powerful enough to weld the tribes into a nation even prior to their settlement in Canaan, that the stresses of the long migration through the wilderness might be sufficient to induce a collection of proud and willful nomads to accept the Mosaic unification. If Moses did achieve such a success, it was temporary, and had to be repeated at a later time, for in the books of Joshua and Judges we read story after story indicating that a state of disunity had returned.

Whatever view of the history we accept, the story of the Mosaic formation of a new nation is to be found in Exodus, chapter xxiv. Moses created a new religious partnership by the making of a covenant between God and the tribes. The text as we have it is probably modified from the original, but the outlines of the covenanting ritual are clear, and the meaning of the ritual is comparatively easy to discover. The blood is the life, the vital fluid. Two parties, independent of each other, are to be united into a single whole. As an intermediate step in achieving the desired union, a third party, the sacrificial animal, is introduced. Its life is taken from it by the draining of its blood; this common life-blood is thus made available to the two original parties. Half the blood is poured over the altar that represents God; the other half is flung over the heads of the people. Now the same vital essence covers both parties. They are no longer independent, but are one in a blood relationship. God and Israel have become, by the ritual, continuous parts of an indivisible life. Furthermore, Israel is now more than a merely human community, as it is one with God.

What is unusual about this ceremony is that the relationship that is set up by means of the blood ritual is not a natural relationship but a contractual one. In early religions, the god or gods are natural members of the people to whom they belong. A god is inconceivable apart from his people. If his tribe is destroyed, the god loses his reason for being. He may remain a deity; Henry Thoreau said "No god ever dies." But he becomes a wild and homeless hobo among the spirits, keeping some of his powers while losing his prestige. Usually, the god is as dependent upon his people as they are upon him. Unlike this ordinary relation was the relation of YHVH to Israel, for He was an *adopted* God. He had existed as a God independent of the existence of Israel and He could, if necessary, exist so again. Just as Israel had adopted YHVH, other peoples might do the same. He could extend His concern and His influence to other nations.

The relationship, then, was not a natural one. It had a definite beginning in time, and it might as readily have a definite ending in time. It depended upon a contract, a covenant, a deed of agreement, and if at any time either party violated the terms of the agreement, the other might declare the partnership at an end. The formula "I will become their God and they shall become My people" expresses the acceptance of the offered contract. While there is a similar contractual bond between Jacob and God in the story related in Genesis xxviii, 20–22, in which the terms of the contract are presented in detail, the probability is that all or part of the itemized contractual obligations are later insertions into an older story. Biblical scholars have recently sought the original idea of the covenant or contract in a type of treaty that was usual in the ancient Near East, a treaty between a superior king ("king of kings") and the minor kings who were his vassals. In this theory, that God should be presented as giving law to the people who have accepted the obligations of the covenant comes alive with meaning. Here, however, we should take note that implicitly in Exodus and explicitly in Deuteronomy vi, 5, what is insisted upon in the Biblical account is not so much the power of God as His grace. God's benevolence has been bestowed freely upon the children of Israel. Their obedience to Him and His law should be rooted in thankfulness and love rather than in fear.

In addition, however, to this contractual theory of the Divine origin of law, the Bible presents, side by side with it, a second theory according to which law had a human origin. In this alternative account, Moses rather than God is the lawgiver. The story goes that Jethro, the father-in-law of Moses, came to the Israelite camp to visit his daughter and her husband. He found Moses spending the entire day sitting in judgment upon particular cases that were brought before him for decision. Jethro reproved Moses for spending his time in this fashion, and recommended that he set forth a code of laws and appoint inferior judges for each division of the people to adjudicate cases that arose under this code. Thus Moses' time could be devoted to leadership of the people, with his only judicial responsibilities being to decide cases that were appealed from the decisions of the inferior judges. Moses was, it seems, impressed by Jethro's suggestion and proceeded to formulate just such a code of laws. This "secular" account of the origin of law breaks off at this point, and is followed by the theological theory that we have already presented.

Though there were two theories, there were many codes of law. To some extent, it may be said that these different codes bear with them indications of their origins. Some emphasize obligations toward the priesthood, and these patently arose, not in the

Mosaic period to which the Bible attaches them, but in a far later period when the priestly class had become large and powerful. Others stress ritual regulations or the responsibilities of a settled, agricultural community. Still others seem to preserve rules of an early nomadic stage of existence ("Thou shalt not seethe the kid in its mother's milk"). But even when there are these special concerns, the codes introduce, to a greater or lesser extent, elements of personal morality and of social welfare. It is notable that in some instances an action that is reported of one of the Patriarchs is forbidden explicitly by one of the later codes. Thus the Bible itself tells us of the marriage of Jacob to two sisters, Leah and Rachel, yet the "Holiness Code" in Leviticus xvii-xxvi specifically forbids the marriage of a man to two sisters. The reason for this is that, whatever its origin, human or Divine, law must change to keep pace with the social and cultural development of the people for whom it is law. The changes may be made piecemeal, by insertions of new provisions in old codes, or they may be made by the substitution of an entirely revised code. To the extent that the sacredness of law is insisted upon, old codes and obsolete provisions might be preserved in a sacred literature. This would explain their presence in the Bible. They would not, however, still be enforced in the ongoing life of a progressive people.

PROPHETIC ETHICS

The high point of Biblical ethics is to be found in the writings of the literary prophets. On the day when, at a harvest feast at Bethel, some time about 750 B.C., the prophet Amos asserted, with irresistible spiritual authority, that in spite of her national prosperity Israel had been doomed to destruction by God Himself, a new era began for the religion of the Hebrews. Their monotheism was transformed into an ethical monotheism. Amos was not a man of learning, not a member of the priestly or upper classes. He was a simple peasant from the hills of Judah, a shepherd and a cultivator of sycamore trees. He had no previous relations with the existing guilds of what might be called "official" prophets. Visiting Samaria, the capital city of the monarchy of Jeroboam II of Israel, he was struck by the profound contrast between the lot of the wealthy upper classes, living in urban style, and the desperate poverty of the masses of the people. He was struck, too, by the extent to which ceremonial religion flourished among the wealthy; he thought of them as trying to bribe God even as they bribed judges and court officials.

Returning to his hill village, he had brooded over what he had seen in the wicked city and had come to the conviction that it was his calling to bring the word of God to His wayward servants. Again he turned his steps to the north, to declare publicly what he could no longer hold within his breast, the conviction that God had weighed the people of Israel in the balance and found them wanting. In particular, he stressed a new and moral interpretation of the doctrine of Israel's election by God. No longer was it to be assumed that the choice of Israel meant that God showed favoritism to the people, and that, no matter what they did, He would pardon them. The choice was not a special privilege to make the children of Israel, the people of God, an arrogant and haughty nation. Rather, the election imposed upon the people a special responsibility. They had to be better than other peoples. It was, therefore, no defense of corruption in Israel to declare that other peoples were equally corrupt. The people of Israel had been chosen to illustrate to the world God's purity and justice. They had, therefore, to live a purer and more just life both as individuals and as a nation.

The prophetic morality to which Amos called the people of God takes little account of ritual purity and ceremonial observances. Outward religion, the religion of sacrifices and offerings, is of no value in itself; its only value is as a secondary sign of inward religion. No matter how meticulously external observances are fulfilled, they are not acceptable to God unless they have been preceded by a turning to Him. An offering from an impure heart is an offense to God, not an honor to Him: "I hate, I despise your feast days, and I will not smell in your solemn assemblies. Though ye offer me burnt offerings and meat offerings, I will not accept them: neither will I regard the peace offerings of your fat beasts. Take thou away from me the noise of thy songs; for I will not hear the melody of thy viols" (Amos v, 21–23).

What God loves and asks of men is social morality. "Let judgment run down as waters, and righteousness as a mighty stream" (Amos v, 24). The people must be just, because God is just. They must be compassionate, because God is compassionate; righteous, because God is righteous. The gods of the pagan religions were not concerned with justice among men; perhaps they could be turned away from anger by sacrifices that were really bribes. Not so the God of Israel. He demanded justice between man and man; He hated oppression and despised idleness and luxury. There is no doubt that in this denunciation Amos was giving voice to a lower class, rural protest against an urban style of life. But he was also setting the tone for what became, in his successors, the dominant ethical strain of the prophets, and in remoter followers the social ideal of most Christian and Jewish moralists down to the present.

It is noteworthy that, although Amos thought of social unrighteousness as the special guilt of the upper classes, he emphasized that punishment was to be directed not merely against the guilty individuals but against the whole nation. It is possibly a survival of an older corporate way of thinking that led Amos to consider the entire nation guilty of the sins of its nobility. There is, accordingly, an important ethical advance still to be made in the substitution of a theory of individual responsibility for that of communal responsibility. Yet it must be remembered that the idea of corporate responsibility cuts both ways; the community is to be saved by individual righteousness if it is to be saved at all, just as it will be doomed for the sins of individuals if the judgment of doom stands against it. In addition, a close reading of the book of Amos suggests that all the specific guilty acts that he lists may be summed up under one head. The people of Israel substituted adoration of the idol of national glory for devotion to the ever-living God. Because their nationalism was national pride, it was appropriate that their punishment should be in the destruction of that of which they were proud. National humiliation was to be the fit penalty for national pride.

A few years later, perhaps about 735 B.C., there arose a prophet who substituted a gentle, warm-hearted, tender tone for the rugged notes of Amos. Hosea had an unfortunate married life, and he transferred his feelings about his unfaithful wife to God and His feelings toward the "unfaithful" children of Israel. Hosea was no less convinced of the immorality of the people of Israel, and he regarded the people of Judah as only slightly better. But where the emphasis of Amos on the righteousness of God had been the central feature of his interpretation of the relation between God and the people, Hosea's stress fell on God's lovingkindness and readiness to forgive. Thus Hosea was led to value love above the practice of cult and the maintenance of the sacrificial ritual. Hosea attacked the priests directly. He insisted that it was their duty to teach the people a morality based upon pure religion. Instead of this, he charged, they had promoted a form of worship that followed other Eastern cults in including at least one form of gross immorality, sacred prostitution. In addition to this charge, Hosea also accused the priests of having welcomed the spreading canker of sin because the sin offerings that were made in atonement were profitable to the priestly group. Hosea's philosophy led him to be anticlerical.

The particular "sins" to which Hosea called attention were of various sorts. He was concerned, of course, as Amos had been, with the squeezing of the poor by the rich and by instances of personal immorality. But he also included theological sin in his list of reprehensible actions; he resented the attempt to combine features of the Canaanite worship of the god, of the place, the Baal, or master of the land, with the pure worship of God. In particular he objected to the representation of YHVH as a bull in small images that were prominent in the local worship in the smaller shrines in the Kingdom of Israel. A third type of "sin" that concerned Hosea might be described as nationalistic, not so much in the sense in which Amos had attacked national pride, but in a somewhat different fashion. Hosea argued that Israel's foreign policy, relying on a system of alliances with surrounding powers, was sinful because it showed a lack of reliance upon God's care for the people. He also attacked the internal separation of the people into the two kingdoms of Israel and Judah, a separation that had followed the reign of King Solomon. In the eyes of God, he said, Judah and Israel are one kingdom, not two. Their union was a religious one; only this could be the safeguard of national existence. Israel and Judah should have but One God, YHVH, but one altar, the Temple at Jerusalem, but one ruling house, the descendants of King David. He stated explicitly that the existence of rival dynasties in the two countries involved the establishment of rival divinities. It is clear from this that Hosea's thought never quite encompassed the conception of YHVH as the universal God, the God of all nations. In this respect, his thought is a step backward from that of Amos, although his presentation of God as a God of love marks some advance over Amos' conception of a punitive God.

While Hosea was still active in the Northern Kingdom, there arose in Judah the first of the three prophets whose literary production has led to their being called "major." In the case of Isaiah, the designation major is appropriate to the quality of his work as well as to its quantity, even though only a part of what we have in the book of Isaiah was actually the product of Isaiah of Jerusalem. The basic and most fundamental quality to be noted in the prophecies of Isaiah is an overwhelming sense of the holiness and the majesty of God which led him to assert and to maintain the strictest of monotheistic outlooks. In the whole body of his work there is not a phrase, not even a word, to suggest that he allowed any sort of real existence to the heathen gods. It is in contrast to the absoluteness of God's holiness and glory that all humans, but especially the Hebrew people, and among them most particularly Isaiah himself, seemed impure and sinful. Here we come to the paradox that was noted earlier: the more God is glorified, the smaller and meaner and less worthy do human beings appear.

Isaiah's idea of God was truly and completely universal. God was alone; there was none beside Him to detract from His power and His majesty. Therefore He must be regarded as the undivided Sovereign of the universe; nothing that takes place on earth can occur in independence of His will. From this point, Isaiah developed a most remarkable theistic philosophy of history. If nothing that takes place can do so independently of God's will, he thought, then everything that does actually occur must do so because God wishes it to occur, and to occur in precisely the way and with precisely the consequences that it had in actuality. All of history must, then, be the gradual realization of a Divine purpose. God's Providence has as its object the progressive achievement of His goal, which is the manifestation of His own glory and the establishment of the kingdom of righteousness upon earth. One of the most noteworthy passages in the whole book of Isaiah describes his vision of the kingdom of righteousness (Isaiah ii, 2–4).

One of the charges that Isaiah brought against the leaders of his people was that they failed to perceive the working of the Divine intention through history. The attempts to play Egypt against Assyria or Assyria against Egypt seemed to Isaiah incredible folly from the perspective of the God's-eye view of history that he expounded. Despite his stress on the absoluteness of God's transcendent majesty, his philosophy of history made it possible for him to bring the idea of God into a close and immediate relation with the events of his time. Thus, instead of his transcendental

23

view of God diminishing the impact of the Divine on human life, he was able to make that very theory of transcendence, of majesty and glory, into the living and practical principle of an actual and universal Divine sovereignty. Like many other later thinkers who accepted a theistic philosophy of history, Isaiah thought that the end of history was close at hand. He envisioned history as a drama rapidly approaching its climax. The political world of his time was being shaken by great convulsions which he interpreted as the footsteps of the Lord marching onward to a day of crisis, out of which the final hope of humanity would emerge.

If there is any weakness to be noted in the thought of Isaiah, it is that in his tremendous vision of the world as unified by the single, overarching Divine plan, he lost sight of the immediate moral message that is central to the other prophets of his time. When he spoke of the transformation of the moral character, it was not in terms of a moral revival sweeping over the whole nation, but rather of a "saving remnant" that would be left after the storm and stress of the era had passed. Apparently he did not believe that repentance and a return to God could root the evildoers out of the community. Calamity and disaster, he felt, would destroy the sinful, and virtue would be triumphant among those who are left. Thus Isaiah's thought, for all its nobility, lacks the immediate personal relevance of Amos and Hosea, or of Micah, who was his contemporary. Isaiah, too, was moved by the plight of the poor and needy, but he pushed relief into the messianic future. Amos, Hosea, and Micah all insisted on the need for an immediate reformation and purification for the relief of the suffering.

PROPHETIC INDIVIDUALISM

Thus far, in discussing the ideas of the prophets, we have seen that their conception of sin and its redemption was connected with a theory of group responsibility. As we move to consider the thought of the prophet Jeremiah, after the year 626 B.C., we find a new outlook in which the role of the individual is stressed. Jeremiah himself stands out as more of a person than any of the other prophets; we have more information about his life than we do about the others. The reason for this is that the book of Jeremiah was written by a scribe who was an intimate friend of the prophet. Baruch, the scribe, was an educated man of noble family who was deeply devoted to Jeremiah, accompanied him through most of his journeys, even to Egypt, and visited him when he was in prison. Baruch supplied a framework of biographical information to surround the messages of the prophet delivered over a period of forty years. There is no explicit dating of the material, as there is in the book of Ezekiel, but there is sufficient information to enable Jeremiah's career to be dated with considerable probability.

Far more importantly, the message of Jeremiah stresses an individual, rather than a corporate, response to God and His will. The most remarkable passage is dated by scholars after the year 586 B.C. (Jeremiah xxxi, 31–34), in which the prophet announces a new covenant with God, taking the place of the covenant made at the time of the Exodus. The new covenant was to differ from the original covenant in being permanent, and more significantly was to differ in the principle by which its permanence was to remain unbroken. The Law, the covenant of the wilderness, consisted of obligations that the people were, in effect, forced to accept out of fear of God. The new covenant enunciated by Jeremiah did not differ from the old in substance; the requirements of the Law remained unchanged. It did, however, depend for its acceptance upon a different motive. Love of God, not fear of God, was the basis for its acceptance. Thus conformity with the Law was to stem entirely from inner, and therefore personal, motives.

The emphasis placed here upon personal acceptance of the covenant is the key to a prophetic individualism that adds an essential note to the ethical teachings of Jeremiah's predecessors. The wilderness covenant had been given to Israel as a national group; as we have seen, the earlier prophets had implicitly agreed to this view and had, therefore, felt that punishment for the violation of the covenant and disobedience to the Law should fall upon Israel as a national group. Jeremiah changed the approach by interpreting the obligations assumed as individual obligations, rather than as group demands. He pushed behind the Law and its formal expression to the individual heart. In the individual rather than in the group Jeremiah thought the root of evil lay. When, in his heart of hearts, any individual recognized his relationship to God, the external actions and attitudes that he would display would be in accordance with the right and the good.

Jeremiah was penetratingly shrewd in his psychological analysis of human motives. He realized that conformity to a law that is imposed from without does not necessarily imply any acceptance of that law, and is, indeed, usually accompanied by an inward hostility both to the law and to the external force by which it is imposed. When forced conformity is changed to inward acceptance, the law is no longer an outside affair. It has become internalized, part of the personality of the individual. The law becomes not what the external authority demands but what the person himself wants. When this change of attitude has taken place, the law and the individual have become one. The Divine will and the human will are identical. Only when this has occurred, Jeremiah thought, is religion truly national in the highest sense. Each individual making up the nation is spiritually reborn and renewed, and in this individual renewal the nation is religiously regenerated.

The prophets before him had reached out to a higher conception of God; Jeremiah seems to be reaching out toward a higher conception of man's relation to God, man's service to God, religion. His predecessors had laid a foundation for this development of Jeremiah's thought in their scornful attitude toward the corporate manifestations of the cult in ritual and sacrifice. Although Jeremiah came of a minor priestly family, he shared the antagonism of his predecessors to the cult. He never gave the opposition to formal cult the superb statement that Amos or Micah did, yet he was as fully convinced as were they that God had not commanded sacrifice or ritual, but only obedience to the moral law. When he called for a return to the "old ways" (Jeremiah vi, 16), it was, in fact, not an old way at all but the new way of inward and individual religion to which he summoned his people.

In this connection it is interesting to note that Jeremiah is presented as the first Bible figure who habitually engaged in personal prayer to God. There are, of course, earlier instances of prayer recorded, but these are occasional and exceptional; so much so that when the priest Eli sees the lips of Hannah moving in a secret, personal prayer, he wonders if she is drunk. Jeremiah's recourse to God in prayer is reported as frequent. His reflections on the spiritual relationship between the individual heart and the Supreme Being apparently led him to a feeling of great closeness and intimacy with God. Several of Jeremiah's personal prayers are cited in his book; it is impressive to note that in them he shows that he is considering one of the continuing questions of religious philosophy, the question of God's moral government of the universe. In Jeremiah's prayers lies the important consequence of his shift from collective religion to individual religion. If God writes His law in the heart of each man, then He must deal with each man singly. Prophetic religion culminates in the recognition that both virtue and vice, both innocence and guilt, pertain to men, not to nations.

THE DAY OF DOOM

Isaiah's philosophy of history was essentially hopeful. The universe, under the care of God's special Providence, was thought of as moving toward the fulfillment of God's designs. Local and temporary disasters might occur, but in God's master plan these were intentional steps in the working out of the final victory.

Even the conquest of Judah by the Babylonians, in 586 B.C., was part of God's design; as He is the universal God, He may use the Babylonians or any other people as His agents. When, after the downfall of Babylonia at the hands of the Persians, some members of the exiled Jewish group returned to the land of their fathers, they found deep disappointment, both on the way and in the homeland. Some of the prophecies—not Isaiah's—incorporated into the book of Isaiah had foretold a triumphant return, but none of the glorious events that this great anonymous prophet had predicted had come true on the homeward journey. When the return had been completed, the situation of the returnees in Judah was less fortunate than they had hoped. There was a drought and their crops failed. Those who had inhabited the land during the years of exile were not friendly to the returned Jews. On the whole, they became disillusioned and began to lose hope and faith.

In this situation, two trends may be observed among the later group of prophets. The first, and for our purposes less interesting, is the call to return to the Temple cult. Haggai told the people that the Lord had not come back to dwell in their midst because they had not rebuilt His house in their preoccupation with rebuilding their own. Joel, who has been called "the sacramentarian among the prophets," believed that the most terrible disaster that could befall the people was for the daily sacrifices in the Temple to be stopped. He considered the sacrifices as the daily renewal of the bond between God and the people. An oracle incorporated in the book of Malachi urges the people to be strictly honest in consecrating the tenth part of their income to the Temple. The extreme anti-cultic emphasis of Amos, Micah, and Isaiah is followed by the return to formal religion.

The second aspect of post-exilic prophecy involves a transformation of Isaiah's philosophy of history into an apocalyptic concern with the last days, the day of judgment, the day of doom. The shift of emphasis is heralded by a shift in the view of the agents of God. In Isaiah, God carried out His intentions through men. In the later writers, God does not depend on human powers; He sends out heavenly or demonic beings to do His work. The consequence of this shift in perspective is that where the earlier prophet was producing an interpretation of events on earth in terms of a Divine program, the later writers have lost faith in human agents and resort to the attempt to lay bare the secrets of heaven. The writers of apocalyptic prophecy followed the universalism of the early prophets, whereas the spokesmen for the Temple cult reintroduced a particularistic Jewish nationalism. But apocalyptic transformed the moral emphasis that is the glory of early prophecy into a cult of other-worldliness.

The word "apocalyptic" means, literally, "uncovering." Perhaps the best English translation would be "revelation." Apocalyptic writings purported to reveal the secrets of the supernatural world; with respect to the natural world, the view of these writers was pessimistic and hopeless. Most of the writings, both in the Bible and in the immediately post-Biblical period, that are classed as apocalyptic show a considerable influence of Persian thought. Persian religious ideas were dualistic; their concern was to show the world as the ground of contest between two divinities, Ahura Mazda (Ormuzd), the god of light and good, and Ahriman, the god of darkness and evil. These two divinities were conceived as equally matched; neither could achieve a final victory over the other. Man's moral choices were, then, important, for in the way each man chose, he added strength to one or the other of these two gods. The apocalyptic writers, too, saw the world as a battleground of the forces of good, God and His heavenly allies, and the forces of evil, Satan and his demonic hosts. Where Jeremiah had, we may say, envisioned the struggle between good and evil as taking place within the human heart, in apocalyptic writing the struggle is transferred to a cosmic arena.

The distinction between earlier prophetic and apocalyptic writings can best be seen by comparing the two conceptions of the Day of God. The prophets had spoken of a day of judgment; a magnificent passage of this sort is to be found in Isaiah, chapters xxiv–xxvii. The first faint hints of an apocalyptic revision of this theme are met in Ezekiel, chapters xxxviii–xxxix. The distinction appears first in the fantastic symbolism of the Ezekiel passage; exaggerated symbolism is a feature of apocalyptic. The second distinction is in the interpretation of the day of judgment as a great day when all the nations of the world shall be gathered against Israel, when God will destroy the enemies of His people and thus vindicate His power. Both prophets and writers of apocalyptic foretold the future, but the prophets regarded God as achieving his purpose by regular, "evolutionary" means, whereas the writers of Apocalypse thought of God as achieving his ends by sudden supernatural interventions, causing unpredictable events in history.

Both prophets and writers of apocalyptic were giving expression to an intense supernaturalism. But the prophetic view of the supernatural was more orderly and rational, tied to a view that God gained his goals gradually, and the apocalyptic version of supernaturalism was irrational and geared to the image of catastrophe. In its original sense, the Day of God meant no more than a fateful day, decreed by God; in the apocalyptic imagination it acquired the meaning of "the end of all days." The prophetic Day of God is the day of judgment for the present age of world history; it is to be followed by more history and other days of judgment. The apocalyptic phrase that corresponds to the Day of God is "in the latter end of all days"; it is the day of final judgment for all ages, coming at the end of time and of history. In the book of Daniel, the clearest case of an apocalyptic work included in the Bible, there is a description of the Divine judgment in heaven, in which the "ancient of days" is pictured as sitting upon His throne while the books in which the records of the lives of men are written lie open before Him (Daniel vii–ix).

There is no doubt that the apocalyptic transformation of history was a development out of the prophetic view. It is not, however, strictly speaking, a continuation of the prophetic view. The apocalyptic theory of history is an offshoot, a branching out from the prophetic philosophy of history which becomes very different. In the foreground of the prophetic writings are the present circumstances of the Jewish people; the prophet looks to the Divinely guided, providential course of history to lead to a better era for all mankind, an era of truth and justice and peace, when "they shall beat their swords into plowshares and their spears into pruning hooks." In apocalyptic writings, the present retreats into the background; apocalyptic works are usually written as if from a standpoint in the remote past; often they are presented in the name of an early heroic figure or of one of the Patriarchs. By this misrepresentation of standpoint, the actual writers of apocalyptic were able to put into the form of prediction many things that were, in fact, historical. These "successful" prophecies lend an air of assurance and credence to their foretelling of the transcendental future to come about by the direct and visible intervention of God.

FROM WISDOM TO PHILOSOPHY

The exciting world of apocalyptic speculation is altogether foreign to the dictates of common sense. Apocalyptic is for the few who can penetrate beyond the literal interpretation of its excesses to the spiritual kernel that lies behind. Common sense is for the many and it provides a practical direction for the everyday life of the average man. Unfortunately, most of the practical wisdom by which men must be guided in the ordinary course of life is not very exciting. Common sense at its best is commonplace. It seems profound only to the very simple. Yet even the deepest of thinkers disregards the homely simplicity of folk wisdom at his peril.

The book of Proverbs is the chief collection in the Bible of common-sense wisdom. There are occasional proverbial sentences elsewhere, such as "The fathers have eaten sour grapes and the

31

children's teeth are set on edge" (Ezekiel xviii, 2). But the book of Proverbs is actually a compilation from eight different earlier collections by various writers or editors, dating from various times. That it has been attributed through the ages to King Solomon is testimony to the place that that king held in the popular mind as a master of wisdom rather than a serious claim of authorship. Proverbs were meant as educational materials, chiefly for the young, but incidentally for their seniors. For the most part, they are expressed in a terse and epigrammatic style, though occasionally they take the form of longer homilies. The book of Proverbs contains acute observations and realistic appraisals of the human world, reinforced by emotional pleas designed to instill convictions about the art of living well.

Proverbs, when they have not passed so far into currency that any attribution of authorship would be superfluous, are generally assigned to an indefinite group referred to as "the wise" or "the sages." The teachings of the wise cover all phases of life. They treat of manners as well as of morals—indeed, did not Thomas Hobbes, in the seventeenth century A.D., go so far as to say that "Manners are little morals"? Proverbs deal with family affairs, the relations between parents and children, husbands and wives, masters and servants. They teach the accepted way of conducting one's social life, whether with friends or with enemies, as well as proper conduct in business and professional matters and in public life. There is no field to which proverbs do not contribute a great deal of prudential guidance, through penetrating examination of life, expressed often with gentle humor and occasionally with mordant irony.

The ideal of the proverbial wise man is not very lofty. The book of Proverbs is not a design for saintly living. Its intention is to show how a clever, honest man can use wisdom to guide his conduct in order to be happy and honored for his worldly success. Personal happiness is the invariable motive given in the book; there seems to be no feeling for the higher ideal of concern for others. When the welfare of others is mentioned at all, it is always with reference back to oneself. Self-interest dominates the entire book of Proverbs. Nor is goodness ever advocated for its own sake. The idea of personal gain is central. The fundamental moral idea of the book of Proverbs is not that goodness is good and wickedness evil, but that goodness is rewarded while wickedness is punished. This is the principle that a wise man understands, and as a result he achieves happiness. A fool fails to understand, refuses to act properly, and perishes.

Often in the Hebrew literature of wisdom there is a feeling that the writers regarded most men as fools of various sorts. There is a scheme of classification for fools, with different names given to their various types of folly. One is the open-mouthed fool, "He that goeth about as a tale-bearer" (Proverbs xx, 19). He is not wicked, merely stupid in his folly. The type of fool most frequently mentioned in the wisdom literature hates knowledge and is, therefore, incapable of appreciating what is good. He "hath no delight in understanding" (Proverbs xix, 1). He lacks self-control; "A fool uttereth all his anger/But a wise man keepeth it back and stilleth it" (Proverbs xxix, 11). He delights in wrongdoing, is quarrelsome and deceitful. He is altogether dangerous; "Let a bear robbed of her whelps meet a man, rather than a fool in his folly" (Proverbs xvii, 12). Still another type of fool is morally bad; he makes sin the business of his life. Then there is the man who takes a delight in wrongdoing, who refuses to listen to good advice and retaliates if he is reproved. The worst of all fools is the out-and-out wicked man. One of the main purposes of the wisdom literature of the book of Proverbs is to try to redeem all these types of fool from their folly.

The first section of the book of Proverbs introduces a somewhat more profound conception of wisdom. Here Wisdom is personified and declared to be the supreme principle in creation as well as in the moral life of man. Because Wisdom is a principle that pervades the universe, truly right living consists of the attempt to live in harmony with those glimpses of Wisdom that the sages have had. God alone truly knows the way of Wisdom; man by his own efforts could never find it out. Hence it is that "The fear of the Lord is the beginning of Wisdom" (Proverbs i, 7). These chapters at the beginning of the book of Proverbs speculate about wisdom itself and its relation to man, rather than trying to set forth the conclusions to which popular wisdom has come. They elaborate a conception of wisdom as a Divinely created person who existed before the creation of the world. At the creation, Wisdom was with God. From God, Wisdom descends to earth to plead her own cause, to win all men, even the simple and foolish among them, to the prudent, righteous life. In this idea of Wisdom we have reached a philosophic conception that ties together the metaphysical plan of creation and the ethical or prudential wisdom that brings wealth, success, and happiness to men.

CHAPTER TWO

The Judeo-Greek Temper

WE HAVE SEEN that the Bible, for the most part, expresses typical Hebrew attitudes based on deep and abiding faith in God and His Providence. The Bible sets forth a challenging demand to reach high levels of ethical living, but it does not encourage men to the speculative questioning of ultimate principles. In some parts of the prophetic literature and in the books of Wisdom we found the faint beginnings of a more characteristically philosophic approach to the universe. There are, in addition, two books included in the Old Testament that we have not yet discussed. These two, Ecclesiastes and Job, might well be ornaments of the philosophic literature of any people. The general view of scholars today is that both of these books are relatively late products, written when the influence of Greek thought had already been felt in the land of Palestine. Thus Ecclesiastes and Job tend to be considered as the first products of a combination of Hebrew and Hellenic modes of thought, a synthesis of Jewish and Greek attitudes toward the ultimates of life and death.

Yet it is not altogether accurate to suggest that the books of Ecclesiastes and Job required a wedding of Hebrew faith and Hellenic skepticism to come into being. There is evidence in the recently rediscovered literature of Mesopotamia and of Egypt that skeptical attitudes occurred among other peoples besides the

Greeks. In addition, as there is evidence on other matters that the Hebrews were affected by the traditions and the literature of the nations that surrounded them in the ancient Near East, we have every reason to surmise that skeptical currents were felt in the Hebrew intellectual world as well. We should, perhaps, take the two books of Ecclesiastes and Job as the surviving representatives of a class of philosophic works in which Hebrew writers develop ancient skeptical themes. The two survivors, in their present form, at least, are late specimens of their type and reveal, therefore, a Greek influence.

THE GENTLE CYNIC

Morris Jastrow, Jr., entitled his English version of the book of Ecclesiastes *A Gentle Cynic*. This title is a very accurate statement of the prevailing tone and temper of the book. The "Preacher" of the title (*Koheleth* in Hebrew and *Ecclesiastes* in Greek may both be translated as "The Preacher") wrote some time about 200 B.C., at a period when the entire world of Greek thought had undergone a shaking of its foundations. All accepted values were suspect and doubted and, as a result, there was a general loss of faith in the purposefulness of life. The Preacher, an old and wise man, was surely deeply infected by this pervasive doubt. He reviewed the events and activities of his own life and failed to see any evidence of an all-inclusive purpose or meaning in it. His ceaseless strivings, typifying those of all men, were empty and repetitious, a mere "chasing after wind." The note of hopeless emptiness, "vanity" in the original sense of that word, is struck in the repeated refrain: "Vanity of vanities, says the Preacher, all is vanity."

The author of Ecclesiastes was a man completely without illusions, willing to submit any and all beliefs to critical testing and judgment of value. Certainly he was not a builder of philosophic systems, concerned with the problems that have traditionally engaged the attention of technical philosophers. He was, however, concerned to discover a way of life for the unillusioned, for those like himself, and to see life consistently and to see it whole. His profundity may be questioned. His vision of ultimate meaninglessness may be challenged as superficial and unconstructive. It may be said of him, as it has been said of every other writer who has tried to banish illusion, that he was shallow in his failure to recognize the value of illusion itself as a motive force in human life. Man's life becomes meaningful, we might say, in the very measure in which he manages to believe in his illusions, to take his illusions seriously. All these strictures can justly be applied to the Preacher. What should not be called into question is the sharpness and shrewdness of the writer's observation of life and the brilliance of the poetic expression he lent to the statement of his observations and conclusions.

The Preacher was impressed by the eternal recurrence of the moments of life, the endless return with no apparent advance, no apparent goal. "One generation passeth away, and another generation cometh: but the earth abideth forever. . . . All the rivers run into the sea; yet the sea is not full; unto the place from whence the rivers come, thither they return again." The sun and the wind—all the phenomena of nature—follow this same pattern, this endless cycle. When we ask ourselves what the meaning of it all is, we can find no answer. All we can discover is this incessant, cyclical departure and return, ebb and flow. "The thing that hath been, it is that which shall be; and that which is done is that which shall be done: and there is no new thing under the sun." Nothing that men can do will alter in any way the fore-ordained regularity of nature's ways. If this is the case, if human activity can make no difference in the world, then our lives cannot be thought to have purpose or meaning. When each of us has lived his course and returns to the dust from which he arose, the world will go on unchanged. All our doings, our sufferings, our agonizings are without cosmic significance.

THE SEARCH FOR SATISFACTION

What, then, is left for man? If, in a cosmic perspective, his life is purposeless and vain, he can at the least seek out the pleasures and satisfactions of earthly life. Surely there are values of the here-and-now that are open to human achievement. If one cannot live with a sense of ultimate purpose, one can find delights and joys in present living. Satisfaction can replace significance, pleasure can replace purpose, as a center of vitality for the living out of one's destined term. With this thought in mind, the Preacher describes, ostensibly out of his own experience, his attempts to find out what satisfactions life had to offer. The quest for possessions, for wealth and what wealth could buy, proved to be empty of any lasting satisfaction. Frivolity and debauchery were found to be equally vain. The search for power and prestige yielded no fruits to the spirit. All these common ways of men for seeking out the most satisfactory courses of earthly life came to seem to the Preacher ways of folly.

Folly having failed, he now set himself the task of seeking out wisdom—human wisdom, we should remember, rather than the Divine or half-Divine Wisdom of other Biblical books. He became, by his own account, the master of all human wisdom; in this assertion and in his statement that he had been "King over Israel in Jerusalem" lies the basis for the tradition that the book of Ecclesiastes was written by King Solomon. Wisdom, however, proved to be no more satisfying than folly. True, "Wisdom excelleth folly, as far as light excelleth darkness." Yet, when all is done, the fate of the wise man is no better than that of the fool. "Then I said in my heart, that this also is vanity. For there is no remembrance of the wise more than of the fool for ever; seeing that which now is in the days to come shall all be forgotten." Indeed, it might well have been said that wisdom was the greatest folly, for wisdom, rather than folly, leads to the realization that "all is vanity and vexation of spirit."

To what can man give his allegiance? What course of life brings with it some satisfaction of the spirit? The Preacher suggests that it is a course of moderation, of enjoying all the opportunities that life has to offer, but expecting from these enjoyments nothing beyond the momentary good they provide. Nothing in life can yield a meaning beyond itself. Nevertheless, "it is good and comely for one to eat and to drink, and to enjoy the good of all his labor that he taketh under the sun all the days of his life, which God giveth him." One must be neither too wise nor too foolish; too wealthy nor too poor; too great and powerful nor too humble. Men are given a brief interval of life and light between two eternities of darkness: the Preacher indicates no belief in immortality; death is the end of all men's strivings. With one exception, the end of the Preacher's reflections is what all those who are called after the name of Epicurus have taught: "Let us eat, drink and be merry, for tomorrow we may die."

The one exception accounts for the inclusion of the book of Ecclesiastes in the Bible. Whether these words were in the original text or whether they are later additions, as some scholars hold, the last verses of Ecclesiastes suggest a new thought, one that appears nowhere else in the book. This new thought provides a perspective from which human life is ultimately meaningful rather than meaningless. For they introduce the idea of a Divine judgment of the works and ways of men: "Let us hear the conclusion of the whole matter: Fear God, and keep his commandments: for this is the whole duty of man. For God shall bring every work into judgment, with every secret thing, whether it be good, or whether it be evil."

THE TOUGH-MINDED SKEPTIC

It is precisely the justice of this Divine judgment that is put to the question in the book of Job. We might say that the Preacher, in his gentle cynicism, casts doubts upon the value of man's life and its activities, while the author of Job, in his more hard-headed, tough-minded skepticism, calls God Himself to account. The problem presented in the book of Job is one facet of the general problem of evil. If God is just, as He is said to be, why do the righteous and the pious suffer, while the wicked and impious flourish? We are all aware that, as John Dewey once said, "While saints are engaged in introspection, burly sinners run the world." [n] How can this be so, in a world watched over by the Providence of a just God? This is the central problem of the book of Job, and the final answer that is given is that we do not know any answer; we can only accept God's goodness and ultimate justice on faith.

The perspective from which this question is raised and illustrated in the book of Job lacks a doctrine of future life. Judgment and retribution are here; but rewards and punishments are consistently presented as belonging to this-worldly life rather than to any other-worldly future state. Now, if it is the case that there is no future life, all rewards and punishments must occur in this world, under the eyes of other men. Conversely, the state in which we find any man must be a true indication of his just desserts. If he is poor and cast down, then it is clear that he must somehow have offended God; if he occupies the seats of the mighty, then it is equally clear that he has earned the Divine favor. This is the popular belief that prevails generally in the Wisdom literature. Prosperity is taken as a sign of virtue and Divine approbation, adversity as a sign of sin and punishment. The book of Job hurls a vigorous challenge at this popular half-truth. The theory of ultimate justice is confronted by the fact of Job's unquestionable righteousness and, in spite of this, his miserable state.

Whatever else comes of the book of Job, then, its incidental result is to show how untenable and inadequate is the naïve popular belief. "Your wise maxims are proverbs of ashes; Your bulwarks turn to bulwarks of clay." Man's happiness or misery in this world bears no direct relation to his religious or moral character. From this point it is but a step to the assertion either of the ultimate arbitrariness and inscrutability of Divine decisions, preserving God's power at the expense of His justice, or of a doctrine of future life, allowing an eternity for the justice of God's decisions to work themselves out and saving both Divine power and Divine justice. The second course is the one that Jewish doctrine in later times has taken; the book of Job takes the alternative path of declaring the judgments of God inscrutable to human understanding.

In this connection we should note that the terms in which retribution is presented in the book of Job make it clear that the book is of a fairly late date, rather than of the supposed time of the story it tells. For, if it belonged to a period earlier than that of the major prophets, and especially of Jeremiah, retribution would have been presented as a group or social affair, rather than as a matter of concern to each individual. In the pre-prophetic view, the innocent suffered with the guilty, as they belonged to the same social group, and responsibility rested with the entire community. Only after the idea of individual responsibility had been proclaimed by the prophets, only after the "new covenant" had been announced by Jeremiah, could it have been asserted that the apparent punishment of any individual must be the consequence of his own guilt, and his apparent rewards the fruit of his own virtue.

THE DRAMATIC VEHICLE

The book of Job is not, however, a wholly new and original composition in its present form. The author who put it into the form in which we have it now used earlier materials, probably quite well known. At its base, scholars have supposed, there is an ancient and popular folk tale, raising the problem of evil. To this has been added a series of dialogues between Job and his friends in which various statements of the prevalent naïve belief in retribution are given by the friends, to each of whom Job offers a rebuttal. There has also been added a dramatic framework, taking place in heaven, providing the reader with a knowledge of what was going on that neither Job nor his would-be consolers had. By the addition of these elements, the final author of the book has been able to penetrate more deeply into the idea of retribution and to criticize the popular theory by means of Job's passionately voiced insistence on his own innocence, rather than by a logical dissection of the inadequacies of theoretical belief to account for observed fact.

Job is shown to the reader, at the beginning of the book, as a very pious and prosperous old patriarch. The scene shifts, then, to heaven, where God and Satan—not the Satan of later Jewish and Christian belief, the Devil, but the earlier Biblical Satan, a messenger and agent of God—talk about Job. God is literally conceived here in terms of a special Providence; He is aware of Job as an individual and He watches over Job. He calls Satan's attention to Job as a man of piety and virtue. Satan, however, raises a very interesting philosophic doubt: truly Job is a pious man, Satan admits, but he questions the motives of Job's piety. If Job is pious for the sake of the rewards of piety, then he is not, properly speaking, to be regarded as a pious man at all, but rather as a man of prudence, a utilitarian. "Doth Job fear God for nought? Hast not thou made a hedge about him, and about his house, and about all that he hath, on every side? Thou has blessed the work of his hands, and his substance is increased in the land." Thus, as the American philosopher Caleb S. Henry once pointed out, in a whimsical essay entitled "Satan as a Moral Philosopher," Satan proved that he really understood that morality is a matter of motive rather than of outward manifestations.

Then Satan suggests that Job be tested. "But put forth thine hand now," he says to God, "and touch all that he hath, and he will renounce thee to thy face." Try Job, Satan suggests, by withdrawing the rewards of his piety, and it will then appear that his devotion to God goes no deeper than his possessions. God agrees to this test, and He places Job's family and his other possessions completely in Satan's hands for the trial by ordeal. It is clear from the context that Job's wife and family were regarded by the author of the book as mere assets, like the property and the animals he owned, rather than as themselves moral persons. There is, however, a charming sidelight on the relationship between Job and his wife; when adversity has struck, she cannot bear to see him suffer and urges him to curse God and die. He scolds her for the suggestion that one should accept the good that comes from God and be unwilling to accept the evil. In this little vignette, Job's wife emerges from the obscurity of impersonality and becomes, for the moment, a real character in the story. The Christian philosopher and theologian Augustine, Bishop of Hippo (354–430), never too kindly disposed to the female sex after his conversion, accused Job's wife, on the basis of her suggestion that he curse God, as "the Devil's assistant." The rabbis, in a far more kindly fashion, interpreted her suggestion as indicative of her love for Job.

The first series of tests succeeded admirably—from God's viewpoint—in proving the devotion and genuine piety of Job. Whatever happened, he preserved his faith in God. Satan, however, proves unwilling to concede the point; he quotes a well-known proverb, "Skin for skin, everything a man has he will give to save his life." Job's final testing can come only if God permits Satan to attack Job at this central point of human vulnerability. "But put forth thine hand now, and touch his bone and his flesh, and he will renounce thee to thy face." To this, once again, God agrees, but limits Satan to power over Job's body, excluding his soul from Satan's jurisdiction. Now Job is made to suffer in his own person, and still he remains steadfast in his faith.

Job held to this faith under the vicissitudes of supernaturally induced trials. He was fated, however, to undergo an even more difficult test of resolution, at the hands of his friends. These friends, Eliphaz, Bildad, and Zophar, come to pay Job a visit of condolence—and now Job curses the day he was born. To these friends the author of the book entrusts the task of speaking for the proverbial wisdom. Eliphaz asserts the prevalent view as the fruit of his own experience: "According as I have seen, they that plow iniquity and sow trouble, reap the same." With this cheerful consolation, he urges Job to consider the troubles that have befallen him as "the chastening of the Almighty" and not despise them. Job is unwilling to accept the implication of the speech of Eliphaz, that he must have sinned in some respect, but he insists upon his innocence. Then Bildad speaks for another phase of common-sense wisdom, asserting that all the good and evil accruing to man is determined and arranged by God with justice. Only to man's finitely limited view does it appear that the innocent are visited by evil; in the larger view of God these apparent evils are known to be good. In reiterating his freedom from any and all wickedness, Job denies that he has any intention of questioning God's justice.

Now Zophar chimes in with the insistence that Job must have sinned, for he is being punished. Zophar's application of the prevalent belief rests upon an interesting extension of its general principle. For, he says, God judges man on the basis of man's individual capacity, rather than of any routinely applied yardstick. Perfect virtue consists in living up to what God knows to be the full measure of the individual's ability. As a result, a man of less capacity may completely satisfy God's demands by doing far less than a man of greater capacity. Men cannot know what degree of perfection God expects of them and cannot, therefore, understand the decrees of Divine justice. Job's reply again challenges the proverbial wisdom: "No doubt but ye are the people, and wisdom shall die with you. But I have understanding as well as you; I am not inferior to you." Thus he sets up his own observations and the consequences he deduces from them as equal in merit to the saws and maxims of tradition. On the basis of his own experience he asserts that "The just, the perfect man is a laughing-stock," whereas "the tents of robbers prosper and they that provoke God are secure."

This pattern of dialogue, of challenge and response, is repeated through two more cycles of speeches by the three friends and Job. The new speeches introduce minor variations in the presentation of the theory of retribution, but no major differences. Then a fourth speaker, Elihu, a younger man than Job or any of his friends, enters the lists. The chief purpose of Elihu's contribution is to reassert, in a new context, the view of the three friends which Job has answered effectively enough to silence them. The subtlety of Elihu's presentation is that he now uses the very replies that Job has made to his friends as proof that Job does, in fact, place himself and his own judgment on a level with God. This would be, if it were true, the sin of pride, what the Greeks called *hybris*, which was the tragic flaw leading to the downfall of the central characters of Greek tragic drama.

JOB'S CHALLENGE

Truly, this is the most fascinating philosophical question to arise out of the book of Job. For there is no possible doubt that Job does fling a challenge at God; and it may be argued that this indicates that he does consider himself on a plane of equality with God. "Surely I would speak to the Almighty, and I desire to reason with God." What presumptuousness on the part of a mortal it is to suggest that his presentation of the case will be so thoroughly reasonable as to convince God. From a perspective steeped in the study of legal philosophy, Dr. Max Laserson [n] spoke of Job's challenge to God as "the contraposition of God and Man as two equal parties in the everlasting trial between rightless might and mightless right." Job, Laserson argues, is a "natural-law radical," who insists upon his day in court even though he knows in advance

45

that the scales of judgment are so weighted against him that he cannot win. It is not equality with God, in any general sense, then, that Job is asserting, but the very special "equality before the law," which might better be rendered as "equivalence" rather than "equality."

At no point does Job actually claim equality with God; his claim is only that he has a right (even over against God) to have his case heard. Job knows that God is not merely the defendant in the case but the judge and jury as well. Job is aware that God's power is beyond challenge; precisely because this is so, he recognizes the danger of injustice. "If it is a test of strength, He is surely superior; but if it is a matter of justice, who can arraign Him?" If God is beyond arraignment, then man's dream of heavenly justice is futile. Furthermore, Job explicitly denies that a Divine answer that avails itself of the fact of superior Divine power is a valid answer to his complaint. "Will he plead against me with his great power? Withdraw thine hand far from me: and let not thy dread make me afraid. Then call thou and I will answer: or let me speak, and answer thou me." Job's one demand is that the question of the justice or injustice of the punishment meted out to him be fairly judged, and on this point he is confident of favorable decision. "I have ordered my cause; I know that I shall be justified."

Job's radical and well-nigh blasphemous demand produces an effect, although it may be argued that God does violate the stipulation set forth by Job in asserting His absolute Eminence. God answers Job "out of the whirlwind." This is, in itself, another of the ways in which the Bible avoids claiming that at any time was God actually seen by man; it must also be read, however, as an indirect assertion of God's power, even over the mightiest and most destructive forces of nature. Job, the Voice declares, has been criticizing God's moral government of the world, God's theodicy. Who is he to question God's actions? What does he know of the creation? Was he there to see how the monsters of land and sea were brought to the birth? Does he have the wisdom of God? Job is forced to the admission that he cannot answer the Lord's questions. God returns to the attack: if Job is lacking in wisdom comparable with God's, does he have power equal to God's? If so, let him give a display of his power. Under this barrage of Divine thrust and question, Job confesses that the mysteries of Divine Providence are, indeed, beyond his comprehension, and he says that now he realizes more fully the omnipotence of God.

In an Epilogue, of the nature of a happy ending, God rebukes the three friends for having presented an inadequate account of His Providence, and says that Job was more nearly correct than they. He restores Job to his former prosperity, and He yields to Job's prayers by extending prosperity to the friends, mistaken though they were. Job's submission establishes the orthodoxy of the book, but it must still be acknowledged that Job's challenge has been evaded, not met face to face. God has not justified His ways; He has, rather, denied Job's right to question them. The basic question remains today, as it has through history, whether Absolute Justice and Absolute Power can coexist, even in God.

SOME MINOR EXAMPLES
OF GREEK INFLUENCE

There were writings of the last few pre-Christian centuries that, for one reason or another, were left out when the canon of the Bible was fixed. Included among these so-called "apocryphal" books were several that, in part, indicate the spread of Greek philosophic thought among the Jews. In the Fourth Book of Maccabees, for example, a work certainly composed before the fall of Jerusalem in A.D. 70, there is a remarkable passage in the form of a discourse, or possibly sermon, on the relation of reason and passion. This was a favorite subject for discussion among philosophers of the Stoic school. The approach of the anonymous author of this discourse is philosophic: "We must determine," he begins, "what reason is, and what emotion is, how many types of emotion there are, and whether reason holds the mastery over all of them." He continues with a definition of reason as the intellect choosing correctly the life of wisdom, a definition that would not have seemed strange in the least to a philosophically trained Greek. Next, however, he equates this wisdom with learning in the Jewish Law, the Bible, bringing together the two strains. This he illustrates by suggesting the virtues of prudence, justice, courage, and temperance—again a very Greek list—as those inculcated by the study of the Law. Then he adduces various Biblical stories to show how it is the aim of the Bible to train men in the practice of these virtues. In the end, the homily rises to a strangely passionate conclusion: "The temperate intellect is able to vanquish the compulsion of the emotions and quench their flaming goads, to surmount the sufferings of the body, however extreme, and through the nobility of reason to scorn and reject the tyranny of the emotions."

Another similar attempt to span the gap between Greek philosophy and the wisdom of the Bible is to be found in the Wisdom of Solomon. In this work, an oration on the superiority of Hebrew wisdom, especially as it is found in the books of Proverbs, Ecclesiastes, and Job, over various pagan beliefs is put into the mouth of King Solomon. Of particular interest is the way in which the author of this work—needless to say, not King Solomon—uses the history of the people of Israel, as that history is narrated in the Bible, as the strongest evidence that the Jewish religion is superior to the religions of the pagan world. The "Wisdom" of this little work reveals how close the Jewish thinkers of this period came to a dual divinity, having God as its male aspect and "Wisdom" as its female aspect. "With thee is wisdom, which knoweth thy works, and was present when thou wast making the world. . . . Send her forth out of the holy heavens, and from the throne of

48

thy glory bid her come, that being present with me she may toil with me."

PHILO OF ALEXANDRIA

There was, certainly, every justification for such attempts to bring about a synthesis of Greek speculation and Biblical religion. With the popular religion of the Greeks, of course, even a poorly trained Jew would have nothing to do. The popular religion was explicitly polytheistic and the many gods it celebrated were obviously forces of nature. But Greek philosophic thought had early reached out to a much purer and more abstract conception of the unity of God, and it was to this higher form of Greek thought that the Jews turned when they tried to interpret their religion to the Greek-speaking world. The need to provide such an interpretation was particularly acute in the city of Alexandria, the intellectual and cultural capital of the Hellenistic world. Here in Alexandria the Jews were not in confrontation with a lesser culture but with one as profound, in its own way, as their own. The leaders and spokesmen for the Jewish community of Alexandria— one of the very large Jewish groups outside Palestine—could not merely dismiss the challenge to their religion. They had to defend Judaism both in its own terms and in terms of the very best that the Greek world had produced.

It was this challenge to which Philo of Alexandria (about 20 B.C. to about A.D. 50) dedicated his life work. There is no doubt that others were also devoted to the same pursuit; we might even speak of a "school" of philosophic interpreters of Judaism. Only fragments survive, however, that can be attributed to other members of this school, whereas many volumes of the works of Philo have been preserved. Philo was thoroughly familiar with the works of earlier Greek philosophers, from the predecessors of Plato through the centuries to his own time. He refers explicitly to previous schools of philosophic thought and to many individual authors. His chief debt was, however, to Plato and Plato's successors in the Academic school.

Except for some short pieces that are usually assigned to his early years, Philo did not write his work in the form of systematic treatises. Instead, he followed a form current in the Hebrew literature of interpretation of his age and later ages, the form of the *midrash* (exposition), a verse-by-verse explanation of the Scriptures. We may say, therefore, that the works of Philo constitute a running philosophic commentary on the text of the Bible. This enormous enterprise was undertaken in order to show the consistency of the philosophic religion of Judaism with the ideas of the Greek philosophers. But even a superficial reading of the Bible shows that, along with much that is profound and elevated, and that may be made the direct object of philosophic study, there is much that is trivial and even objectionable. There are passages, too, that were regarded by the Greek writers as ludicrous; Philo reports that there were some who laughed at the Biblical story that God made clothes of skins for Adam and Eve. In order to overcome the effect of such passages in detracting from the full impact of the Bible as a philosophic document of a high order, Philo followed other Judeo-Greek writers by interpreting such texts allegorically.

The use of the allegorical method was especially important in the explanation of passages in which the Bible speaks of God in too human terms (anthropomorphically). Greek philosophic culture, especially as it had developed in the school descended from Plato, had achieved a very abstract conception of God, comparable to the highest reaches of Biblical thought in the greater prophets. Minds accustomed to this exalted God-idea, but without any sentimental or historical connection with the Jewish people, might well scorn the tribal God with whom they made acquaintance at the very gates of the Scriptures, in the book of Genesis. The use of allegory to soften the impact of anthropomorphism was essential to Philo's success as an interpreter of Judaism.

Moreover, much of the earlier part of the Bible expresses a narrow and parochial sense of the relation of God to the Jewish people. Later, again in the greater prophets, this particularism decreases and God is conceived as the God of all men, the universal God and Father, rather than the special protector of a small and politically insignificant nation. Here is another context in which the use of allegory to make the Biblical concepts acceptable to advanced minds among the Hellenistic Greeks was essential. Finally, Greek science, developed from the pre-Socratic philosophers through to the outstanding mathematicians and astronomers of the Alexandrian schools, had worked out a generally accepted theory of the heavens and earth. The outlines of this theory were common to all the scientists of Philo's time, although they might dispute many details. The Bible presents a theory of the universe which is no more in accord with Greek cosmology and astronomy than it is with that of the twentieth century. Philo had to allegorize the Bible cosmology in order to gain a hearing in his sophisticated Alexandrian environment.

Before entering into the discussion of any specific aspects of Philo's thought, we should emphasize the fact that, according to his lights and those of his time and place, he was a pious and devoted Jew. He made, at the very outset, an assumption that is not part of his philosophy but that lies at its root—namely, that the Five Books of Moses contain the absolute truth, as revealed by God. We may take note of the fact that this truth did not lie on the literal surface of the Biblical books; Philo was neither a literalist nor a fundamentalist. But he was firmly convinced that anything that was true could be discovered in the Bible by allegorizing, and, conversely, that anything that could be read into the Bible by allegorical methods was true.

Thus Philo did not come to philosophy with, so to speak, a

completely open mind. Philosophy was not the basic study to which all other belief must conform, but was secondary to the revealed truth of Scripture. There were eight principles that Philo thought to be essential to the religion presented in the Bible. These were the roots out of which his philosophic interpretations had to grow. Fortunately, most of the basic principles had been matters discussed in the Greek philosophic schools, so that Philo's task was one of defending a particular version of the principle in question against alternative views, not of creating a philosophic justification out of whole cloth.

For example, the first principle of Scriptural religion is the existence of God. Evidently, in accepting the existence of God, Philo had to deny the views of atheists, who rejected the idea of God's existence. He also attacked the school of Skeptics, whose general principle of asserting nothing as certain led to their reserving judgment concerning God's existence. In addition, there was, in the tradition of Greek philosophy, a view tending toward an extreme humanism, in which the qualities and powers that, to Philo, properly belong to God were attributed to the human mind. This view, too, came in for special attack in several of Philo's works. One of the fascinating allegoric and symbolic expositions given by Philo ties his rejection of this humanistic philosophy to the Biblical verse (Deuteronomy xxiii, 4) "An Ammonite or a Moabite shall not enter into the assembly of the Lord."

Besides the first principle of the existence of God, Philo found in Scripture justification for belief in God's unity, Providence, and His creation of the world; the unity of the world; and the existence of incorporeal ideas. For these six principles, Philo could find support in Greek philosophy without difficulty. He also held to two further principles, that the Law is revealed, and that it is eternal, for which no philosophic support was available in the Greek tradition. Here he was compelled to make his own way, though some of his arguments are similar to those used within the Rabbinic tradition of Biblical interpretation.

PROVING THE EXISTENCE OF GOD

Despite his acceptance of the existence of God as a first principle and unshakable assumption, Philo thought that the truth of this assumption could be proved with comparative ease, even though he acknowledged that it was easier to construct an argument to prove the case to oneself than to flesh it out with verbal formulations that would be convincing to others. The first of the proofs that Philo presented was of a Platonic cast: Plato had argued that anything that comes into being must have been brought into being by something else; as the world has come into being, it must have a cause that existed before the world and could bring it into being. Philo adopted this argument as his own and found in the book of Isaiah a passage that could be stretched into an allegorical argument to show that the cause had to be external to the effect and therefore that there must be an independent creator. For, in the book of Isaiah (lxvi, 1), the prophet reports God's saying, "The heaven is my throne and the earth is my footstool." Now, both a throne and a footstool are products for which there must be a maker, effects for which there must be a cause. Since the cause must be distinct from its effect, God must be distinct from the heavens and the earth.

Another of the philosophic proofs that Philo adapted to his own use was drawn from the work of Aristotle. Aristotle had considered the possibility that the world might be eternal, and that the Platonic argument, based upon its having come into being, would, as a result, not be adequate. This possibility Philo categorically rejected, on a Scriptural basis, but the second part of the Aristotelian argument, basing a proof of the existence of God on the need for an original agent, or Unmoved Mover, to account for the observed motions of the universe, Philo was ready to accept. Aristotle had thought that this argument proved only

53

that God existed as the cause of motion; Philo declared that an Unmoved Mover must also be the creative cause of that which He moved.

Philo also adopted, probably from Stoic sources, an argument that is found in many other Greek sources. This argument has become famous under the name of the argument from design. When we look at the world around us, we see many evidences of uniformity and order in the natural processes that are going on. But when we see similar examples of order in the products of human activity, we reason from the orderliness to one who established the order. By analogy, the order of the universe proves that there is an Orderer, God. "Should a man see a house carefully constructed . . . he will get the idea of the artificer, for he will be of the opinion that the house never reached that completeness without the skill of the craftsman; and in like manner in the case of . . . every smaller or greater construction." Professor Harry A. Wolfson [n] has noted the use of this argument in the Rabbinic literature:

> It is like unto a man who was traveling from place to place when he saw a mansion all lighted up. He wondered: Is it conceivable that the mansion is without a caretaker? Thereupon the master of the mansion looked out and said to him: I am the master of the mansion and its caretaker. Similarly, because Abraham our father wondered: Is it conceivable that the world is without a caretaker? Thereupon the Holy One, blessed be He, looked at him and said: I am the master of the universe and its caretaker.

There is a fourth argument that is used by Philo to prove the existence of God and that is generally similar to an argument found in philosophers of the Stoic school. In this argument, instead of looking out at the world and finding there the analogies upon which proof of God is based, men are urged to look within, to their own natures. This introspection will reveal that they have a mind which is within their body, but distinct and separate and of a different character from their body. Again applying the method of analogy, men will then see that in relation to the universe, yet distinct from it, there must be a Universal Mind, which is God, who governs the universe even as the mind of man governs the body. God is, of course, not "within" the universe in the same sense as the mind of man is within his body. Even the human mind may, in certain situations, such as those of dreams and of inspiration, exist apart from the body; what the human mind does at these unusual and rare moments, God does always. God is always outside the world, although His powers are exerted in the world.

All of these proofs, however different they may be in detail, are of the same order, since all depend upon reasoning by analogy or reasoning from an effect to its cause. There is a fifth proof of which Philo writes which is of a different order completely, since it does not rely upon discursive reasoning but upon immediate intuition or direct knowledge. This is the kind of immediacy that is gained by revelation or in prophetic inspiration. Once again, as has been pointed out by many students of Philo, one can see in the account of the possibility of a direct knowledge of spiritual reality by the mind a distinction that Plato had made between true knowledge and the information that we gain from experience. The use that Philo makes of this fifth proof is to glorify Moses and the prophets as vessels of revelation. Even here, however, we must remember that Philo claims for Moses only a clear vision and direct knowledge of the *existence* of God. What God is, the *essence* of God, is forever unknowable.

THE THEORY OF INTERMEDIATION

Although men cannot know the essence of God, nevertheless they are constantly aware of events and objects in the world around, indeed, of that world itself, as the products of Divine activity. Both philosophically and theologically, Philo's thought moves in two directions, which are never completely reconciled. On the one hand, especially insofar as his philosophy is so deeply influenced by that of Plato, he pushes the God-idea toward an ever more abstract, remote, idealized concept. Plato had exalted the Ideas, and of all these he had most stressed the Idea of the Good as above all the rest. Philo goes farther; above even the Idea of the Good is God: "Superior to virtue, superior to knowledge, superior to the good itself and the beautiful itself." On the other hand, at the same time as Philo is elevating the concept of God thus far above the Ideas, which were themselves so far above the things of sense which we experience in our day-to-day activities, he is eager to preserve the Biblical view of God as a force immanent in the daily lives of men. The God-idea must be exalted to satisfy the demands of philosophical theology, yet God must be thought near at hand to satisfy the religious needs of His servants.

To reconcile these two demands is one of the still unsolved riddles of religious thought; the distinction lies behind the oft-repeated references to the difference between the "God of the philosophers" and the "living God." The way in which Philo tries to bring the two together depends upon his transformation of the Platonic Realm of Ideas into a personal being, the Logos, which represents symbolically God's activity in the world, God's immanence, and can be separated in thought though not in actuality from God Himself. First, the Ideas of Plato have a double aspect given them by Philo. Under either aspect, the Ideas are not independent existences (as they are in Plato), but rather are Divine products. When Philo refers to the Ideas as patterns, he thinks of them as the thoughts of God, existing in the mind of God before the creation of the world; indeed, they had to be combined into an idea of the world before the world could be created: "We must suppose that, when He intended to found one great city, He conceived beforehand the models of its parts, and that out of these He constituted an intelligible world."

But there is also a second way in which Philo discusses the Ideas; in addition to being patterns, they are also powers, or causes. It is the Ideas under this aspect, as powers active in the universe, that account for the actual physical creation we see around us. These Ideas are powers of God; they do not have efficacy through their own nature. Even their activity is not of themselves, but is derived from God: "To act is the property of God, and this we must not ascribe to any created being; the property of the created is to be acted upon." Thus any active force in the Ideas is merely a force bestowed upon them by God to enable them to do His will. This course of reasoning allows Philo to retain the belief that everything that is is dependent upon God, while at the same time preserving the abstract and elevated eminence of God, unsullied by direct contact with material things.

We have seen above that when Philo speaks of the patterns as an organized whole, he uses the expression "intelligible world" to refer to their organization. The corresponding term used by him to refer to the powers as an organized whole is "Logos," the Greek word translatable as "word" or "speech" or "mind" or "wisdom." In the main, Philo uses the term as the equivalent of "mind." The collectivity of Ideas is the Logos, or Mind of God. But we have also seen that the Ideas, conceived as powers, do not remain merely as the content of the Divine Mind. They are invested with an agency in the external world. They assume a sort of independence in their activity. This activity is not, however, haphazard and disorganized. The Ideas as agents of God in the world constitute a sort of task force, each with its specific duties and its specific relations to every other. The universe, which was a pattern of Ideas in the Divine Mind, is projected forth and becomes a created universe; but it retains the organization and pattern that it had prior to its actual creation. Philo applies the term

"Logos" to this organized existence outside the Divine Mind. First Logos is the Mind of God; then it becomes mind embodied in the created universe.

One of the few preserved fragments attributed to the Judeo-Greek philosopher Aristobulus, about a century earlier than Philo, suggests that he, too, was in search of the same sort of differentiation between God as eminent and God as active in the world. For Aristobulus is reported to have said, "We must understand the Word of God not as a spoken word, but as the establishment of actual things, seeing that we find throughout the Law that Moses has declared the whole creation to be words of God." Philo continued to give his concept of the Logos the same emphasis; Logos is speech as well as mind. "God speaks not words but things," said Philo in his treatise on the Ten Commandments. In his discussion of the Creation of the World, Philo noted that, "God, even as He spake, at the same moment created."

But Logos may have still another meaning: wisdom. Philo was thoroughly familiar with the Scriptures and knew of the many passages in the later Biblical writings in which Wisdom is personified and raised to a rank only below God. He was probably familiar, too, with such very late, non-canonic works as the apocryphal Wisdom of Jesus Son of Sirach (often called Ecclesiasticus), in which Wisdom is said to be identical with the revealed Scripture. Besides all this, Wisdom was frequently personified in Greek writings and there too it was used as a synonym for mind. Treating Logos as Wisdom, in all these various senses, gave Philo an additional avenue of approach to the Greek mind in his undertaking to convince it of the philosophical character of the Jewish religion.

There is a danger in Philo's treatment of the Logos as intermediate between God and the world, between God's mind and our minds, between God's Wisdom and human wisdom. The danger is that what starts out as an aid to the conception of God as both eminent and immanent, and as, so to speak, a ladder whereby the mind of man may move from a consideration of the things of the world he perceives to an intuition of Divine reality, may become so separated from God in its independence as to be a second—even if secondary—divinity. The greater the emphasis that is placed upon the immateriality and the holiness of God, the greater is the danger that the Logos, God's intermediary instrument, will be taken as the actual creator. Philo himself avoided this trap by retaining his belief that it was within the ability of God to act directly upon the material being of the created world, a belief founded upon passages in Scripture such as the description of the bringing of the plagues upon the Egyptians. Later writers, who lacked Philo's complete faith in the truth of the Bible, transformed the Philonic Logos into an independent divinity, and thus distorted the limited Philonic theory of intermediation.

ETHICAL IDEAS IN PHILO

In the ethical ideas of Philo the attempt to bring together the insights of Greek philosophy and Hebrew Scripture produces a distinctive and interesting product. For the most part, the terms Philo uses are borrowed from the Greeks, but the content introduced into these terms is dominated by the ideas derived from the Bible. Like the philosophers, and especially like Plato, Aristotle, and the Stoics, Philo expresses the goal of the ethical life in terms of striving for happiness. Other expectations, such as gain, glory, and pleasure, are mentioned by Philo as goods for which men hope. Happiness is, however, the highest good and the most fitting object of desire and hope for the philosophically oriented person. "It incites the devotees of virtue to study philosophy," says Philo, "believing that thus they will be able to discern the nature of all that exists and to do what is agreeable to the perfecting of the best forms of life."

Again in agreement with the Greek philosophers, Philo regards happiness as the product of two kinds of virtue, an intellectual virtue, which he calls wisdom, and a moral virtue, which he calls prudence. Whereas wisdom or intellectual virtue can be taught, prudence or moral virtue is the fruit, not of teaching, but of habitual practice. The state, or the representatives of the state, can train the young in moral habits, but cannot teach these habits, since they have no intellectual content. The role of law is to serve as the guide to proper habits of conduct; the legislator is an important part of the system of moral training. The ideal should be the making of laws that are most closely in accordance with nature and practical reason. Here Philo's distinctive emphasis, resulting from his Scriptural basis, appears. For Philo argues that laws which are in accordance with nature cannot be devised by men who follow the dictates of their own reason.

Laws that are in accordance with nature must come from that One Who knows what nature truly is, because He is the Creator of nature. Only the revealed law of God can be the kind of law for which the philosophers have been seeking. Such a law would be, like nature itself, changeless, because it is the product of a Divine legislator to whose nature all change is foreign. The Bible, then, the Law of Moses, is for Philo the true pattern and model of a law that is in accordance with nature. Prior to the Sinaitic revelation, some of the Patriarchs had gained an insight into the law of nature. Noah and Abraham are noted especially for their following of natural law. They "gladly accepted conformity with nature, holding that nature itself was, as indeed it is, the most venerable statutes." There is a shift here in the meaning given to the term "nature." For here what is meant is not that man follows the leadings of his own impulsive nature, but rather that there is a law, a body of statutes, incorporated in the world itself. This, it may be recalled, is one of the characteristics of the Logos. Philo says, then, that the Patriarchs followed the Logos which they discovered in nature. Later men, more fortunate than the Patriarchs, have a superior law, the Law of Moses, as their guide.

Starting from this point, Philo next attempts to demonstrate that the Biblical commandments are designed to instill in men the very same virtues that the Greek philosophers had seen as the basis of the ideal law. He argues that the Ten Commandments, divided into duties to God and duties to other men, constitute the general heads under which all other commandments and prohibitions included in the Bible can be properly classified. The Ten Commandments set forth the universal virtues; all other positive and negative commandments he presents as "special laws." In classifying the virtues, Philo combines Greek and Hebrew ideas in a most detailed and complete fashion. Basically his classification is Greek; it divides virtues into the intellectual, the moral, and the practical. The intellectual virtues are wisdom, piety, godliness, holiness, and faith. The first four of these had been spoken of by the Greek philosophers, but faith, especially as the term is used by Philo to mean belief in truths of revelation as opposed to truths discoverable by reason, is not at all characteristic of the rational ethical approach of these philosophers. We must remember, too, that Philo finds Scriptural passages to serve as warrant for those virtues that are common to his work and that of the philosophers as well as for faith.

The moral virtues are, again, those that the Greek philosophers had stressed. The four chief virtues are prudence, courage, temperance, and justice; lesser virtues are philanthropy, fellowship, peace, equality, grace, mercy, and nobility. It is in the interpretation of these virtues that Philo's Jewish background comes to the fore. This is especially the case with regard to philanthropy, which does not appear as a major virtue in the Greek writers, but is treated by Philo as one of the leading virtues. In the Jewish tradition, philanthropy is regarded very highly; observing the virtue of philanthropy is said by the Rabbinic literature to counterbalance failure to observe all the other commandments. In addition to his supplementing the list of Greek virtues by including philanthropy, Philo also lists prayer, repentance, and study as virtues. Here the influence of the Hebrew tradition is notably clear, and particularly, we should add, the influence of the Pharisaic branch of the Hebrew tradition. For it was among the Pharisees and their later descendants, the Rabbis, that the emphasis was placed upon prayer, rather than upon sacrifice, and upon study of the Law as a guide to and constant reminder of what ought to be done.

Philo's effort to justify Judaism philosophically in terms of the philosophies current in his time and place typifies an attempt that we shall find repeated often in the course of our story. The nineteenth-century scholar James Darmesteter once wrote, "The most remarkable feature of Judaism is that without a philosophical system it had reached a philosophical conclusion about the government of the world and the nature of God." Whenever the Jews found themselves in an environing society that had a philosophical system (whether or not that society had reached philosophical conclusions), there were those who tried to expound their philosophical religion in terms of the alien system. Philo is the first major thinker to have made the trial. Professor Wolfson believes that Philo did his work so well that all later religious philosophy in Judaism, Christianity, and Islam until the seventeenth century was an extended postscript to Philo; not every student of the man or the period would offer so favorable a judgment. All must agree, however, even on the basis of the incomplete summary here, that his was a truly remarkable achievement of synthesis and interpretation.

CHAPTER THREE

The World of Rabbinic Thought

PHILO'S SYNTHESIS of Greek and Jewish elements in his philosophic interpretations of the Bible represents one of a number of alternative possible ways of meeting a recurrent problem in the development of any long-standing tradition. Life and its conditions change and move for any cultural group. A tradition, especially a tradition written down in sacred and unalterable documents, regarded as the very word of God, is fixed and static. If provisions of some sort are not made for the continuous reinterpretation of the tradition in terms suited to the new conditions of life, the tradition itself is bound to become a dead letter and those who adhere strictly to its literal words to become a fossil people. Philonic allegorizing kept the Jewish tradition alive in an environment that was foreign to the surroundings in which the tradition had developed.

We do not know how early the process of writing down the Hebrew traditions began. Certainly it was under way by the year 621 B.C., when the Deuteronomic document was discovered in the Temple at Jerusalem. By the time of the return from the Babylonian Exile, the traditional writings had the force of a code of laws for the government of the Jewish people; it is significant to note that Ezra is linked with Moses as lawgiver to the Jewish people. The tradition was quite early, then, well on the way to being fixed and unalterable. Soon after the return from the Exile, we hear of a new class of men, the Scribes, whose distinctive function in Jewish society was to serve as experts in the Law. In effect, we may say, they were lawyers and judges, rather than legislators, but we may assume that, as in every legal system, it was the lawyers and judges who determined the meaning of the law, who created the enforced law out of the general language of the legislator. The role of the Scribes was dual: at one and the same time they were the preservers of the tradition and its modifiers. Yet these two roles were really one, for it is beyond question that the way to preserve a tradition is by modifying it. But it is still worth while to distinguish the two roles, for they lead to two attitudes in interpretation. One attitude places the preservative or conservative function first, and introduces modifications only when they are absolutely necessary in order to preserve. The other reverses the order of importance; adaptation of the tradition is its major concern, and, secondarily, it seeks justification in the tradition itself for the modifications that are introduced.

We do not know enough about the historical development of Jewish law to detect these two strains in the period of Scribes. We are told of the "Men of the Great Synagogue," who were probably those who followed Ezra in the process of developing the religion of Judaism out of the materials of the tradition. They are supposed to have had as their maxim the words "Be deliberate in judging, and raise up many disciples, and make a hedge for the Torah." The first of these principles is a good rule for judges under any legal system; the second suggests that the Men of the Great Synagogue regarded themselves as a teaching group as well as a court of law; the third has been variously interpreted, but behind all the interpretations there lies the determination, never abandoned, to preserve the Bible for future generations.

At some point about 200 B.C. the account of the transmission of the heritage of the Scribes speaks of the leaders in pairs. Possibly this is the point at which the two attitudes toward interpretation begin to be evident, though our knowledge of the teachers linked together in pairs is still too inadequate to enable this judgment to be made with certainty. It is not until the fifth (and last) pair, Hillel and Shammai, dating about 30 B.C., that the two schools of interpretation become clearly distinguishable. Indeed, from this time on, the tradition itself speaks of the School of Hillel and the School of Shammai. These men and their followers engaged in constant controversy; precisely what the nature of the controversy was, we do not know. It seems likely that the School of Hillel followed rather loose principles of interpretation, while that of Shammai was far stricter in its dealings with the tradition. At all events, we do know that the School of Hillel became dominant among the rabbinical interpreters, down to the year A.D. 415.

The rabbis—the word means "teacher"—were the successors of the Scribes. They continued the pattern of detailed study of the Written Law and also of the growing body of precedents and interpretations making up what was called the "unwritten law." The rabbis served primarily as legal experts; but since the Law had replaced the Temple as the center of Jewish religious concern after A.D. 70, they must be regarded as religious experts, too. Unlike Philo, the rabbis developed their interpretation of Judaism in the midst of the Jewish community, first of the homeland, in Palestine, and then of the largest of the communities outside the homeland, the Jewish community of Babylonia. They were not so much striving for a synthesis of Jewish ideas with those of an alien system of thought as to make explicit the contemporary meanings of the Jewish system itself. They were working from within. They were trying to preserve the Law as a "well of *living* waters" by discovering ways in which the words of the Law could be applied to the situations met by generations of Jews in attempting to face the day-to-day problems of living.

LOGIC AND RABBINIC INTERPRETATION

Since the process of interpretation was carried on by the rabbis for so many hundreds of years, it was inevitable that there should be a formulation of accepted techniques of interpretation. Without these, the process would have ended in chaos, for each individual and each school could have used private and highly individualized methods of treating the sacred text. If the word "logic" is used very loosely, we may say that the rabbis developed a logic for dealing with the text of the Bible. Some writers have gone farther, and have exercised great ingenuity in showing that rabbinic interpretations were, in a strict sense, based on the canons of Greek logical theory. The success of these critics in demonstrating this point is more of a tribute to their cleverness than to the logic of rabbinic interpretation. For essentially, as Max Kadushin has pointed out, the connections established in rabbinic thought were organic and psychological, rather than logical. If any connection is to be established, it is between rabbinic modes of interpretation and Greek rhetoric, not Greek logic.

Hillel, of whom we have spoken above, compiled, from previous usage, the earliest list that we have of acceptable procedures of textual interpretation. He furnished seven rules that are the basis of later rabbinic interpretation down to the twentieth century. The first of Hillel's rules is that an inference may be drawn from the less important to the more important, or the reverse. For example, if a type of activity is forbidden on a less important holiday, but nothing is said of its being forbidden on a more important holiday, such as the Day of Atonement, it is possible to draw the inference that this type of activity is prohibited on the Day of Atonement, too. On the other hand, if some activity is permitted on so important a day as the Sabbath, then we may infer that it is also permitted on a lesser holiday, even though the

Scriptural text does not say so explicitly. This is known as the rule of Lightness and Heaviness (*Kal Va-homer*).

A second permissible type of inference, according to the Seven Rules of Hillel, is by analogy. When, in two passages in the Bible, there are found words of identical meaning, the laws given in the two passages, however different they may otherwise be, are subject to the same limitations and applications. Thus the same word, meaning "in its season," is found in connection with two offerings, the Perpetual Offering and the Passover Offering (Numbers ix, 2 and xxviii, 2). In connection with the Perpetual Offering, it is specifically stated in the text that this obligation sets aside the command to rest on the Sabbath; this is not said with respect to the Passover Offering. Because "in its season" occurs in both passages, however, Hillel inferred, by analogy, that the obligation to sacrifice the Passover Offering also sets aside the command to rest on the Sabbath. This type of analogical inference is called "Similar Regulation" (*Gezerah Shawah*).

Third, Hillel allowed a type of inference in which a specific regulation found in one principal Biblical passage is held to be applicable to a whole group of passages that are united by virtue of some part of their content. Thus the expression "if there be found" (Deut. xvii, 2) is followed (Deut. xvii, 6) by the expression "at the mouth of two witnesses, or three witnesses." The requirement of two or more witnesses is extended to all passages in which the expression "if there be found" is present, even where the explicit text does not mention anything about the acceptable number of witnesses (e.g., Deut. xviii, 10; xxii, 22; xxiv, 7). Thus, a protection for the accused that occurs once is generalized by this constructive inference. This type of inference is called "Building a Family on the Basis of One Passage" (*Binyan ab mikkathub ehad*). A fourth rule is closely similar, save that the "family" is built on two passages rather than one: "Building a Family on the Basis of Two Passages" (*Binyan ab mishshene Kethubim*).

Hillel's fifth rule concerned legitimate deductions from the order in which particular and general terms were arranged. It is called "The General and Particular, and the Particular and General." If the general term, for example, "all living creatures" comes first in the text and is followed by an enumeration of particular terms, such as "cattle, sheep and goats," the particular terms are to be considered as a restrictive list of illustrations, and the law in the text is to apply only to them. If, however, the particular terms come first and the general term follows them, the law in the text is to be applied generally and to extend beyond these particular illustrations. The sixth rule, exposition by means of analogy with a similar passage, is regarded by many scholars as of doubtful authenticity; to make up the number of seven, they treat the fifth rule as two separate rules. The seventh rule is that of legitimate deduction from the total context.

Ishmael Ben Elisha (probably about A.D. 60 to about A.D. 130) found it necessary, in his generation, to reformulate the rules of interpretation. Between Hillel's time and Ishmael's, there had apparently developed an exaggerated and strained method of interpretation, relying too much upon the extension of meaning of single words and even of single letters. Ishmael tried to restrain this tendency by placing his emphasis upon more direct and simple types of textual interpretation, based upon the assumption that the Biblical text was written in ordinary language. In Ishmael's name there has come down to us the aphorism, "The Torah speaks the language of the children of men," expressing this assumption as a basis for simplified interpretations. The correct principles of legal interpretation, in Ishmael's version, numbered thirteen; only one of them is completely new, however. All the rest are included in Hillel's seven rules. Indeed, eight of them are a detailed expansion of Hillel's one rule concerning the general and the particular. The new principle that Ishmael introduced is that when two Scriptural verses contradict one another, their contradiction is to be resolved by adducing a third Scriptural verse. Ishmael's statement of the rules of legitimate inference

have had so great an authority among the Jews that they are included in the daily morning prayers.

For legal purposes, the rules according to Ishmael have continued to supply rabbinic interpreters with the norms, even
though a few other techniques of interpretation have been used,
from time to time, by one authority or another. But legal interpretation is only one of the ways of using the Biblical text. It is also
used for the stimulation of appropriate religious attitudes, to in-
spire men and women to virtue and devotion, and to exhort to
proper behavior. It is a source for sermons as well as for legal
treatises and decisions. For non-legal purposes, a far more extended list of proper modes of interpretation was developed within
the Jewish tradition. The most highly regarded list of these rules
was transmitted in the name of Eliezer ben Jose Ha-gelili (about
A.D. 130 to A.D. 180). There are thirty-two rules given in Eliezer's
list, and these are much more obviously rhetorical than those in
the legal listings of Hillel and Ishmael.

RABBINIC IDEAS OF GOD

The techniques of inference of which we have been talking
were not used to develop a theology. In many respects, Judaism
is the least theological of religions, if by theology we mean a
systematic and consistent body of doctrines. There was, inevitably,
a system of law drawn from the Bible, and, as we have said, legal
interpretation was the chief function of the rabbis. What the
rabbis said about God, however, although it was equally founded
on the interpretation of Biblical verses, lacked the general authority of their legal comments. Rabbinic Judaism prescribed a great
many details of conduct, but allowed considerable latitude of
thought. Each man was expected to read and study the Bible for
himself; some more learned men were widely respected for their
Scriptural knowledge, and what they said in application of Bibli-

cal passages to thoughts about God and man was carefully listened to and remembered by their hearers. But their remarks did not constitute a standard of orthodoxy—and, of course, where there is no defined orthodoxy, there can be no heresy.

The rabbis did not draw their ideas of God indiscriminately out of the Bible. It is evident to any reader of that sacred Book that it combines conceptions of incredible simplicity and primitiveness with ideas of a most exalted kind. The rabbis unconsciously made a selection out of the variety of possible passages and, to the extent that they used other texts at all, did so by assimilating the God-idea of these texts to the higher idea which stirred their own religious imaginations. Max Kadushin [n] is probably right in suggesting that the basic emphasis of the rabbis was on the experience of God in daily life, or, as he calls it, "normal mysticism," rather than on intellectual formulations. Once an idea of God had emerged out of personal experience within the social group, the Bible could be searched for texts that could be interpreted to suit this experience of God. Instead of the ancient Book's being the source of later ideas, it seems to have been the case that the later ideas were the source of meanings that were read back into the ancient Book. The rabbis certainly did not think in terms of the evolution of the idea of God, but when they read the words of the Bible, they did so in the light of their own more highly developed ideas.

There is no attempt in the vast body of rabbinic literature to prove that God exists. Philo had to look for such proofs because he was confronted by an intellectual atmosphere in which philosophers had called God's existence into question. The rabbis knew of men who doubted God's Providence (as Job did) and they thought of the atheist as one who did not really doubt God's existence but only His providential concern for men. They had the Bible as their fundamental truth, and God is not only the Revealer of the Bible but also He Who is revealed therein. Philosophers might say that to read the Bible is to learn how to discover God through His effects. The rabbis, never questioning

God's existence, would have said that the Bible teaches men how to discover God's effects.

Similarly, Philo found it necessary to argue metaphysically that God is one, and he identified the unity of God with uncomposed, simple Being such as the Greek philosophers had discussed. The rabbis had nothing of this sort in mind when they talked of the oneness of God; all they meant was that there is one God, and that He is the Creator and Governor of the universe. In asserting God's unity, they were denying polytheism, not deducing metaphysical consequences from the nature of the universe. Moreover, the rabbinic insistence on the Divine unity was closely tied to the belief in the moral government of the world. The attribute of righteousness is stressed by the rabbis as the supreme force in the world. To be directed toward one moral goal requires that there be one moral will behind all events that take place. That one moral will is the will of the one God.

George Foot Moore[n] regards the rabbinic emphasis on the Divine unity as chiefly directed against the "currency of the belief that there are 'two authorities'" or two powers in the universe. This might be, for example, a dualism of the Persian type, making God responsible for the good in the world and some other force responsible for the evil, or it might be an implied dualism suggested by a doctrine of intermediation such as we have seen in Philo's own theory of the Logos. Thus one of the chief rabbinic commentaries on the book of Exodus, *Mekhilta*, explains "I am the Lord thy God," by saying that in various places in the Bible God appears before the people in different guises, so to speak. At the Red Sea, He shows Himself as a man of war; at Sinai, He appears as "an old man full of mercy"; in still other places under different aspects. The text continues: "Scripture, therefore, would not let the nations of the world have an excuse for saying that there are two Powers, but declares, 'I am the Lord thy God.' I am he who was in Egypt, and I am he who was at the sea. I am he who was at Sinai. I am he who was in the past, and I am he who will be in the future. I am he who is in this world, and I am he who will be in the world to come." Whether the point of this emphasis on unity is as clearly directed against believers in duality as Moore thought, there is no doubt that what is being talked about is an actual living unity, not a philosophical concept.

Again, the problems that philosophers and philosophical theologians have debated, in consequence of the religious need to assert both the infinite remoteness of God in His heaven of heavens and His infinite closeness to each and every worshiper, did not disturb the rabbis. Because He is the true God, He is near at hand when He is called upon, even though He may seem to be remote. Indeed, the very measure of His greatness and supremacy is His availability. Though the Bible speaks of His dwelling-place on high, it speaks, too, of his presence in the human heart and in the humblest of the things of earth. God can be experienced, not only in the sublime moments of the awesome revelation at Mount Sinai, but also in the everyday activities of the ordinary human life. The rabbinic literature provides formulas of blessing to be used on all the occasions of life, as a constant reminder that every moment of man's life is under the direct care and guidance of Divine Providence. When bread is to be eaten, a man should recite the formula of blessing reminding him that the bread he eats came forth from the ground because God willed it to be so. When he is to drink wine, he reminds himself that wine is also a gift of God. Each and every joy and each and every sorrow has its appropriate blessing because every event of life is Divine in its origin and is an occasion for direct experience of God. Beside this sense of the omnipresence of God, theoretical arguments about transcendence and immanence pale into insignificance.

DIVINE SERVICE

This attitude of complete devotion destroys, too, the sharp differentiation between the sacred and the profane. In many cultures, studies have shown that certain places and times, certain persons and certain activities are set apart from all the other activities of men. These are the sacred things, forbidden to ordinary men at ordinary times. All other activities are profane. There seems to be little ground for doubting that the priestly religion of the Hebrew people, of which we read in the Bible, maintained just such a distinction between the sacred and the profane. There was even an inner core to the priestly sacredness; the Temple at Jerusalem contained a "Holy of holies," the holiest of all places on earth. This was so extremely sacred that it could be entered only once a year, and then only by the High Priest himself. The rabbinic emphasis on the sacredness of the everyday life of men went to the other extreme. All was sacred and all was profane. There was no special class of men qualified to serve in the holy places; all men were servants of God. Perhaps this was no more than to take literally the "kingdom of priests." The rabbis themselves were known to be superior in their knowledge of the Bible and the oral tradition or in their abilities as interpreters; but many of them made their livings in the most humble trades. The principle behind this may be expressed theoretically; God should be served by the hands of men as well as by their minds. Eleazar ben Azariah (about A.D. 70 to about A.D. 130) was an extremely wealthy man as well as a noted scholar. In his name there is handed down the maxim "If there is no Torah [here to be understood as meaning not the revelation itself but its study], there is no worldly occupation, and if there be no worldly occupation, there is no Torah."

All men are servants of God. Diligence in study was one way in which men served; faithful performance of one's ritual and ceremonial obligations was another; honest pursuit of a trade was still a third. In the rabbinic tradition, prayer was recognized as "service with the heart." The mere routine repetition of a ritual form was not, however, what the rabbis meant when they spoke of prayer as service with the heart. Proper prayer requires a proper

73

attitude on the part of the one who prays; the rabbis called this proper attitude "intention." They meant by this a deliberate and conscious turning of the mind to God, a purposive awareness of Him to Whom the prayer was addressed. If the words of the prayer were those of a standard ritual expression, this attention to the meaning of the words and to their intended Hearer would bring the words to life. If the words were one's own, "intention" was, so to speak, a guarantee of sincerity and intensity.

So important was this concentrated attention in prayer that the rabbis advised at least the learned men of the community that they should wait until they could concentrate properly before they prayed; it was worse to go through the empty recital of a formula than not to pray at all. A rabbi who had participated in a discussion of a difficult legal case and in whose mind the issues of that case were still present should not pray until his thoughts had settled down. Some of the rabbis used to sit in silent meditation for an hour before their prayer in order to drive out all that did not belong in their minds and to establish an absolute concentration of their thoughts on the Hearer of prayer. The same intensity of concentration, of course, could not be required of everyone; each in his own way, however, was to make his prayer in the proper spirit of devotion.

The forms of public prayer were fixed by the rabbinical leaders, and their work has survived as the core of twentieth-century Jewish worship. The Eighteen Benedictions (*Amidah*, or *Shemoneh Esreh*) may have originated even earlier; some scholars believe it to have been part of the liturgy of the Second Temple. It consists of a series of brief paragraphs of praise and thanksgiving, joined with petitions in which the common hopes of the Jewish community were expressed. Individuals were supposed to supplement this common core with their own private petitions. One of the principles of prayer on which the rabbis were in agreement was that these private prayers should be both brief and silent. "Let a man's words before God always be few." Despite this, both in the Bible and in the rabbinic literature, there are examples given of prayers that were both long and successful. Excessive zeal in thinking up exaggerated litanies of praise of God is reproved, since the Bible (Psalm cvi, 2) has said: "Who can utter the mighty acts of the Lord? Who can show forth all his praise?"

The rabbis firmly believed that, in His own way and in His own due season, God always hears and answers the prayers of His children. That their own prayers and the prayers of their communities were not answered when they were offered did not disturb their confidence in the least. Experience was irrelevant, for the principle was not that God answers men's prayers in the way and the time when men think they ought to be answered, but in *His* way and at *His* time. There were, of course, a great many legends of successful prayer; some of the "saints" of the rabbinic tradition were particularly effective with one or another type of special prayer. One Honi Ha-Meaggel was reputedly most successful in praying for rain. Hanina ben Dosa was supposedly particularly apt at prayers for the restoration of health. For the most part, however, these legendary materials supplement a view that allows specific prayers to be unavailing for one of two reasons: either that the true spirit of prayerful intention and concentration was not as great as it should have been, or that, in the completeness of God's wisdom, He knew that the time was not right for the granting of the prayer or that what was being prayed for was not in the best interest of the man who prayed. God's wisdom, in such matters, is always to be relied on. It is said that the proper prayer of a truly pious man will include a formula of submission to the wisdom of God. Often the formula was "May it be Thy will, O Lord." At the dedication of the Temple, King Solomon is supposed by the Rabbis to have prayed: "Lord of the World, when an Israelite comes and prays . . . , if it be suitable give it to him, and if not do not give it to him, . . . but if a foreigner comes and prays in the temple, give him whatever he asks."

THE LAW AND THE PROPHETS

A considerable part of the fascination of this story and of the prayer itself lies in its inversion of the usual account of the Jews as a particularly arrogant and nationally centered group. The doctrine of the Chosen People, the idea that one nation had a peculiarly favored position in relation to God, has been one of the most cherished points at which the Jewish people have been subject to attack throughout the centuries—for, as each of the attackers has known, his own people, not the Jews, were the peculiarly favored people of God. In this prayer reported in the name of King Solomon, the doctrine of the Chosen People is latent but seemingly turned upside-down. God should always answer the prayer of the alien, because his faith is weak and limited and unable to withstand disappointment. If his prayers are not immediately answered, he will retreat from the worship of God. The Jew, on the other hand, has a firmer basis for his faith. His faith rests upon God's revealed Law. For this reason, he does not require that his prayers be answered; he reposes his trust in God's justice and His mercy, as these are revealed in the Scriptures.

It is the possession of the Bible, God's revealed word, then, which makes the Jews the Chosen People. Such a possession entails the obligation to cherish and to preserve the Bible, but it also demands the continual study of the Bible. Study of God's Word is a way of Divine service. One of the religious duties of the Jew is to study the Bible and to "meditate therein day and night." Fulfillment of this religious obligation is on a plane with, perhaps superior to, observation of all other religious commandments. The Law is God's most precious gift to all mankind; His love for the Jews is manifested by the great number of commandments He has given them, thus showing His infinite concern for their welfare both in this world and in the Hereafter. "Intention," the concentration and direction of the mind toward God, the Revealer, in the study of the Law, the revelation, is as important to proper study as we have seen it to be to proper prayer. The underlying motive of study is love of God.

The rabbis, however, were neither Literalists nor Fundamentalists. Indeed, the very measure of the respect and regard that they had for the Bible is their recognition that it could not be studied without aid. Part of the assistance that a man needs in studying the Bible comes from the living words of his teacher; one of the most engaging features of the Jewish attitude through the centuries has been the deep feeling for the teacher as a Divine agent. In addition to the actual teacher, there are those others who have contributed over the years to the interpretation of the Biblical revelation, especially in its application to everyday life. These men, and the fruits of their studies in the form of legal rules and moral lessons, are also entitled to respect as, one might say, extensions of revelation. Finally, as other knowledge, whether of Jewish origin or not, becomes available for application to the study of the Scriptures, it, too, gains the status of Scripture. One of the charming Rabbinic stories tells how Rabbi Levi introduced a discussion of astronomy and celestial distances in an assembly of his colleagues when the subject about which they were concerned was the nearness of God. It is not recorded that the other rabbis objected; any information that could be applied to the understanding of the Bible was worthy of consideration. All wisdom comes from God. All study engaged in with proper "intention" is service to God.

As a result of this attitude, the concept of "Law" (Torah) cannot be limited to the Pentateuch. The works of the Prophets, the miscellaneous writings of the Bible, the historical sections of the Bible, all share with the Pentateuch the character of sacred writings. Even beyond the Bible, Divine inspiration was thought to have rested upon especially gifted rabbis. In general, however, the idea of inspiration by the holy spirit is limited to the writers of

77

the Biblical books. To those on whom the holy spirit had descended the rabbis gave the distinguished name of Prophets, and they claimed that forty-eight Prophets and seven Prophetesses had prophesied to Israel. After the last of the Biblical Prophets, the rabbis thought, the holy spirit no longer visited the people, and later revelations were given by a mysterious voice from heaven (*Bat Kol*). "When the last prophets, Haggai, Zechariah, and Malachi, died," says one of the Rabbinic sources, "the holy spirit ceased out of Israel; but nevertheless it was granted them to hear communications from God by means of a mysterious voice." The rabbis were too deeply infused with the advanced conceptions of their own age to say that it was the Voice of God that was heard; they used the indirect expression, which means literally "echo of a voice," to suggest what they would not say.

Side by side with the written Law there had existed for many centuries an unwritten law. There are Biblical indications of certain regulations that were known by oral transmission to the priests, for example, but were never included in the Scriptures. Furthermore, many of the laws included in the Bible are of such generality that there must have been a supplementary knowledge of the specific ways in which they were to be applied. Certainly a large part of the activity of the rabbis in the development of the legal codes consisted of the introduction of novelties to meet the needs of new situations that had grown up in post-Biblical times, but some of the rabbinical work must have been the preservation of older unwritten traditions. After all, the Temple was no longer in existence when the rabbis codified the Jewish law, yet their codification includes much detail concerning the priestly purifications which could not be new. The unwritten law shared with the Bible the sanctity of revelation. Whether written or unwritten, all law was God's law. The expression "the Law of Moses" as used by the rabbis had no historical significance; it expressed a canon of authority rather than a fact of history.

The rabbis often introduced new legislation. For some of it

they were able to provide Biblical sanctions by the use of the various legitimate methods of interpretation that have been discussed. Some of it could not be supported in this way, and for this unsupported law the authority of tradition dating back to Moses was called upon as its sanction. For this purpose, it was important to maintain the existence of a continuous chain of tradition (*shalshelet ha-kabala*). *Fathers* (*Aboth*), one of the most widely read sections of the rabbinic code, begins with a statement of the chain of tradition: "Moses received Torah from Sinai and delivered it to Joshua, and Joshua to the Elders, and the Elders to the Prophets, and the Prophets delivered it to the Men of the Great Synagogue. . . . Simeon the Just was of the survivors of the Great Synagogue. . . . Antigonos of Socho received from Simeon the Just . . ." and so on. In addition to the rabbinic laws supported by textual interpretation and those justified by the appeal to tradition, there were also fairly numerous occasions when the rabbis, usually as an authoritative group but occasionally individually, introduced completely new decrees and enactments to meet completely new situations, or even set aside laws plainly written in the Bible when these were clearly outdated. In such cases, there was no attempt to introduce Biblical authority, yet the laws thus enacted had as much force among the people as those justified on Biblical grounds. The rabbinic attitude toward the Bible as God's revelation is a far more complicated and subtle attitude than any literalism could possibly be.

ETHICAL TEACHINGS OF THE RABBIS

We have had occasion, in speaking of the ethical ideas included in the Bible, to notice the close relationship there set up between ethics and law. Unlike the ethics of the Greeks, which was primarily justified by rational arguments, the Biblical ethics was presented as the will of God expressed to man in the form of law. The

79

THE STORY OF JEWISH PHILOSOPHY

legal context of ethical principles is preserved in the ethical teachings of the rabbis. Unlike the civil and criminal law and the law of religious observance, however, the rabbis did not systematize and codify the ethical law. A reason for this may be assigned; in matters of ethics, which are matters of quality, it is impossible to reach the same degree of precision of statement that can be readily achieved in other matters that are more susceptible of measure. This reason is not given by the rabbinical writers, but it is suggested by a favorite phrase, "committed to the heart," which the rabbis use as roughly equivalent to "left to one's own conscience."

Although, in reference to other commandments and prohibitions in the Bible, the rabbis seemed to exercise their greatest ingenuity in increasing the number of laws, with regard to the moral life they seem to have sought simplification. They found 613 commandments and prohibitions in the Pentateuch; but they hunted through the rest of the Bible for texts in which the moral demands on man were reduced to far fewer numbers. "David came and comprehended them [the 613 commandments] in eleven (Psalm xv). Isaiah came and comprehended them in six: 'He that walketh righteously, and speaketh uprightly, he that despiseth the gain acquired by oppression, that shaketh out his hand from the holding of bribes, that stoppeth his ears from hearing of blood, and shutteth his eyes from looking upon evil; he shall dwell on high' (Isaiah xxxiii, 15). Micah came and comprehended them in three: 'He has told thee, O man, what is good, and what the Lord requireth of thee. Only to do justice and to love mercy and to walk humbly with thy God' (Micah vi, 8). Isaiah further comprehended them in two: 'Observe justice and do righteousness' (Isaiah lvi, 1). Amos came and comprehended them in one: 'Seek me and live' (Amos v, 4)." This is not the only example; there are many others in which the rabbinical writers seem to be searching for a way of reducing the general principles of the ethical life to a simply understandable and observable formula.

It is easy to understand why this should have been so. For the men of learning, the delights of careful and precise legal distinctions may have been a perpetual joy. For the average person, concern was less with the joy of learning and more with the provision of a rule of life; the simpler the rule of life, the more readily it could be carried in the mind and used as a guide to action in the situations that a man might meet, the more effective it would be. The ultimate purpose of any ethical teaching is practice, not theory. A single general rule or criterion can never be the whole answer to questions of moral practice, but it can and does serve as a ready and available touchstone for deciding among alternative courses of action when immediate action is necessary.

For most men, the distinction between morality and prudence is hard to comprehend and harder to maintain. Following a good path for the sake of its rewards or of the favor of God, or avoiding evil ways in order to escape Divine retribution is prudence, not morality. Yet the primary emphasis in the Bible is placed upon the rewards and punishments that are visited upon the individual (or the group) for good or evil conduct. The rabbis, too, emphasized the factor of rewards and punishments. Here again it is important to remember that this emphasis does not necessarily mean that the rabbis themselves considered the rewards and punishments as the reason for doing good and avoiding evil. They were teachers, and as teachers they knew the difficulties of placing moral conduct on the level of abstract obligation to God. In consideration of the limitations of those they taught, the rabbis stressed the factor of rewards and punishments, although they knew of higher moral sanctions. Thus the story is told of Johanan ben Zakkai that he asked his disciples, "Which is that good way to which a man should cleave?" One replied, "A good eye"; a second, "A good associate"; a third, "A good neighbor"; a fourth, "One who sees the event." The fifth disciple, Eleazar ben Arach, earned the praise of his teacher by responding, "A good heart." Here we see a moral sanction, that of unselfish love, replacing the hope of reward or the threat of punishment. Once more, we are told that Antigonos of Socho said, "Be not like servants who serve their master on condition of receiving a gift, but be like servants who serve the master without receiving a gift." This, too, suggests a disinterested criterion of moral conduct.

Ideally, all the commandments of the law should be fulfilled for their own sake, not for the sake of any advantages to be derived from obedience. This is a pure moral motivation. But it was one of the greatest of the rabbis, Rab, who said, with profound psychological penetration, that one should occupy himself diligently with the study of the law and with the doing of the commandments, "even if not for their own sake; for out of doing it not for its own sake comes doing it for its own sake." Prudential motives should not be scorned, for they have educational value. A later rabbi, named Safra, is reported to have prayed, "May it be Thy will that all who labor in the Law for other motives may come to labor in it for its own sake." Furthermore, we must remember that the Jewish law was the core and center of a religious civilization, so that a pure religious motivation would certainly be as highly regarded as a pure moral motivation. This pure religious motivation, frequently referred to, was of a double character: love and fear of God. Of the two, the rabbis regarded love of God as higher than fear of God. Simeon ben Eleazar said, "Greater is he who acts from love than he who acts from fear." But the rabbis also pointed out the uniqueness of those emotions in the relation between man and God. In other relations, they noted, fear and love are mutually exclusive. Only in relation to God can man feel both of these emotions toward the same object.

The primary ethical imperative is expressed by the rabbis under the term "hallowing the Name of God." The cardinal sin opposed to this is "profaning the Name of God." Both concepts are post-Biblical. In the Bible there is no equivalent; the Bible speaks of God's hallowing His own name by the performance of deeds that lead all men to acknowledge His divinity. The rabbis based their new concept of the chief obligation of men on the text (Leviticus xix, 2): "Ye shall be holy, for I the Lord your God am holy." When the people of Israel acted in ways that led others to acknowledge the power of God to make men righteous, they were hallowing the Name of God. They were not, of course, adding to God's holiness, but they were demonstrating the influence of the God they worshiped to change their lives for good. Martyrdom for the sake of religion is the supreme form of hallowing the Name of God. Profaning the Name of God includes any acts performed by Jews which tend to discredit their religion and thereby to lead other men away from God. It is the only unforgivable sin.

PHILANTHROPY

The Biblical and rabbinic injunction to love of one's fellow men is neither an invitation to sentimentality nor a suggestion of almsgiving whether on an individual or a social scale. It is more than either, because it is a way of hallowing the Name of God and because it is the fulfillment of a Divine command. In serving these two religious and ethical purposes, the performance of acts of philanthropy is a source of spiritual vitality. One word, meaning both righteousness and justice (*Zedakah*), is used in the Bible for philanthropy. The concept is one of restoration of a social and moral equilibrium that has become upset by individual unrighteousness or by social injustice. There is no sense of condescension in the Biblical idea of philanthropy. To help the poor and needy is one of the duties of men. It is a man's obligation to give to others out of the bounty that God has conferred upon him.

The rabbinic concept of philanthropy is a refinement of the Biblical idea. The Biblical commandments remained in force, and were perhaps even more stringently insisted upon. The stress in the rabbinic literature is on the spirit of both giver and receiver. The spirit they required was one of humility; the attitude of both giver and receiver was to be one of a humble sharing of the goods which God has given to his children. Those who are able to give and those who are able to receive are to consider themselves as brothers, members of one family. God, Who is the loving Father of both, wants them to help each other, just as an earthly father might want his sons to help one another. Philanthropy can make one household of the entire human race.

In accepting from the Bible the obligatory character of philanthropy, with its stress on restoration of a balance, on justice, the rabbis laid equal stress upon the concept of mercy or love (*hesed*), a term they used to suggest the mental attitude with which acts of philanthropy should be undertaken. The concept of giving which is most prominent in the rabbinic writings is "deeds of loving-kindness" (*gemiluth hasadim*). This was not limited to the rich; it might be practiced by rich and poor alike, for it is a concept of giving that includes the idea of the giving of personal service and encouragement as well as the giving of material aid. Acting in loving-kindness embodies the ideal of "intention" which we have met in other contexts. It is far removed from thoughtless or routine donation, or the mere fulfillment of an injunction of the law. To act in loving-kindness requires the engagement of a heart full of love for one's fellow beings; one must first understand the need and only then can he truly move to satisfy it. The rabbis thought that acts of philanthropy should be judged by the extent to which they were based on loving-kindness; "Greater than almsgiving is acting in loving-kindness; and the act of giving alms can be valued only by the measure of loving-kindness that is contained therein."

In the rabbinic literature, a great deal of attention is given to providing ways to save the recipient of alms from any embarrassment and to save the donor from ostentation. Various devices were worked out to insure that anyone who was in need could get assistance without making public profession of his need. One of these devices—some scholars believe it to have been established first in Biblical times—was the setting-up of a room in the synagogues where pious men could leave donations for the poor without being seen to do so, thus avoiding making a parade of their virtue in giving, and where the needy could take what they needed from the contributions in cash or in kind, thus avoiding the shame of pauperism. In addition, there were special funds that were collected through the officers of the community, and the synagogues provided facilities for the feeding and lodging of needy strangers as well as the unfortunate of their own community.

These institutions were embodiments of an interpretation of the nature of philanthropy. Philanthropy, whether it is given in gifts or loans or services, is not a favor from giver to receiver, for a favor is an act of grace which can be given or withheld. Philanthropy is an obligation to God arising from elementary considerations of justice and brotherhood. It is significant that the rabbis give a great deal of attention to the idea of giving beyond the subsistence minimum. So, they say, a man who had been well-to-do and who had been so unfortunate as to lose his fortune should not be kept merely at a level at which he could stay alive. True philanthropy called for him to be maintained at the level of his former prosperity. It would be only a slight exaggeration to say that the rabbis felt that no one should be forced by poverty to lower his standard of living. In a fourteenth-century code preserving the rabbinic tradition, the learned author wrote: "If he is hungry and needs food, he must be fed; if naked and in need of apparel, he must be clothed; if he lacks household utensils, these must be secured for him; and even if he has been used to ride a horse and to have a servant wait upon him when he was well-to-do, a horse and servant must be provided for him; and so on with everyone, according to his needs."

There were, of course, priorities. One passage of great interest reports that Huna (died A.D. 297) thought that applicants for food should be checked to see whether they were really needy, but that applicants for clothing were to be given covering without examination, because one who has no clothing is exposed to contempt, while one who lacks food is not. This shows clearly the concern for more than the physical welfare of the recipient. On the other hand, Huna's contemporary, Judah (died A.D. 299), argued the reverse position; applicants for clothing are to be checked, but not applicants for food, because those who are in need of food are actively suffering, while those who need clothing can wait. Beyond such questions, the rabbis were agreed that women's needs and those of orphan children took priority over the needs of men and that the needs of scholars were to be met before the needs of the ignorant. There were certain acts of high thoughtfulness that earned special commendation and merit, such as providing dowries to enable poor girls to marry, or providing funds to ransom those who had been taken captive.

The high regard in which the rabbis held philanthropy may be judged from this saying of Rabbi Judah:

> Ten strong things have been created in the world. The rock is hard, but iron cleaves it. The iron is hard, but the fire softens it. The fire is hard, but the water quenches it. The water is strong, but the clouds bear it. The clouds are strong, but the wind scatters them. The wind is strong, but the body bears it. The body is strong, but fright crushes it. Fright is strong, but wine banishes it. Wine is strong, but sleep works it off. Death is stronger than all, and charity saves from death; as it is written, *Charity delivereth from death.*

THE DOCTRINE OF A FUTURE LIFE

What the Bible meant by "Charity delivereth from death" should be apparent from what has been said earlier. There is no Biblical belief in a life after death. When rewards and punishments are spoken of, as in the book of Job, prosperity or adversity in this world is what is meant. To speak, then, of deliverance from death could mean only that the day of death was to be delayed, that man would be granted, for the sake of his deeds of charity, a longer period in which to enjoy the life of this world. During the immediate post-Biblical period, however, possibly under the influence of Greek, Persian, and Egyptian speculation about a future life, there begin to appear Hebrew works in which rewards and punishments are transferred from this world to the World-to-come. Moreover, in the tradition for which the rabbis are spokesmen, the doctrine of a future life came to include the idea of a resurrection of the dead to bodily life. These ideas appear in some of the apocryphal works of the second and first centuries B.C.

One of the distinctions between the Pharisees and Sadducees, attested to by the ancient sources, was that the Sadducees did not accept the newer ideas of a future life, whereas the Pharisees believed, according to the historian Josephus, "that souls have a deathless vigor, and that beneath the earth there are rewards and punishments according as they have been devoted in life to virtue or to vice. For the latter everlasting imprisonment is prescribed; for the former capability of coming to life again." The rabbis continued the traditions and beliefs of the Pharisees. They accepted the idea of a life after death and they agreed that, for the righteous, at least, this life after death would include the revivification of the body.

There seems little reason to doubt that the emphasis placed on speculations concerning the future life in the rabbinic literature was tied to questions of national prestige and the consolatory doctrine of the coming of a Messiah. It was during a period in which the national pride of the Jewish people was most abased that the idea of a future life began to flourish in Jewish circles. The promise of the Bible that the Lord would overthrow the oppressors of the Jewish people had not been fulfilled. The messianic hope that through the agency of an anointed agent of the House of David, God would usher in an era of truth, justice, and mercy seemed most unlikely soon to be fulfilled. Meantime, the devotion of the Jews to their God and to their tradition was unabated. They believed firmly that the messianic age would come; how could they not believe, for it had been promised by God Himself? Yet, as the fulfillment of the promise receded farther and farther into the mists of the future, they could feel no hope that they might be among the fortunate ones who would live to see the coming of this golden day.

It was inevitable that, once the idea of a future restoration to bodily existence had begun to make its way among the Jews, it would be welcomed by many as the road to the fulfillment of their great hope of seeing the wonders that God would perform. In this context, the belief in a future life took on a distinctively national character. No longer did they hold that only the righteous would be returned to life; now the belief was that all Jews, with but a handful of exceptions, would be revivified. "All Israel have a portion in the world to come. . . . But the following have no portion therein: He who maintains that resurrection is not a Biblical doctrine, the Torah was not divinely revealed, and an Epicurean. Rabbi Akiba added, One who reads uncanonical books. Also one who whispers a charm over a wound. . . . Abba Saul says: Also one who pronounces the Divine Name as it is spelled." Thus the rabbis elevated the doctrine of the future life into one of the very few dogmatic teachings of their system. It was given a place in the prayers of the synagogues and became the pillar of hope in the Jewish religion.

CHAPTER FOUR

From Gnosticism to Kabbala

Sir Gilbert Murray, in his perceptive book *Five Stages of Greek Religion*," speaks of a change of tone that occurs in Greek literature between the time of the classical writers of the period of the glory of Athens and the beginning of the Christian era. The alteration he finds in the way in which the writers relate themselves to the world about them. The new attitude is one in which spirituality and emotionality are intensified, sensitiveness is increased, and humility in the face of the universe replaces confidence in man's powers of discovery. Murray summed up his impression of the change in these words:

> It is a rise of asceticism, of mysticism, in a sense, of pessimism; a loss of self-confidence, of hope in this life and of faith in the normal human effort; a despair of patient inquiry, a cry for infallible revelation; an indifference to the welfare of the state, a conversion of the soul to God. It is an atmosphere in which the aim of the good man is not so much to live justly, to help the society to which he belongs and enjoy the esteem of his fellow creatures; but rather, by means of a burning faith, by contempt for the world and its standards, by ecstasy, suffering, and martyrdom, to be granted pardon for his unspeakable unworthiness, his immeasurable sins.

In a pungent phrase, Murray characterized the era as one of "failure of nerve."

Although the attitudes to which Murray refers were particularly evident in early Christian writers, they can be found in many other groups as well, widely distributed geographically and representative of many nations and many religions. In post-Biblical Judaism this temper of mind is best revealed in the writers of apocalyptic works that are included among the non-canonical "apocrypha" and "pseudepigrapha." An additional trove of material showing how prevalent the altered mood was among Jews has become available with the discovery of the Dead Sea Scrolls. Whatever the reason for the change that Murray describes, its pervasiveness is beyond question, since even a people like the Jews, who struggled so intensely to maintain their separateness and to keep the influence of the external world on their thought to a minimum, succumbed to its influence.

One of the movements of thought that the new era brought to birth is called Gnosticism (from Greek *gnosis*, "knowledge"). There were many sects, pagan, Christian, and Jewish, that bear this common name, and they maintained a rich variety of doctrines and adopted an amazing diversity of often discordant ideas out of Zoroastrianism, the Hellenistic mystery religions, and ancient Egyptian and Babylonian beliefs, as well as Jewish and Christian elements. What all these sects had in common was the belief that salvation comes through special knowledge (*gnosis*), not through faith, or through observance of the Divine law or even through good works. The Gnostic scorned faith, mere belief, as far inferior to his special knowledge. This was not knowledge in any ordinary, everyday sense of the term, in which one sets out to learn something and gradually, piece by piece, does acquire the information he seeks. *Gnosis* knowledge is "the knowledge of the ineffable greatness," given in instantaneous revelation. Knowledge of God (*gnosis theou*) is not an intellectual acquisition; it is a union of the human and the Divine. To *know* God is to *become* God.

Understood in these terms, it is clear why knowledge is salvation, "Gnosis is redemption of the inner, spiritual man."

JEWISH GNOSTICS

Spiritual thinkers among the Jews, however deeply they may have been infected by the Gnostic attitude, retained the ancient Jewish feeling for the absolute eminence and inaccessibility of God. The closest they came to mystical union with God was absorption into the "Throne World," the superior realm in which God's throne was the central feature. Speculative thinkers of great spiritual insight whose names are lost to us elaborated the hints contained in the Bible or passed down by word of mouth from earlier Jewish mystics into an elaborate geography of the "Throne World." The first chapter of the book of the prophet Ezekiel incorporates a puzzling and remarkable description of the "*Merkabah*," a sort of combination of chariot and Divine throne. The interpretation of this difficult passage had long been the favorite theme of Jewish mystics—even among the leaders of the rabbinic teachers whose work entered into the Mishnah. Chief among the representatives of speculative mysticism in the first century before the Christian era was Johanan ben Zakkai, and it was among his disciples that early discussion of Throne mysticism, "*Maaseh Merkabah*," was carried on. During the next few centuries elements of the tradition stemming from this group were preserved and probably modified from other sources. Between the fourth and sixth centuries of the Christian era occurred the classical period of Jewish Gnostic speculation on the Throne World. From this period come the major literary remains of this tradition.

If Robert Grant,[*] one of the most recent scholars to be concerned with Gnosticism, is correct in his claim that this movement in its general form suggests "an extremely heterodox Judaism or even, one might say, Judaism-in-reverse," then we might add that the Jewish Gnostics were those who managed to retain a foothold within Judaism, whose heterodoxy was somewhat less extreme. The non-Jewish Gnostic tradition discussed the sphere of divinity under the name of the *Pleroma,* or "fullness." In it were to be found angels and archangels, divided into groups bearing such names as "potencies," "aeons," "archons," and "dominions." In Jewish Gnosticism the "fullness" becomes the Throne World. This realm consists of seven halls or palaces (*hekhaloth*), in the last of which God's throne is to be found. It is interesting to note that Gershom Scholem, the outstanding authority on the history of Jewish mysticism, points out that originally, in the early literature, the visionary journey into the Throne World was spoken of as an "ascent," while later, after about A.D. 500, it is called the "descent." Those who pursued this mystic course were referred to as "descenders to the chariot" (*Yorde Merkabah*), and apparently constituted groups with rigid admission requirements.

MYSTICISM OF THE THRONE

Jewish Gnostics were, then, organized groups, not isolated individual seekers after mystical experience. They passed down through their members a special knowledge (*gnosis*) which was not permitted to become public. There is some indication that the primary requirements for admission to these groups were maturity and good moral character. It seems probable, too, that some conditions of social standing had to be met. In addition, the literature indicates that postulants seeking admission were submitted to examination by the pseudo-sciences of physiognomy and chiromancy—the reading of character from the face and hand, respectively. Those who satisfied all requirements were considered worthy of receiving the secret tradition and, ultimately, of being helped by this knowledge to make the descent to the Throne World. The chief subjects of the *"hekhaloth"* books, which survive in fragmentary form, are the techniques of preparation for the descent, the description of what is to be seen along the way, the heavens through which the mystic passes before reaching the Throne World, and the precise portrayal of the seven palaces, the attendants and gatekeepers in each, which magical seals or formulas are to be used to enter each palace in turn, and, finally, a description of the heavenly throne itself.

A striking feature of the thought of Jewish Gnosticism which emphasizes its kinship to other forms of Gnostic speculation is that, generally speaking, the heavenly beings are regarded as antagonistic to men. This is the factor that makes the descent to the Throne World so dangerous; the angelic guardians and gatekeepers are reluctant to grant a living soul admittance, which implies liberation from the bonds of earthly existence. The voyager must equip himself with secret names, magical seals, and ever more complicated formulas to compel the gatekeepers to comply with his aspiration. As the descent moves inward, from palace to palace, toward the throne, the magical "passport procedure" becomes more complex. Scholem points out the psychological validity of this increasing difficulty, basing his statement on the literature:

> Sunk in his ecstatic trance, the mystic at the same time experiences a sense of frustration which he tries to overcome by using longer and more complicated magical formulae, symbols of a longer and harder struggle to pass the closed entrance gates which block his progress. As his psychical energy wanes the magical strain grows and the conjuring gesture becomes progressively more strained, until in the end whole pages are filled with an apparently meaningless recital of magical key-words with which he tries to unlock the closed door."

The idea of God that is implicit in Jewish Gnosticism stresses His majesty. The seeker must pass through tremendous dangers to approach even His throne. The thought of God's indwelling in the world is completely absent from the literature of *Merkabah* mysticism. Not only is there no suggestion of God's love of man; even the conception of man's love of God is almost altogether absent. God is, to borrow Rudolf Otto's phrase, "wholly other." * His magnificence and His sublimity strike awe into man's heart. The gentler qualities of the Creator which might produce love and a sense of union are barely mentioned. We might even say that this is a power mysticism, emphasizing, on the one hand, God's eminent power and, on the other, the power of the mystic, by his mastery of the secret magical names, to break through all but the last of the veils of mystery that surround the Divine glory. This ultimate, cosmic veil, it is said, prevents even the angels from seeing God directly.

THE MYSTERY OF CREATION

In the non-Jewish varieties of Gnosticism, there is a close connection between the description of the Divine realm of saving knowledge and the unfolding mystery of creation. In Jewish Gnosticism, as we have seen, there is little reference to creation or to the creative aspect of God. The few references to the cosmos that are found in the literature of *Merkabah* mysticism direct attention to the order of the universe rather than to the dramatic process of its creation. Yet there is fragmentary evidence that there were Jewish mystics of this period whose speculations centered on the mystery of creation. So, for example, the Babylonian Jewish teacher of the third century A.D., Rab, is reported to have said, "Ten are the qualities with which the world has been created: wisdom, insight, knowledge, force, appeal, power, justice, right, love and compassion." On the one hand, this statement may be taken as a list of the characteristics of God, the Divine attributes; on the other hand, a less literal reading suggests that these "qualities" or attributes were, so to speak, solidified and trans-

94

formed into the materials of creation. What is important is not the particular interpretation that we give to this passage and others like it, but the evidence it gives us that Jewish speculative mysticism did not totally neglect the theme of creation. Parallel to "*Maaseh Merkabah*," Throne mysticism, there was "*Maaseh Bereshith*," Creation mysticism.

The most interesting literary survival of Jewish Creation mysticism is a little treatise, *The Book of Formation (Sefer Yetsirah)*, which probably draws on both philosophic and mystical sources and was itself the subject of later philosophic and mystical commentary. *The Book of Formation*, short as it is, is thought to consist of a basic text written between the third and sixth centuries of the Christian era, with later insertions and additions. The text is enigmatic, especially since we know so little of the cultural situation within which it was written. Despite its brevity (in the longest text, *The Book of Formation* contains only 1,600 words), it presents evidence of Parsi, Greek, and Gnostic influence as well as indicating continuity with older Jewish tradition.

In the creation stories of the Biblical book of Genesis, one account may be interpreted as an assertion that creative force was exerted by the words of God. "And the Lord *said* 'Let there be light,' and there was light." *The Book of Formation* suggests that the elements out of which God formed the world were the numbers and letters that make up the speech of God—the ten basic numbers and the twenty-two letters of the Hebrew alphabet. The total is thirty-two. "In thirty-two mysterious paths of wisdom did the Lord write. . . . He created His Universe by the three forms of expression: Numbers, Letters, and Words." The ten numbers are called *Sefiroth*; they are primary and elementary, suggesting that the decimal system is part of the constitution of the universe, yet at the same time presenting the ten "corresponding to the ten fingers," a simple natural way of counting. Ten is also the number of the attributes of God; we have seen above a list of ten Divine attributes asserted as the basis and material of creation,

95

and we shall later have occasion to see how the Kabbalists brought
together the notion of ten *Sefiroth*, representing ten attributes of
God, with a theory of emanation making of the *Sefiroth* themselves the matter of creation. *The Book of Formation* asserts that
God has ten infinite attributes, but does not assert the identity of
these with the *Sefiroth*, which are ten in number and infinite: "the
infinity of the Beginning and the infinity of the End, the infinity
of the Good and the infinity of the Evil, the infinity of the Height
and the infinity of the Depth, the infinity of the East and the infinity of the West, the infinity of the North and the infinity of the
South." Only a few verses later, the last six *Sefiroth* remain the
same, but the first four are changed to "one—the Spirit of the Living God; two—Air from Spirit; three—Water from Air; four—Fire
from Water." Furthermore, each verse concerned with the *Sefiroth*
associates with the term an adjective *belimah* whose meaning is
obscure and uncertain. *Belimah* might even be taken to mean, as
Scholem suggests, "out of nothing," a translation that would show
an attempt on the part of the unknown author to pay some heed
to the orthodox version of creation out of nothing (*ex nihilo*).

When the anonymous author of *The Book of Formation* comes
to discuss the twenty-two letters, in his second chapter, his treatment begins as a discourse in phonetic science, but swiftly moves
into a mystical phase. Three letters, the initial letters of the Hebrew words for air and water and the final letter of the word for
fire, are designated as "Mothers." Seven letters (those which may
be doubled in Hebrew) are called "Doubles." These seven are
representative of the seven known planets: Saturn, Jupiter, Mars,
Sun, Venus, Mercury, and Moon. They also represent the seven
days of the week, the seven heavens, and many other "sevens,"
including "seven gateways in Man—two eyes, two ears, two nos-
trils and the mouth." Finally, there are twelve "Simple letters"
corresponding to twelve basic activities of man, to the twelve com-
pound directions (NE, SE, E by N, E by S, N by E, N by W, NW,
SW, W by N, W by S, S by E, S by W), to the twelve signs of

the Zodiac, the twelve months of the year, and the twelve chief members and organs in man. There is a fertile soil here for later cultivation, the suggestion of a multiplicity of occult interpretations of the three realms of man, space, and time.

The principle of combination of *Sefiroth* and letters into creation is referred to in different ways. In the first chapter, the author hints at an executive function for the *Sefiroth*: "His word is in them when they emanate and when they return; at His bidding do they haste like a whirlwind; and before His throne do they prostrate themselves." When the letters are being discussed, we are told that God "drew them, hewed them, combined them, weighed them, interchanged them, and through them produced the whole creation and everything that is destined to be created" —a passage that suggests, at the very least, that God first formed words (letter combinations), and the objects signified by the words came into being or are still to come into being because their names exist. Still a third passage hints at a mathematical theory of permutations, as well as the use of the letters as, so to speak, building blocks: "How did He fuse them together? Two stones build two houses, three stones build six houses, four stones build twenty-four houses, five stones build one hundred and twenty houses, six stones build seven hundred and twenty houses, seven stones build five thousand and forty houses. Make a beginning from this and calculate further what the mouth cannot pronounce and what the ear cannot hear." This is not an exaggerated claim; interpreting "stones" to mean "letters" and "houses" to mean "words," the text suggests the incredible total of possible words as 1,108,564,632,972,646,080,000!

Another mystical and perhaps numerological concern of the Gnostic period has come down to us in various versions of a tract known as *Measure of the Body* (*Shiur Komah*). Taken literally, this little book is a strange, blasphemous description of the Body of God; it is small wonder that among Jews who were unsympathetic to mysticism it was regarded with antagonism and horror.

Later mystics, however, considered *Measure of the Body* as emblematic and symbolic rather than literal and therefore believed it to be a revelation of rare spiritual intensity. Just as Throne mysticism had its Biblical source in the first chapter of Ezekiel and Creation mysticism its source in the first two chapters of Genesis, *Measure of the Body* was based upon the fifth chapter of the Song of Songs. In the Song of Songs, it is the body of the beloved that is described; for this, *Measure of the Body* substitutes the Body of God. There seems to be no way of making sense out of the inconsistent jumble of the enormous numbers given for the size of the various Divine organs; even the units of measurement themselves are neither standard nor consistent. If there ever was a key to unlock the meaning of the mystery, if it was not merely an attempt to give concrete expression to the infinite majesty of the Lord, we have lost the key.

BEGINNINGS OF THE KABBALA

In the twelfth century, in Provence, a book was compiled in which many of the elements of earlier Jewish Gnosticism were preserved together with a substantial part of an otherwise lost Eastern text, *The Great Mystery* (*Raza Rabba*), which was well known and highly regarded in Babylonian Jewish circles by the tenth century. This twelfth-century Provençal work, entitled *Brightness* (*Bahir*), must be regarded as the earliest of Kabbalistic treatises, the source through which older Gnostic speculations became a part of the mystical philosophy of medieval European Jewish life. In this little book, we find a doctrine that must be regarded as transitional between the *Sefiroth* of *The Book of Formation* and the fully developed *Sefiroth* of later Kabbala. The term "Sefiroth" does not appear; there are, however, ten fundamental emanations. The first three are called "Words" and are given a rank in the chain of being; the latter seven are called "Voices" of

God, and are interpreted as symbolic rather than as actual existents. These "Words" and "Voices" are equated with members
of the Divine body. Man's creation in the likeness of God and a
doctrine of correspondence between the universe, the macrocosm,
Primal Man (*Adam Kadmon*), on the one hand, and human life,
the microcosm, Lower Man (*Adam Tahton*), on the other, is expressed symbolically by the relations of the members of the Divine
body to those of the human body. The Glory of God (*Shekhinah*),
a term that had been earlier used as a means of avoiding direct
reference to God and thus avoiding blasphemy, now, in *Brightness*, takes on a separate existence as the feminine counterpart of
God. In this way *Brightness*, like much of the later Kabbalistic
literature, introduces a sexual element into the cosmic scheme,
probably following in this respect non-Jewish Gnostic originals.
Despite the intense and unchallenged monotheism of the Jewish
tradition, the doctrine of the Glory (*Shekhinah*) achieved a great
and lasting popularity, not only among mystics, but among all
Jews. It gives expression to a basic and inescapable sense that
somehow the universe cannot exist without the union of male
and female. The true unity of God Himself consists in His union
with the Glory.

THE PIOUS OF GERMANY

This European work based on Eastern sources must be taken as
a fair representative of the way in which the Kabbala came into
being. It was probably as early as the ninth century that the fruits
of Eastern speculation came to be known in Europe. Certainly
as early as the tenth century Sabbatai Donnolo in Italy wrote a
commentary on *The Book of Formation*. In Germany, in the
Rhineland, a twelfth-century Jewish pietist sect, the Pious of Germany (*Haside Ashkenaz*), flourished for about a century and had
a profound influence on Jewish thought for a far longer period.

These pietists were far less speculative in their thinking than later Kabbalists of Southern France and Spain. Perhaps the more homely, down-to-earth character of the pietistic writings accounts for their greater persistence and influence with the average man.

The Book of the Pious (*Sefer Hasidim*), a collection of literary remains of the three leading lights of the group, betrays the influence of the Christian mysteries of its time as well as that of earlier Jewish sources. All three of the authors whose works are included were of the Kalonymid family: Samuel ben Kalonymus, his son Jehudah the Pious (d. 1217), and Jehudah's close relative, Eleazar of Worms (d.c. 1225). Eleazar was the editor of *The Book of the Pious*; in fact, much of his other work also took the form of compilations. Jehudah the Pious is the figure of this group who stands out most clearly. Yet since he became the hero of a vast number of legends, what we know of him is how he appeared to the popular mind, as a wonder-working saint and even a prophet, rather than what he truly was.

Not yet in a strict sense Kabbalistic, the pietism of the German group added to the Gnostic speculations a development of number and letter mysticism carried far beyond that of *The Book of Formation*. The mystery of the names of God was the subject that attracted Eleazar of Worms; he considered the initiate who had mastered the knowledge of the Divine names as one whose magical powers were of guaranteed effectiveness. Jehudah had emphasized a moral interpretation of piety, but he too believed in magic though he renounced its practice. Eleazar preserved his teacher's moral stress but went further in allowing the practice of magic. Not surprisingly, it was the belief in magic that captured the imagination of later generations. The well-known legend of the Golem, so often retold and dramatized, is part of our heritage from the German pietists. It is ironic that Jehudah, whose own thought had so stressed the idea of selfless renunciation of power, and even asceticism, should survive in legend as one who succeeded in achieving magical power because of his mastery of the ineffable Name of God.

German pietism also developed an intense prayer mysticism which had a double aspect. On the one hand, it was an application of letter and number techniques and interpretation to the fixed text of the prayers. On the other, it was an attempt to achieve a concentration of spiritual force through the prayer. Undoubtedly these two aspects, the magical and the spiritual, were connected in the thought of the Pious, but the connection is missing from the literature. The spiritual aspect appears as a substitute for the "descent" of the Throne mystics; instead of concentrating the spiritual force of the initiate into a personal experience of visiting the Throne of God, the effort now is to provide a motive force that will be sufficient to carry the mystic's prayer before the Divine King. Unfortunately, however, we know less about this inner feature of the theory of prayer than we do about the external and magical features.

The Pious attached great importance to the fixed form of prayers. Their stress on the need always to recite precisely the same words in precisely the same order suggests, especially taken in combination with the interest in other types of magic, that they considered the liturgical prayers as magical formulas. In other words, the proper recitation of a prayer was a method of compelling and controlling supernatural forces. To justify the exact traditional wording of the prayers, the Pious used three techniques that appear among the rhetorical modes of Scriptural interpretation and that were especially beloved by later Kabbalists. These modes are known as *gematria*, *notarikon*, and *temurah*.

Gematria is the technique for calculating the numerical value of Hebrew words. In many ancient languages, including Hebrew, there is no separate set of symbols for indicating numbers. Instead, each letter of the alphabet represents a number. Any word of the Hebrew language can be read as a number rather than as a word. Many words would, of course, be composed of letters whose numerical equivalents added up to the same total. This, in turn, suggests the possibility of interpretation by substitution of numerically equivalent words. In the Middle Ages, this was often toyed with as a form of entertainment, but mystics in the Jewish tradition employed it as a serious technique for extracting secret meanings from a sacred text.

Notarikon is a method of acrostics. Its basic technique is to treat each letter of a word that is being studied as the initial letter of another word, so that a three-letter word may be taken as a "shorthand" representation of a three-word phrase. All languages have such conventional abbreviations; the distinction of *notarikon* is its assumption that every word may be so treated. This technique was also applied in reverse; instead of expanding a word into a phrase, mystical interpreters sometimes contracted a phrase into a word by taking only the initial letters of each of the original words of the given phrase. Again it is easy to see how *notarikon* might be played as a "parlor game" by some people and yet be used seriously by others as a productive method of discovering occult significance in a traditional prayer. *Temurah* is a method of letter transposition. It is based upon a conventional and very complicated system for using the Hebrew alphabet as a code according to a strict set of substitution rules. This method, too, can be extremely fruitful as a source of new interpretations of old materials.

MYSTICAL SPECULATION IN PROVENCE AND SPAIN

At about the same time as these views—way-stations on the road to Kabbalism—were being developed in Germany, a development even closer to Kabbalism was taking place in Provence. We have already had occasion to mention the book *Brightness* (*Bahir*) as an example of the transportation of Middle Eastern occult speculation into Europe. This book was one of a number of surviving literary products of the activity of a group of mystics usually called the "school" of Isaac the Blind, who is often referred to as the "father" or founder of the Kabbala. A commentary on *The Book of Formation* (*Sefer Yetsirah*) is often attributed either to Isaac or to his father, Abraham ben David of Posquieres. Some scholars in the nineteenth century thought that Isaac the Blind was the compiler of *Brightness*. They based this judgment on the sentimentally valid but not necessarily sound argument that, in the beginning of the book, a contrast is posed between the inner light and external darkness. These words could have been written by one who was blind; there is no reason to assume that they must have been written by such a one. Isaac is also thought to have been responsible for introducing the doctrine of the *Sefiroth* in the form that it took in later Kabbalistic speculation. He was an adherent of the doctrine of transmigration of souls, a factor in later Kabbalism.

Two disciples of Isaac the Blind, Ezra and Azriel, after studying with this master, returned to Spain. Azriel tells us, in his commentary on the ten *Sefiroth*, that he traveled all over Spain trying to interest the philosophers in his mystical doctrine, but that they did not accept his logical demonstrations. Somewhat discouraged by his failure to win adherents, Azriel returned to his native town of Gerona and established a school. He was the author of a number of Kabbalistic works, including the commentary already referred to and a commentary on the Song of Songs. In addition to the purely Kabbalistic elements in his thought, Azriel shows clearly the influence of neo-Platonic ideas, which he probably knew through the *Fountain of Life* of Solomon ibn Gabirol. This influence is revealed in many ways. For example, Azriel denied the possibility of our attributing any positive quality to God. His theology follows the "way of negation." Then, too, he describes the creation as taking place by the issuance of pure spiritual substance from God. All the elements that were later to make up the universe were present potentially in the Godhead. What is spoken of as creation was the transformation of these potential elements into actual existents by successive emanations from the Supreme Being. The imperfect and finite features of the world of actuality could not be conceived as the results of the direct action of God the Infinite (*En Sof*), for if imperfection proceeded directly from Him, He would be imperfect. The ten *Sefiroth*, therefore, are explained as intermediary steps in the process of creation by emanation, the stages in the course of which pure spirit becomes matter.

Moses ben Nahman (Nahmanides, c. 1190–c. 1270) studied for a time with Azriel and he, too, is often referred to as a Kabbalist. It is perhaps fairer to describe Nahmanides as a mystical philosopher who dabbled in Kabbalism among other occult systems. Nahmanides' greatest distinction was as a student of Talmudic law; his greatest fame came as a result of his appearing as spokesman for the Jewish people at the notorious disputation of 1263, at Barcelona. But of all his many works, there is not one that presents a Kabbalistic view in its entirety. Nahmanides does share with the Kabbalists a belief in transmigration of souls, but he differs about the method of creation out of nothing. "God," he says, "first created a fine, light matter, without firmness, but with a potentiality for taking on form; this is prime matter." The term Nahmanides used for "prime matter" was the Greek word "*hule*," a word ancient in the philosophic tradition. That Nahmanides' theory of creation owes far more to the Greek physicists than to Kabbala is shown, beyond this, by the way in which he discovered the four elements (earth, air, fire, and water) in the first few verses of Genesis.

It was not, then, because of doctrinal similarities that Nahmanides was so often listed among the Kabbalists. The reason was his insistence, as a commentator on the Bible, that there is no knowledge that is not contained in its sacred pages. Not every

aspect of knowledge may appear on a simple and superficial reading of the text. It is necessary to apply various techniques of interpretation, literary and numerical, and even to draw inferences
from the physical form of letters and words in the traditional
manuscripts. There is, Nahmanides says, a primordial Torah
which God created before ever He created the world. Moses
translated this Torah into the language of the people and this
is the literal text. But God revealed all the content and all the
meaning of the primordial Torah to Moses; and this content is
available to us today if we know the techniques for reaching the
meaning behind the text. Thus the Bible addresses two groups of
people, each on its own level; to the mass of humanity it speaks
directly, while to mystical students it whispers the secrets of creation and redemption as well as answering the questions of science
and philosophy. Better by far than the Kabbalists themselves,
Nahmanides justified the application of mystical technique of
interpretation to the Biblical text.

ABRAHAM BEN SAMUEL ABULAFIA

The term "Kabbala" means "tradition"; it is clear that the
view of Nahmanides allows of a special tradition of mystical interpretation, just as the early rabbinical leaders had claimed to
follow a special tradition of legal interpretation. Many of the
early Kabbalistic writers attributed their works to great leaders
of the past, especially to those who had a reputation as mystics.
In fact, since whatever tradition there was had been handed down
by word of mouth from master to pupil, great differences of interpretation arose, even among Kabbalists who owned the same
master. But there is another source besides tradition that contributed greatly to the development of the Kabbalistic system:
revelation. Scholem [n] quotes from the Kabbalist Isaac Hacohen
of Soria, "In our generation there are but a few, here and there,

who have received *tradition* from the ancients . . . or have been vouchsafed the grace of divine *inspiration*."

Abraham ben Samuel Abulafia (1240–c. 1291) had no hesitation in proclaiming himself a vessel of Divine revelation, a prophet and a messiah. One of his most remarkable adventures, one that narrowly escaped being fatal, came about when, at the age of forty, he set out to convert the reigning Pope, Nicholas III, to Judaism. The Pope died suddenly, before Abulafia could talk with him; who can tell how the course of history might have been changed had the Pope lived on. Abulafia was imprisoned for about a month, but then set free. He resumed the wandering life that he had led before this great adventure, becoming more prone to visions and to prophecy. He himself declared that the highest form of Kabbala was prophetic.

Abulafia's introduction to the mysteries of Kabbala took place when he was about thirty years of age, through a group which emphasized the use of *gematria, notarikon,* and *temurah* as methods of access to secret knowledge. In addition, he studied with care *The Book of Formation* and a number of commentaries. Thus he was well grounded in both the doctrine of the *Sefiroth* and the letter-and-number mysticism that entered into the Kabbalistic tradition. In his own writings, however, he paid far less attention to the doctrine of the *Sefiroth* than he did to number-and-letter mysticism. His concern for the latter differed greatly from what we have already seen, for his mysticism is meditative rather than truly speculative, leading to ecstasy and prophecy rather than to a rational system. Meditative mysticism focuses upon an object to the exclusion of all else, even of the immediate physical surroundings, until the spiritual import of the object becomes apparent. The object has thus become a vehicle to transport the soul of man into the realm of pure spirit, the realm of God.

Judaism, however, lacks cult objects suitable for such an intensity of meditation. Abulafia's searching for an appropriate object led him to the Hebrew alphabet, not so much as a physical object, but as the elements that make up the name of God. The letters do not have the mystical meaning in their own right; by meditation upon them we reach the Name, which is the true object of contemplation. The discipline preparatory to this contemplation, Abulafia calls the science of letter-combination (*tsiruf*). Concentration on meaningless letter combinations is the heart of this discipline, which Abulafia himself described as akin to music.

> Know that the method of Tseruf can be compared to music; for the ear hears sounds from various combinations, in accordance with the character of the melody and the instrument. Also, two different instruments can form a combination, and if the sounds combine, the listener's ear registers a pleasant sensation in acknowledging their difference. The strings touched by the right or left hand move, and the sound is sweet to the ear. And from the ear the sensation travels to the heart, and from the heart to the spleen, and enjoyment of the different melodies produces ever new delight. It is impossible to produce it except through the combination of sounds, and the same is true of the combination of letters. It touches the first string, which is comparable to the first letter, and proceeds to the second, third, fourth and fifth, and the various sounds combine. And the secrets, which express themselves in these combinations, delight the heart which acknowledges its God and is filled with every fresh joy."

There is a play of the mind on the possible letter combinations which leads the mind toward God. The Hindu uses the mystical syllable OM as the focusing point of his meditations and is led thereby to a sense of the unity of the self and the transcendent; so in Abulafia's "mystical logic" the combinations of letters reveal the deepest secrets of the universe. As the initiate progresses, he moves from utterance through writing to thought. Finally, when he has become aware of the possibilities of letter combinations, he turns his awakened powers to the Name. ". . . Then turn all thy true thought to imagine the Name and His exalted angels in Thy heart as if they were human beings sitting or standing about thee." Next comes the ecstasy. "Thy whole body will be seized by an extremely strong trembling, so that thou wilt think that surely thou art about to die, because thy soul, overjoyed with its knowledge, will leave thy body. And be thou ready at this moment consciously to choose death, and then thou shalt know that thou hast come far enough to receive the influx." At the very last moment, the reticence of the Jewish tradition in the face of an assertion that God can be seen, even at the height of ecstasy, recurs. Abulafia says, "And then, wishing to honor the glorious Name by serving it with the life of body and soul, veil thy face and be afraid to look at God. Then return to the matters of the body, rise and eat and drink a little, or refresh thyself with a pleasant odor, and restore thy spirit to its sheath until another time, and rejoice at thy lot and know that God loveth thee!"

There are many similarities between Abulafia's "prophetic Kabbalism" and the theories of *Yoga*. How much Abulafia had learned of this ancient Hindu discipline on his widespread travels is unknown, but the likeness is so great that Scholem calls the teachings of Abulafia "a Judaized version" of *Yoga*. Abulafia's own attempts to claim that his doctrine of prophecy is identical with the theory of prophecy of Maimonides are rationalizations, perhaps because Abulafia had been accused of over-familiarity with the mystical doctrines of Christianity. He did recognize the Gnostic character of his system, however, and referred to his doctrine as the true *Maaseh Merkabah*, a punning reference to the theory of combination.

JOSEPH BEN ABRAHAM GIKATILIA

Scholem has translated a very interesting autobiographical manuscript by an anonymous disciple of Abulafia, showing how an individual can develop in mystical powers. For our purposes this is of less importance than to glance at the systematic and well-nigh rational presentation of its doctrines by a younger contemporary and disciple of Abulafia, Joseph ben Abraham Gikatilia (c. 1247–1305). In a book called *The Nut Garden* (*Ginnath Egoz*), Gikatilia wrote of letter-and-number mysticism in a vein as sympathetic as Abulafia's but far more pedestrian. The word "Ginnath" in his title is represented in Hebrew by the three letters "GNT." This word is an acrostic symbolizing *gematria*, *notarikon*, and *temurah*, the three chief techniques employed by those who practiced letter-and-number mysticism.

Gikatilia and Moses de Leon, who was the compiler and perhaps the author of the classic Kabbalistic work the *Book of Splendor* (*Sefer ha-Zohar*), were contemporaries and acquaintances. Gikatilia's influence on his greater contemporary is in the area of letter-and-number mysticism. The deeper and richer contemplation of the possibilities of letter combination which Abulafia had developed appears nowhere in the work of Moses de Leon. De Leon's influence on Gikatilia is to be seen in the shift of Gikatilia's interest to De Leon's favorite subject, the *Sefiroth*. De Leon's *Book of Splendor* was already in circulation, in part at least, when Gikatilia's best-known work, *The Gates of Light* (*Shaare Orah*), was written, in 1293. *The Gates of Light* is entirely given over to a very thorough discussion of the *Sefiroth*, and of the Divine Names associated with them. Possibly the attention paid to the Names of God is a survival of the earlier influence of Abulafia, but except for this, *The Gates of Light* develops precisely those theosophic aspects of Kabbalism that Abulafia had given least attention.

The doctrine of the *Sefiroth* must be regarded, not merely as the play of the Gnostic and theosophic mind on the obscure hints scattered through the Bible, but as a suggestion of a possible answer to the philosophic question of how God can be at the same time the remote and transcendent, awe-inspiring King and the near-at-hand, ever-loving Father. In the formulation given by

Gikatilia, the Supreme God, the Limitless (*En Sof*), by a voluntary self-limitation manifested Himself in the first and highest of the *Sefiroth, Kether Elyon*, the "supreme crown." This emanation is not God; yet God is to be known through *Kether* and the other *Sefiroth*, all of which may be spoken of as "crowns of the Divine King." Further emanations from *Kether* produced the nine other spheres through which the manifestation of God proceeded: *Hokhmah* (Divine Wisdom); *Binah* (God's intelligence); *Hesed* (God's Love); *Din*, or sometimes *Gevurah* (God's Power and Judgment); *Rahamim* (Divine Compassion), to which Gikatilia assigns more often the name *Tifereth* (Beauty); *Netsach* (Eternity); *Hod* (Majesty); *Yesod* (Foundation); and *Malkhuth* (Kingdom). It is clear that these are attributes of God; yet each attribute is presented as a separate step in manifestation, a stage of God's emergence. Seen not from God's viewpoint, but from man's, from below, the "tree" of the *Sefiroth* represents a series of stages of increasing abstractness. Men can meditate successively on each, including in their meditation the Divine Names and symbols associated with each *Sefirah*. With increasing power, the mystic can reach up higher and higher toward the unreachable, the Supreme Source from which all flows.

Reflection upon the *Sefiroth* as a tree, with *Malkhuth* represented by the roots firmly imbedded in earth while the highest leaves, *Kether*, stretch up toward heaven, suggests one of the favorite graphic illustrations of the Kabbalistic tradition. Another is suggested by thinking of the *Sefiroth* as making up the symbolic figure of a man, the *Crown* on his head, and his feet planted solidly on the earthly *Kingdom*. This human-like symbol is "the primordial man," *Adam Kadmon*; all the visible aspects of the actual human body reflect this spiritual reality. Such a cosmic metaphor encouraged the development of a detailed anatomical symbolism that is often offensive to the refined modern mind. But, like the mysticism of *Measure of the Body*, this, too, must be understood in its own terms. As in poetry, a mystic must attempt, through figures of speech, to express the inexpressible, however shocking it may seem to the uninitiated.

Once the idea of a series of stages in the emanation of God has been stated, it soon is realized that the aspect of God as Supreme Being is not sufficiently removed from the immediacy of earth. Kabbalists seized upon Isaiah xliii, 7, to justify a process of ten *Sefiroth* repeated on four levels. The first of these is referred to as the Realm of Emanation (*Atsiluth*); the second, the Realm of actual Creation (*Beriah*), is that described in Genesis; the Realm of Formation (*Yetsirah*) involves the introduction of number and form and is the subject of *The Book of Formation;* the fourth, the Realm of Action (*Assiyah*), is the physical world in which man and his creative activities play a significant role. Each of these realms has its proper complement of spiritual beings: to the Realm of Emanation belongs the *Shekhinah,* the symbolic representation of God's glory. The Realm of Creation contains the souls of the righteous and some of the heavenly beings associated in the Gnostic tradition with the Throne World. Other angelic beings are to be found in the Realm of Formation. In the Realm of Action dwell those angels whose special concern is the prayers of men as well as that angelic troop, led by Sandalphon, which carries on a perpetual war against the forces of evil—that unusual survival in Jewish popular legend of the struggle between the forces of good and those of evil which indicates the strength and persistence of Parsi influence on Jewish thought.

THE BOOK OF SPLENDOR

During the very years, in the last quarter of the thirteenth century, when Abulafia was presenting his doctrine of letter-combination as a technique for ecstatic meditation and a preliminary to prophecy, a younger Spanish contemporary, Moses de Leon, was composing the major classic work of the Kabbalistic tradition, the

Zohar, or the *Book of Splendor.* For a long time it was widely believed that De Leon was not the author of this book, but only its compiler. Recent studies, however, leave no room for doubt that it was an original work, incorporating ideas from many sources, but all brought together and synthesized in the fertile mystical imagination of De Leon. Not immediately, but within two centuries after its composition, the *Book of Splendor* had gained acceptance as one of the major works of the Jewish literary tradition. It is the only book of the Kabbalistic tradition to rank with the accepted classics of rabbinic literature.

The form of the *Book of Splendor* is that of a running sermonic and anecdotal commentary on the Bible (*Midrash*). Its language is not Hebrew, but Aramaic. In style it is diffuse and long-winded. There is nothing about the *Book of Splendor* to suggest a systematic doctrine, carefully expounded. It is rather more like a rambling story whose central figure, Rabbi Simeon ben Yohai, long regarded in the Jewish tradition as the typical mystic, discusses many topics in a haphazard fashion. The thought moves from theme to theme as the mood, or the Scriptural saying, of the moment dictates. The conversation has all the casualness and irrelevancy of good talk anywhere. The method of presentation might be described as controlled free association. What we have here, in the name of Simeon ben Yohai, is a record of the mystical reflection of Moses de Leon. The ideas that touched off the reflections, however, are never stated directly. They must be discovered by reading them back from the illustrations and applications that make up the text of this rare and profound book.

What is called the *Book of Splendor* is not, in fact, a single work, but rather a collection of works of differing lengths. But practically all that is included in the printed editions of the *Book of Splendor* is the work of one author. This judgment is borne out by the language used, which has a great measure of consistency, and the style, which, even in its variety, reflects a single mind, a single personality. Close textual study shows that the use

of Aramaic was an artificial device; the author of the *Book of
Splendor* did not normally use Aramaic and, in fact, did not know
the language well. He is careless about grammatical forms, constantly misuses words, has a small vocabulary, and seems completely unaware that Aramaic sentence construction often differs
from that of Hebrew. He tries to be consistent and to maintain
the illusion of an ancient composition; thus, for example, the term
"Sefiroth" never appears in the *Book of Splendor* although discussion of the *Sefiroth* is a major element of its content. But from
time to time the author slips in a Spanish or Arabic word, destroying the illusion he labored so hard to create.

Inevitably, too, the content of the treatises making up the
Book of Splendor reveals considerable variety. Parts of it read,
not only on first glance, but even after repeated study, like utter
nonsense; other parts, equally obscure to the casual reader, become luminous and suggestive. Very little attention is paid to
letter-and-number mysticism of the type developed by Abulafia,
yet virtually every other theme of earlier Kabbalistic and Gnostic
speculation appears in the *Book of Splendor*. The section called
"The Greater Assembly" (*Idra Rabba*) indicates both the possibilities and the dangers of ecstatic trance. Prayer mysticism is
a major theme of "The Assembly on the Occasion of a Lecture"
(*Idra di-be-Mashkana*). "Palaces" (*Hekhaloth*) reflects the Gnostic concern with the celestial halls of light. "Secret of Secrets"
(*Raza de-Razin*) also suggests a Gnostic concern, the reading of
character from the face and the hand. "The Old Man" (*Sava*)
contains a discourse on the mystery of the soul. "The Head of the
Academy" (*Rav Methivtha*) describes a mystical vision of a tour
of Paradise, in the course of which a celestial "head of the academy" delivers a lecture on the fate of the soul in the world to come.
"Secrets of the Letters" (*Sithre Othioth*) is a monologue on the
letters occurring in the Name of God. These themes and others
recur in the major sections and even in some of the untitled shorter
sections of the book.

The *Book of Splendor* is, then, a gathering of virtually every theosophic and occult doctrine that had occupied the attention of Jewish mystics. It was aptly described by Karppe [n] as a "riot of lush esotericism." When Moses de Leon actually used a literary source, he was usually careful not to mention it, and a great deal of detective work has gone into the discovery of the books from which he derived the ingredients that he stirred into his work. To compensate for his failure to mention his real sources, De Leon invented—and even quoted—a five-foot shelf of imaginary sources. S. A. Neuhausen put together a "catalogue" of these imaginary books under the witty title *The Library of the Upper World (Sifriah shel Maalah)*. De Leon's chief actual sources were the Babylonian Talmud and various midrashic works. He also drew on Scriptural commentaries and philosophic writings of his own time, as well as on prior Kabbalistic literature. He did not merely use this material; he transformed it. It passed through the alembic of his creative mind emerging with new meanings. All was changed into a web of allegorical narrative.

THE IDEAS OF THE BOOK OF SPLENDOR

A completely systematic account of the ideas of the *Book of Splendor* is impossible of attainment. The title itself, with its suggestion of the brilliant radiance of light, is probably the best clue to the basic metaphysical doctrine of the book. Light streaming forth from a central point is the emblematic representation of emanation. The primal spark was infinite, spaceless; yet the rays streaming forth from it, so to speak, "created" space and whatever is in space. The light by means of which we see is the light of the fourth day of creation, derived from the primal light; darkness is a non-luminous light, produced out of the visible light, and it is also the substance of all material objects. To understand the doctrine of the *Sefiroth* properly, to see why each *Sefirah* is equally a manifestation of God and God Himself, it is necessary to keep clearly in mind the analogy of light.

Light, and all that was created after light, was not directly created by God. The immediate creative agent was the Word of God, first introduced in Genesis in the verse telling of the creation of light. The God Who lies behind all is beyond inquiry. His nature is unfathomable. He is the Infinite One (*En Sof*); He is Nothing (*Ain*). Men can name Him only by the question Who is He (*Mi*)? But by transposition, the letters of *Ain* (Nothing) become *Ani* (I); the ultimate God knows Himself as "I," and this is the beginning of His manifestation in the *Sefiroth*. In this sense we may understand the idea of God's limitation or contraction, for knowledge of the self is a limitation; to know oneself is to know what one is not as well as what one is.

A different Name of God is associated with each of the *Sefiroth*. Each Divine Name illuminates one phase or aspect of the Divine Being. Any mystic sage who became master of all the Divine Names and of their interrelations would know completely the manifest God; but the unmanifested God, the God behind all things, *En Sof*, no man can know. In the course of the *Book of Splendor*, the *Sefiroth* are described in many different ways, grouped in different combinations, divided in various fashions. This must not be regarded as a consequence of inconsistency but rather as an attempt to express the clusters of meanings that mystical insight had reached in meditation on the mysteries of creation.

The tenth *Sefirah* (*Malkhuth*) is particularly regarded as the dwelling place of the Glory of God (*Shekhinah*). In less poetic language, this might be interpreted as meaning that the manifestation of God on earth is His Glory ("The whole earth is full of His Glory"). Since, in the sexual symbolism of the Kabbala, the *Shekhinah* is the feminine principle, or consort of God, we may say that earth and heaven are held together by the union of God and the *Shekhinah*. But the sin of Adam broke this union, separated *Malkhuth* from the other *Sefiroth*. "Even as the sun seeks for the moon, so does the Holy One seek for the *Shekhinah*; but He finds her not, for the sins of men separate them." Each sin committed by any man brings into being a demon. These demons stand between God and the *Shekhinah*. God could destroy these demons if he wished to, but this would violate man's free will, which "would be impossible without the demoniacal urge to sin." Man is thus not merely an earthly being; he is a force in the cosmic scheme. Man's freedom of will is cosmically of such importance that God and the *Shekhinah* tolerate separation rather than infringe on human freedom. So great a privilege must carry with it special responsibility. The *Book of Splendor* touches only incidentally on ethical questions, but the cosmic role it assigns to man demands an ethical interpretation and a constant struggle for righteousness.

Zoharic man is a complex of body and soul. His body, at the original creation, was made of light. This is what is meant by the Biblical statement that man was created in the image of God. But after the first sin, man's body became darkened; no longer was he the image of God. Where, before the fall, all creation looked up to man, after the fall even the animals ceased to respect him, and he began to fear them. Yet man's body, though in a fallen state, retains the external form of the universe; man is the "microcosm" corresponding to the "macrocosm." The doctrine of correspondence, beloved of all mystics and all those whose thought approaches mysticism, in every tradition, is present in full measure in the Kabbalistic view as expressed in the *Book of Splendor*. Man's body is the mirror of the Divine realm, symbolized by the Primordial Man, *Adam Kadmon*. The mysteries of the association of the *Sefiroth* with the members and organs of Primordial Man are made manifest in the organs and members of each man.

The human soul, too, is a theme to which the *Book of Splendor* devotes much attention. The soul springs from the *Sefiroth*, for it is a spark of the Divine. There are three aspects of the soul, not

so much different capacities or faculties as three grades of related-
ness. *Nefesh* (life, the vital soul) is present in all living beings; it
is the animating principle without which men and animals would
not be alive. *Ruah* (air, spirit) is distinctively the human aspect
of soul; it is the expression of man's inner life. Finally *Neshamah*
(breath) is the link between man and the spiritual realm. *Neshamah* is most closely akin to God, a spark of the Divine coming
from the third *Sefirah, Binah.* There is an unfolding of latent
powers involved in moving from grade to grade. As a man acquires
merit through study and insight, *Ruah* and *Neshamah,* the higher
grades of soul, emerge from *Nefesh,* the lowest grade. The Kabbalistic devotee alone is capable of fully realizing *Neshamah.*
When a man sins, *Neshamah* leaves him; after death, *Neshamah*
is not punished. For *Neshamah* is the Divine element in man.
Nefesh bears the brunt of retribution, though some passages in
the *Book of Splendor* assert that *Ruah* shares its suffering.

"From the day when God thought of creating the world, even
before it was actually created, all the souls of the righteous were
concealed in the Divine thought, each in its own individual form."
All human souls were in existence before the creation, not just
as a sort of generalized "soul-stuff," but as individuals. In this
creative phase, the pre-existent souls were in the realm of *Sefiroth.*
Next they were stored "in a treasure-house in the upper Eden."
From this place, at the appropriate time, each soul came to earth
and entered, at the moment of conception, into the body it was
to occupy on earth. There are two passages in the *Book of Splendor*
that speak of the soul of the individual meeting with God before
descending to earth. During this conference, the soul vows a life
of piety and mystical penetration. Then it goes off to its destined
body and begins to accumulate good and evil deeds, merit and
demerit; the ultimate balance of these determine its reward or
punishment after death. In a beautiful and striking image, the
Book of Splendor speaks of the embodied soul as weaving the
raiment that it is to wear after death.

MOSES CORDOVERO, SYSTEMATIZER

After the composition of the *Book of Splendor*, there were many writers who developed and expounded the doctrines of the Kabbala. Some ideas at which Moses de Leon merely hinted, or which were mentioned with some distaste, like the idea of transmigration of souls (*gilgul*), received full and sympathetic discussion by later Kabbalists. On the whole, however, there were no considerable advances in the mystical philosophy of Judaism for more than two centuries. Then, as Scholem explains most convincingly, the shock of the expulsion of the Jews from Spain (1492) triggered a new period of creativity among the Jewish mystics, centering in the little town of Safed in Palestine. The most original of these later mystics was Isaac Luria, who truly begins a new era in Kabbalism. His mid-sixteenth-century contemporary, Moses Cordovero, is, however, of more immediate concern for us, because of all the Kabbalists, Cordovero is most systematic and most philosophical in his presentation of the older Kabbalistic teachings.

Moses ben Jacob Cordovero lived for only forty-eight years (A.D. 1522–70). He was a prolific writer; his remains include a commentary on the entire *Book of Splendor* as well as many other works of both legal and mystical content. He was drawn to the study of Kabbala at the age of twenty, when a heavenly Voice advised him to "heal the altar of the Lord which is broken down." Cordovero interpreted this to mean that he should enter into a study of the mysteries of the Scripture. We find him, thereafter, as an associate of a group of mystical students, presided over by Solomon Alkabez, whose sister he married. Though Cordovero himself had a great respect for Alkabez, even to the point of regarding his brother-in-law as an angel descended from heaven for the enlightenment of men, his work led to an almost total eclipse of the writings of Alkabez. The beautiful liturgical poem "Come, my friend, to meet the Bride" (*"Lekha Dodi"*), one of the best loved elements in the Friday-evening ritual, was written by Solomon Alkabez. It is known by many who have never heard the name of its author.

The most important book by Cordovero was his encyclopedic system of Kabbala, *A Garden of Pomegranates* (*Pardes Rimmonim*). The word *Pardes* (PRDS) in the title is a *notarikon*, an acrostic of the four senses in which the Bible may be understood: *peshat*, the simple, literal sense; *remez*, the hinting, allusive, beckoning sense; *derash*, the expository, homiletical sense; and *sod*, the secret, mystical sense. There are thirty-two major divisions of the *Garden of Pomegranates*, corresponding to the thirty-two paths of wisdom—the ten numbers and twenty-two letters of *The Book of Formation*. Cordovero tried to find unity amid the variety and multiplicity of themes that had been discussed by earlier Kabbalists. An excellent example of this comes in Book II, whose central theme is the reason why it was necessary that there should be a realm of emanation (*Atsiluth*). This section begins with an explanation of why there had to be precisely ten *Sefiroth*, neither more nor less. This discussion led Cordovero to note the prevalent traditional idea that the world was created by ten "sayings" or words. He then interpreted these ten words in terms of the ten *Sefiroth*. Another source speaks of ten angels; these ten Cordovero also associated with the ten *Sefiroth*. It was in this way that he found a common basis uniting every group of ten mentioned anywhere in the Scriptures, or in the legal or mystical tradition.

Cordovero tried to describe the stages of emanation in terms of an intellectual process. Viewed from outside, these stages may be regarded as successive moments of the Divine thought; from this standpoint, the *Sefiroth* are progressive materializations of ideas in the Mind of God. Each *Sefirah*, however, may be, as it were, analyzed from within. It becomes distinct from the *Sefirah* that precedes it because of an internal process of development.

Yet this very intellectual process leading to its distinctness moves it toward a new phase or stage, which in its turn becomes differentiated from it. This internal movement, within the Divine idea, was a matter of special concern to Cordovero. His reconstruction of the process is ingenious and subtle. He thought of the *Sefiroth,* not as "substances," "selves," or "beings," but rather as "vessels" (*kelim*) or, in Scholem's translation, "instruments" by means of which the one substantial being, the Infinite One (*En Sof*) acts. In this respect, Cordovero's thought passes over into a pantheism very close to that of Baruch Spinoza. So close is the parallel that many scholars have been led to the over-hasty conclusion that Spinoza was influenced by Cordovero.

Cordovero tried, without signal success, to avoid falling into pantheism. As a mystic, he wished to discover God in everything; as a pious Jew, he wanted to keep a line of distinction between God and His creatures. The formula by which he thought to be able to do both simultaneously is "God is all reality, but not all reality is God." The contradiction apparent in this formula is one into which Spinoza was never trapped, though some critics have seen a similar possibility in Spinoza's more consistent pantheism. Scholem has translated a passage from Cordovero that is far closer to Spinoza. *En Sof* can be called thought of the world "insofar as everything that exists is contained in His substance. He encompasses all existence, but not in the mode of its isolated existence below, but rather in the existence of the substance, for He and existing things are (in this mode) one, and neither separate nor multifarious, nor externally visible, but rather His substance is present in His Sefiroth, and He Himself is everything, and nothing exists outside Him."

We find Cordovero constantly raising questions of a philosophic character despite his adherence to the Kabbalistic tradition. His mind was genuinely speculative. Thus, for example, although he insisted on the limitation of the Divine emanations to the number of ten, neither more nor less, he also raised the purely theoretical question whether God's power was able to emanate more or whether God was inherently limited to ten emanations. The question is more subtle than appears at first glance; if we declare God to be benevolent, as the Jewish tradition does, we must recall that "it is of the nature of His benevolence to overflow outside Himself," provided, of course, that He has power to do so. If we declare, further, that His power is infinite, then His benevolence should have produced "thousands of millions of emanations." Once again we find Cordovero raising a difficulty that he is unable to resolve. Are we to sacrifice God's infinite power or His infinite goodness?

We have sketched here a development of more than a thousand years from the vague yearnings of Jewish Gnostics for an approach to God to the highly structured systematic mystical philosophy of Moses Cordovero. This is a part of the history of Jewish thought that has only recently begun to come into its own. Rationalists and legalists who dominated the writings of Jewish history during the nineteenth century allowed their temperamental dislike of mystical speculation to prejudice their accounts of the development of Jewish thought. In disgust at the crudities of *Measure of the Body* or the sexual imagery of the *Book of Splendor*, they dismissed some of the finest achievements of the mystical spirit in Judaism as trivial, uninfluential, and unworthy.

There is in the literature of Jewish mysticism a deep and rich vein of spiritual suggestion, rewarding to the pious student. There is more, too. In the course of the writings of the mystics, questions that go beyond mysticism to the central core of religion are raised and answers suggested. In the raising of these fundamental questions, however incidentally they may arise, mysticism passes over into philosophy.

CHAPTER FIVE

Rationalism in the Judeo-Arabic Era

BY THE TIME the followers of Mohammed had imposed their militant monotheistic faith throughout the Middle East, the rabbinical party had become dominant in Jewish life. The Talmud, in its Babylonian version, was made the standard authority because the heads of the Jewish academies in Babylonia, the "glories of Israel," the *geonim*, used it as a guide in rendering judgment in cases brought before them for decision. The principle of revelation was enlarged to include the Talmud as a work of Divine inspiration, standing beside the Bible, not below it. Some of the *geonim* went so far as to refer to themselves as "pillars of the world" and to claim that their decisions had the status of revelation, "the word which the Lord commanded Moses." The *gaon* Natronai, in the eighth century, expressed the proud superiority of his class by saying, "Anyone who presumes to dispute any of their decisions is like a rebel against God and His Law." This self-aggrandizement was certainly supported, and may even have been caused by the status that the Mohammedan authorities gave to the Prince of the Exile and the *geonim* as official representatives of the Jewish community.

Some Jews were dissatisfied with the pattern of centralized authority that this official organization of the community produced. The protesters objected particularly because, for the most part, the office of *gaon* as well as that of Prince of the Exile became hereditary. Occasionally, it is true, a very brilliant outsider was chosen to be *gaon*, but this was a rare occurrence. Usually the office was handed down from father to son. Thus a few families controlled both the secular and the religious life of the Jewish group. An aristocracy took control of Jewish life in the empire of the Muslim Caliphs and had the force of that empire, in the last resort, to back up its decisions. Since the Caliph confirmed the selection of the Prince of the Exile, any revolt against the decrees of the Jewish leaders was a rebellion against the Caliph's choice. There were some Jews who had never accepted the authority of the Talmud. Some, perhaps, rejected the whole idea of rabbinic interpretation and believed, with the Sadducees of old, that the written Scripture alone was God's word. Others, as we have seen, read the Bible in a mystical sense, rather than the legal sense that the rabbis had inherited from the Pharisees. Still others resented the accumulation of superstitious and legendary material in the rabbinic literature and exerted themselves to purge the Jewish tradition, and especially the idea of God, of all this impurity. There were rationalists who believed that all Scriptural doctrine had to justify itself to the reason of each individual. Each of these protesting types may have included only a handful of individuals. Together they constituted a fairly large anti-rabbinic minority in Jewish life, waiting for the spark that would weld them into a single force and ignite the flames of revolt against the dominant representatives of official Jewry. The time and the occasion came together in the second half of the eighth century, A.D., in the year 767.

ANAN BEN DAVID

Anan, son of David, the man about whom the long-threatened revolt crystallized, was born in Persia, probably in the town of Bazra, about A.D. 714. He was a scion of one of the aristocratic families. His childless uncle, Isaac Iskawi, held the office of Prince of the Exile. Anan, Isaac's oldest nephew, was heir-apparent to his uncle's office. He prepared himself thoroughly for the office to which he thought himself entitled by studying under the leading Jewish scholar of that age, the *gaon* Yehudai. In addition he is reported to have known the works of the Greek philosophers in Arabic translation. Whether or not this report is true, there is no doubt that Anan was an able student and teacher. This was acknowledged even by his bitterest enemies. He was also a man of a vigorous and independent mind and perhaps also sympathetic to the anti-rabbinic currents of his time. When Isaac Iskawi died, the *geonim* of the academies of Sura and Pumbeditha met together, as was the custom, to select a new Prince of the Exile. Anan and his friends and followers expected his nomination as a matter of course. But the *geonim* passed over Anan and named his younger brother, Hananiah.

Now, Anan's proud spirit would not permit him to submit tamely to this defeat, which he considered an insult. He refused to place himself in subordination to his younger brother and, at the insistence of his followers, proclaimed his opposition to him. Inevitably the Muslim authorities heard of this step and regarded it as open rebellion against the will of the Caliph. They cast Anan into prison, and, in the ordinary course of events, this would have spelled his doom. Anan, however, escaped execution. There is no proved historical account explaining his good fortune. But there is a story which may be true and which, even if it is not, reveals a great deal about the philosophic background of the movement that grew up about Anan and was later called the Karaite (Literalist) movement.

The tale runs that luckily Anan met a fellow prisoner who was a distinguished Muslim thinker, but unorthodox by the standards of that period. This thinker, who has been conjecturally identified as Abu Hanifa, founder of the Muslim sect of Hanafites, advised Anan what to do to avoid punishment. Following this good advice,

Anan set to work to expound all the doubtful passages in the Bible in a fashion different from that of the Talmud and the rabbis. Next, he told his partisans to make sure, by bribing the highest officers of the court, that the Caliph would personally attend his trial. Then, when the Caliph appeared, Anan threw himself down at the feet of this mighty emperor and cried, "O Commander of the Faithful, didst thou appoint my brother to a position of honor in one religion or in two?" Receiving the answer "In one religion only," Anan proceeded most skillfully to argue that his religion differed from that of his brother and the rabbanite Jews. He presented to the Caliph a summary of the divergent interpretations of Biblical passages that he had worked out and, with great tact, expressed his deep veneration for Mohammed and explained how his new religion agreed in many points with Islam. Anan's defense gained him both his freedom and the favor of the Caliph.

This story indicates two chief sources for the views of Anan, and hence for the Karaite movement. One is the thought of some Muslim philosophers contemporary with Anan or slightly earlier. In particular, it has long been recognized that Karaite ideas were similar to those of the Mutazilites. Recent studies of Muslim philosophy place Abu Hanifa among the earliest adherents of this school of thought. The Mutazilite philosophy attempted to remain true to the Kuran and, at the same time, to purify the rather coarse Kuranic idea of God by interpretations that were in line with the higher developments of the Greek spirit. In addition, the Mutazilites firmly opposed doctrines of predestination and argued in support of freedom of the human will.

The second and more central source of Anan's position was opposition to the Talmud and to the rabbis. A later writer declared that Anan's watchword was "Search diligently in the Bible and place no reliance on my opinion." If he did say these words, he was giving expression to a fundamental principle of a minority of Jews in all times. The Bible, for people of this cast of mind, is sufficient in itself. It needs no oral law or authoritative pronouncement of the rabbis to explain or to amplify it. Each individual is obligated to study the Bible himself, and the injunctions that he finds there are binding upon him. Every person, said Anan, will be rewarded or punished in accordance with his own understanding of the Scriptural commandments. If, by his own study, he finds an ordinance in words where other people find none, God will punish him for any violation of that ordinance. This is a principle that can lead to an extreme form of religious individualism as well as to a very high esteem for the capacities of human reason.

Anan's *Book of Precepts*, completed about 770 and known today only in fragments, reveals its author as rather more ascetic than the main stream of rabbinic thought. His asceticism and his firm belief in the coming of a Messiah were related to each other by way of his antagonism to determinism. He could not bring himself to believe, with the rabbis, that the time of the messianic millennium was fixed by an inexorable Divine decree. It was in man's power, he thought, to speed or retard the coming of that day by his own actions, chosen by his own free will. If man's actions were morally evil, the Messiah would come later; if man chose actions that were morally good, the Messiah would come sooner. Anan's asceticism was designed to lead men to avoid all evil in order that the messianic era might begin as soon as possible.

The very rigor of Anan's precepts worked against any large group of disciples. He seems, indeed, not to have had any interest in leading a mass movement but only to have given leadership to a group of city-bred intellectuals who resented the dominance of rabbinical scholarship. Nor was his son, Saul, who succeeded him as leader of the small group of Ananites, any more interested in gaining a mass following. Anan's grandson, Daniel, was a little more active in pressing his hereditary claims to the office of Prince of the Exile, in 825. Though Daniel had no success in proving his right to the succession, his stand led the Caliph of the time to issue a decree granting a wide privilege to groups of "unbelievers" to set up independent communities. This decree gave warrant to the Ananites to establish their own leadership and thus served to make the breach between them and the rabbanites permanent.

BENJAMIN OF NAHAWEND

A few years after Daniel's activity, there arose the second important leader and thinker of the sect, the man to whom, more than even to Anan, later generations of Karaites attributed whatever success their sect may have had. This was Benjamin the son of Moses, from the town of Nahawend, in Media. Benjamin Nahawendi was the first writer to have called the group of which he was a light by the name of Karaites. Benjamin's work, like that of Anan, is known only in fragments and by summaries in later writers. From these sources we learn of the high esteem in which he was held and the outlines of his distinctive allegorical philosophy. In his activity as a judge in his home town of Nahawend, Benjamin apparently found it necessary to relax the severity with which Anan had interpreted the laws of the Bible dealing with religious subjects. He continued the urban liberality of Anan's regard for the legal personality of women in most respects, but he was far stricter than Anan in emphasizing the subordination of children to their fathers or guardians.

The submission of children to paternal authority did not go as far as a break with the Ananite tradition of individual study of the Bible. In this respect, Benjamin, too, steadfastly maintained the duty of every person to do his own thinking, to strive to penetrate by his own efforts to the essence of things. A son may challenge his father's opinion, a disciple that of his master, without opening himself to rebuke. As a judge and leader of the community, Benjamin felt strongly the need for order and restraint; as a scholar, however, he valued highly the independence and freedom of the mind in the search for truth. Intellectual freedom was not, in his view, the special privilege of a limited class of authorized scholars. Every man had the same right and the same duty. Salvation "in the sight of God" was the reward of persistent study, even though the privacy and individuality of the search might lead to mistakes. Benjamin's rationality appears in his insistence that errors justified by reason do not constitute sin.

Benjamin's own commentaries on many of the books of the Bible favored an allegorical and symbolic method of interpretation similar to that of Philo of Alexandria. Anan, too, was probably familiar with Philo's ideas and is reported to have speculated on the possibility of transmigration of souls, but there is no evidence to suggest that he adopted Philo's methods. Benjamin used the method of allegory, and for him the Bible text came alive with new possibilities of meaning. The chief problem that led Benjamin to allegory was the need to explain away the many passages in the Bible in which God is presented as a Being with human qualities. Philo had faced a different problem—how a perfect Being could be the Creator of an imperfect world such as ours—but both found a solution by introducing other semi-divine beings as intermediaries between God and the world.

In Benjamin's view, the process of intermediation was not a creation out of nothing, as the rabbanite tradition maintained. He followed, rather, later Greek (neo-Platonic) philosophers in arguing that creation flowed out of God Himself. The first product of this flow, or emanation, was, according to Benjamin, the Throne of God. From the Throne there issued the Glory, and from the Glory, the Angels. It was the Angels, removed from the exalted eminence of God by three stages, that created the material world. Whenever the Bible seems to speak of God in human terms, it is to the Angelic creators that the terms are to be applied. Benjamin based this whole cosmic theory on his interpretation of two verses, the second and the sixth, in the third chapter of the book of Exodus.

DANIEL AL-KUMISI

A third major leader of early Karaite philosophy was Daniel the son of Moses, known as al-Kumisi or al-Damaghani from the district and town of his birth. He flourished in the second half of the ninth century, in the generation after Benjamin Nahawendi, and he spent some part of his life in the Holy Land. Daniel had little use for speculative philosophy and he insisted that the Bible was not to be interpreted allegorically or by analogies or in any way save the most direct and literal. He showed little regard for any of the sciences, even dismissing medicine on the ground that no being save God is possessed of the power of healing. In spite of this seemingly anti-philosophic tendency, Daniel showed himself a thoroughgoing rationalist as well as an absolute monotheist in the way in which he conceived of the angels mentioned in Scripture. Wherever, he asserted, angels are mentioned in the Bible, we must understand that the term does not apply to living, speaking semi-Divine beings who act as messengers of God. The term refers, instead, to forces of nature, such as fog, fire, and wind, by means of which God performs His works. Daniel's intense monotheism would not permit him to acknowledge any possible subtraction from God's exclusive sway.

"You can scarcely find two Karaites," said Jacob Kirkisani, the distinguished Karaite historian and theologian of the tenth century, "of one and the same opinion on all matters; upon almost any point each has an opinion different from all the rest." Our examination of the views of the first three outstanding intellectual leaders of the Karaite movement certainly supports Kirkisani's comment. If still further evidence be needed, it can be found in Kirkisani himself, for he devoted a chapter of his work to presenting the doctrine of transmigration of souls, in which, he says, Anan believed, and followed this with a second chapter refuting this belief. Yet underlying the diversity of conclusions to which Karaite writers came, there was a community of dedication to the application of critical reason to the study of religious matters. In the main stream of Jewish thought until the rise of the Karaite sect there was no explicit and conscious philosophical theology. Theosophical speculation there had been, and legal reasoning, but it was reserved for the Karaites to take the first steps, under the tutelage of Muslim thinkers, in a controlled and rational speculation on the religious foundations of Judaism.

RABBANITE RATIONALISM

Early in the tenth century, in Muslim lands, two writers within the rabbanite main stream heralded the burst of philosophic creativity for which medieval Judaism is noted. David ben Merwan al-Mukammas was probably a Babylonian, born in Mesopotamia. Nothing is known with certainty about his life, but his contemporary, Kirkisani, reports that David, a Jew by birth, was converted to Christianity and studied in the distinguished Christian schools in Syria. These studies bore double fruit: on the one hand, he is supposed to have made considerable use of Christian writers in his now lost commentaries on the Biblical books of Genesis and Ecclesiastes. On the other hand, by means of his Christian studies he was led to reconvert to his ancestral faith and return to Judaism, apparently because of a philosophic aversion to the doctrine of the Trinity.

David's chief work, written in Arabic and entitled *Twenty Chapters*, is only partially preserved. Enough of it is known to make clear to us that his thought was inspired by that of the Muslim rationalists, the Mutazilites. He was familiar with some of the ideas of Aristotle, not in their original form, but in the modified version, influenced by neo-Platonism, proclaimed by these Muslim philosophers. He divided the sciences, for example, into theoretical and practical. Of these, practical sciences are of a lower order than theoretical, for theoretical sciences have as their goal knowledge for its own sake, whereas practical sciences aim at the application of knowledge to useful production. Of theoretical sciences, physics, the knowledge of nature, is least and lowest. The sciences of logic and ethics, which lead men to understanding and to correct opinions, rank above physics. Theology is the highest of the sciences; the knowledge sought by theology is knowledge of the unity of God, and the understanding to which it leads is understanding of His laws and commandments.

The firm emphasis on the absolute unity of God which David ben Merwan al-Mukammas shared with the Mutazilites was the basis of his rejection of Christianity and his reversion to Judaism. God's absolute unity is unlike any other oneness that we can consider. We may speak of the unity of a class in which many particular things are grouped, or of unity as a number, or of the unity of an individual person. None of these ways of speaking so much as begins to suggest the unity of God, which is a unique kind of unity. In the Divine oneness there is no distinction of parts and no bringing together of elements. We cannot come to the idea of God either through analysis or through synthesis. The Christian doctrine of the Trinity makes a distinction between the three persons in the Godhead and by making this distinction destroys the absoluteness of God's unity. To say that God is first does not imply a beginning for Him, nor does it imply an end to say that He is last. God is "One in his Glory," incomparable, not merely because as God he is beyond comparison, but because there is nothing to which He can be compared. He is beyond resemblance.

To insist upon God's unique unity and incomparability leads, needless to say, to a most exalted idea of God. But to reach this sublime conception brings about difficulties for the philosopher or theologian. For all our ordinary use of the language of description implies comparison and classification. When we try to say what God is, the words we must use are those that we would use at other times about lesser beings. So, if we say God is All-Powerful, a comparison with other beings in respect to power lies behind our statement, and therefore a classification of God in the class of powerful beings. Moreover, comparison and classification, to the extent that both are ways of defining or setting bounds to whatever we compare or classify, are limitations, and God is unlimited. David al-Mukammas thus found himself caught up in one of the central difficulties of religious philosophy, that the higher our idea of God, the more difficult it becomes to express this idea.

For David, as a Jew, there was the alternative of using about God the language of the Bible. According to the current theory, the Bible contained God's self-revelation. Surely, then, if all descriptions of God are couched in Scriptural expressions, there is no limitation of His unique glory. Although this alternative commended itself to David's traditionalism, his rationalism led him to see that this easy way out could not be accepted without further analysis. When, for example, we speak of God as living, we may mean that there is a distinct quality or attribute of life which makes Him live. If this is what we mean, then we imply that there may have been a time when God was not living. Again, if the quality can be separated, it is conceivable that there may come a time when God will lose this quality, a time when God will not live. This must, surely, be wrong! Unlike the "life" which we attribute to ourselves and other limited beings, the "life" we attribute to God must be, like God himself, eternal. But then, if life is a distinct quality and is eternal, there are at least two eternal beings, "life" and God, and this would violate the principle of God's uniqueness; it must, therefore, be wrong to say that life is a distinct quality. The conclusion to which we are driven is that God lives through himself, not through a distinct attribute, "life."

A similar course of argument can be used to show that the other qualities attributed to God in the language of the Bible must be understood in a special way if we are to use them to say what God is. None of these qualities can be thought of as less than eternal; yet if it is eternal, it cannot be separate from God, or God would not be unique. Just as God does not live through an attribute, "life," so God is not powerful through an attribute, "power," or wise through an attribute, "wisdom," or just through an attribute, "justice." All of these, and the many other qualities ascribed to God, must be different ways of saying "God" rather than different things said about God. Each by itself must be a complete expression of the unity of God and therefore identical in meaning with every other; if not, then God is improperly described as composite.

If the upshot of this argument is that any expression used of God is synonymous with every other and with the term "God" itself, what is the reason for the use of these many expressions? If "God," "the living God," "the Divine wisdom," and other such expressions are all synonymous with each other, what is it that we add to our description of God by their use? In positive terms, nothing, said al-Mukammas. But, following a suggestion in the neo-Platonic version of Aristotle known to him, he suggested that each of these terms was to be regarded, not as an affirmation of something about God, but as a denial of its various opposites. Thus, to say God is powerful must be understood as a denial of any weakness in God. David al-Mukammas was the first Jewish philosopher to suggest what later (in Maimonides and his successors) became a central theme in Jewish philosophy, the theory of negative attributes.

Muslim rationalism centered its speculations in two themes: the unity of God and His justice. We have seen how David al-Mukammas pursued the first of these themes. The second David treated, as far as we know from the surviving sections of his work, more briefly, under the head of rewards and punishments. Because both reward and punishment are assigned by God with absolute fairness, it is clear that this subject does pertain to the theme of God's justice. Reward and punishment are defined in traditional terms: reward is the peace and blissfulness enjoyed by the soul in the world to come in return for its endurance of life in this world and for its temperate indulgence in worldly pleasures. Punishment, conversely, is sorrow and lack of peace in requital for overindulgence in sinful delights. The commandments and prohibitions of the Bible have as their purpose to train the soul in self-control. Thus Biblical regulations are related to the ultimate destiny of the soul, and it is for this reason that God associated promises of reward and threats of punishment with the Biblical laws. David saw nothing wrong in suggesting that men will do good and resist evil only when the rewards and punishments of their course of life are made explicit.

Although there were many rabbinic sources that limited the sufferings of evil-doers after death to a period of one year, tempering justice with mercy, David would have none of this. The world to come, he argued, is without end. Any fate, then, whether blissful or sorrowful, in that eternity must itself be eternal. David presented several arguments in support of his contention that both reward and punishment are endless. Of these, one is especially revealing of the exalted view of God that shines through David's philosophy. In doing evil and thus violating God's law, a man implicitly indicates that he lacks the fear of God. This contemptuous scorn amounts to a denial of the absoluteness of God and is, therefore, equivalent to dishonoring the name of God. Eternal punishment is surely the only suitable way of requiting so serious a sin.

Finally, David al-Mukammas argued that retribution is neither purely spiritual nor purely physical. Man's body and his soul share alike in his good deeds and his evil deeds. It is therefore appropriate and fitting that body and soul should participate together in the reward for the one and the punishment for the other. It is difficult for us to understand how this doubleness can take place. But then we do not comprehend what purely spiritual retribution means, either. Unless, without fully understanding, we accept the principle that body and soul share in retribution, we cannot believe in the resurrection of the dead.

Though he was by no means a major philosopher, and though it seems impossible, on the basis of our present knowledge, to consider him as a thinker who exerted great influence, nevertheless David ben Merwan al-Mukammas was a persistent and consistent rational thinker who tried to combine traditional rabbanite Judaism with Mutazilite ideas to produce a systematic Jewish religious philosophy.

ISAAC ISRAELI

His contemporary, Isaac ben Solomon the physician, often called Isaac Israeli (c. 850–c. 953), though far better known than David, was far less successful as a philosopher. It is his medical works to which Isaac owes his fame; these works, translated into Latin, were studied by physicians in the European universities. They retained their status as writings of basic importance as long as the tradition of scholastic authority maintained its force. Incidentally to the translation of his medical works, Isaac's philosophic writings were also translated and read by some of the most distinguished scholastic philosophers. Thus by chance and undeservedly Isaac Israeli was known as the Jewish philosopher second only to the great Maimonides.

Isaac, to whom Maimonides once referred as "merely a physician," was born in Egypt and later went to Kairuan, one of the intellectual centers of his age. He served as court physician to several of the Caliphs of the Fatimid dynasty whose seat was at Kairuan. There is no record of any dramatic changes of fortune in his life, but he provides a ready illustration of the extent to which religious lines were crossed by students of medicine in his time. His teacher, Ishak ibn 'Imram, was a Muslim; Isaac, in his turn, accepted many Muslim students. Though Isaac wrote at least five medical treatises in Arabic, all of which were translated into Hebrew as well as into Latin, his most popular and widely circulated book was a little handbook of practical advice, with some moral counsels interspersed, for his medical colleagues. Isaac's practicality extended to such recommendations as to present the bill for the services of the physician while the patient was still feeling poorly rather than waiting until the patient felt completely better. The moral aspect of Isaac's *Guide for the Physician* lay in his urging his fellow physicians to devote part of their time to unpaid practice among the poor. Like many another Jewish physician of his period, Isaac Israeli had the wisdom not to exaggerate the healing powers of the physician. The work of the physician is adjunct and auxiliary to the work of nature. "The physician does not bring about the cure, but he prepares and paves the way for nature; nature is the actual healer."

Isaac's philosophical works are two in number: *On the Elements*, and *On Definitions*. For the most part, these are tedious compilations of notions drawn from ancient Greek scientists and philosophers. Only when Isaac digresses from the main course of his presentation is there any originality. Questions concerning the existence and the nature of God, the questions that bulked so large in the philosophy of the Middle Ages, do not appear in the surviving works of Israeli. His chief purpose, in *On the Elements*, was to defend the classical Greek theory of the four elements— earth, air, fire, and water—against any other theory, whether classical or Muslim, that substituted atoms ("seeds") or qualities for the classical four. One of the arguments used by Isaac to refute atomism—a view that never gained acceptance among Jewish philosophers—shows our author's mathematical understanding. Just as geometrical "points," which have by definition location but no size, cannot be put together to make a line, so, he argues, discontinuous atoms cannot be the source of continuous substance.

Although this theory of the elements may seem to lead to a

physical, almost materialistic, account of the world, Isaac was, in fact, a traditional believer in a Divine creation out of nothing. In order to hold both these views, he had to make and to keep clearly in mind a distinction between the supernatural creative act and the long series of natural generative acts. The original creative act alone was a creation out of nothing. All later generative acts were productive combinations of already existing elementary substances. The Divine creation out of nothing was not a necessity of the Divine nature, for God is free. God did not create in order that any good might follow in its train or that any evil might be avoided. There was no pattern or exemplar in the Divine Mind which God followed in creation, despite the neo-Platonic insistence that there was such a model. God created the world simply and solely because He wished His goodness and wisdom to be revealed thereby.

Isaac's account of the detailed process of creation was not the simple Biblical one. He was aware of the philosophical need for explaining how a remote and entirely spiritual being could be the source of completely material creatures. His explanation has features in common with the theories of emanation that occur so often among philosophers influenced by the Platonic heritage: God directly created only a splendor, an Intelligence. When this Intelligence was firmly established, a spark of light emanated from it, and this spark became the rational soul, not as bright as the Intelligence from which it proceeded. In due course, a spark from the rational soul became the animal soul, from which in turn there issued a spark that produced the vegetative soul. The sphere of the heavens emanated after the same manner from the vegetative soul. As the sphere thickens and materializes, it becomes visible. With the materialization of the sphere of heaven, Isaac's scheme of emanations is brought to a close.

But with the conclusion of the supernatural phase and the emergence of the visible sphere, Isaac shifts to a physical and naturalistic explanation of the universe: since the nature of the sphere is to be a mover, the outermost sphere moves or pushes its neighbor and fire results. Air comes from fire; water from air; earth from water. The combination in various proportions of fire, air, water, and earth produces the mineral, animal, and vegetable realms of experience. By supplying this dual theory of origins, one accounting for the suprasensible realm of creation, the other for the sensible realm of combination, Isaac may have been trying to reconcile the assertions of theology with his scientific interests.

One of the most interesting questions to examine in the light of Isaac's theory is that of the nature of the soul. The threefold soul, rational, animal, and vegetative, was presented as appearing in three successive stages of cosmic emanation. Soul is clearly spiritual, and, since it precedes the appearance of the sphere of heaven, it is invisible, imperceptible. Man's body, on the other hand, is the highest of the material combinations. The first problem in understanding Isaac's theory of the soul is to see how the cosmic soul is related to the material and individual body. In order to understand, we must realize that although man is individual body, he too contains a Divine spark. Unlike the sparks of the cosmic scheme of emanation, the spark in man is dormant, passive, merely potential, until it is activated by effort, by a conscious striving toward truth and goodness. The reward of this striving is attachment through life to the upper, or cosmic, soul.

There are, it would appear, two distinct types of soul of which Isaac speaks. One is the cosmic soul, existing in complete independence of any body; the other is the Divine spark within the individual which ultimately enables him to strive toward, and be warmed and enlightened by, the cosmic soul. This view is historically of very great interest, for Isaac's cosmic soul is like the conception of soul in the Platonic tradition, whereas his view of the individuated soul is derived from the Aristotelian tradition. Whether he was aware of it or not, Isaac had embarked upon the difficult enterprise of combining Plato and Aristotle. Although the need for scientific explanation rather than religious motives seems to be the source of Isaac's philosophic speculation, the outcome of his thought was deeply religious, for it concerned the relation of man's soul to the universe. Isaac's theories led to a view characteristically (though not exclusively) Jewish by emphasizing the participating role that the individual had to play in the attaining of a relation to the universal soul. Not by faith but by effort could the individual soul rise to the level of its cosmic counterpart. The souls of just individuals could pass without harm through the fire of the heavenly sphere into the upper regions of cosmic soul. But the souls of the unjust, weighted down by their load of evil, could not rise to the ethereal soul. Trapped in the fiery sphere, these souls were, so to speak, burned. The ultimate fate of one's soul depended on the moral character of one's life.

SAADIA BEN JOSEPH

The rationalism of early Karaite thought and the attempts of David ben Merwan al-Mukammas and Isaac Israeli to develop philosophic systems within the rabbanite position were but preliminary flirtations of the medieval Jewish mind with philosophy. The fulfillment of the impulse they record came in the *Book of Beliefs and Opinions* (A.D. 933) of Saadia ben Joseph. Saadia, known as al-Fayyumi because he came from the Fayyum district of Upper Egypt, was born in A.D. 882. He was a brilliant defender of the rabbanite position. One of his first works, written in his early twenties, was a refutation of the ideas of Anan ben David and he continued through his life to attack the Karaite movement. Saadia also was one of the first careful students of Hebrew grammar and the compiler of the first Hebrew dictionary. The Arabic translation of the Bible which is still used by Jews in countries where Arabic is spoken was his work; in most respects, Saadia's translation is very literal, but his rationalism shows through in his use of paraphrase to avoid assigning human qualities to God. He wrote commentaries, of a philosophical as well as linguistic character, on many of the Biblical books and composed a treatise on the Jewish liturgy which is interesting not only for its historical and critical content but also because it preserves many otherwise forgotten religious poems and prayers.

Indeed, so outstanding was Saadia's ability and so widespread his reputation that in 928, although not a Babylonian, he was appointed head (*gaon*) of the rabbinical academy at Sura—the first "foreigner" to receive this recognition. As a result of a quarrel between him and the hereditary Prince of the Exile, Saadia's undisputed tenure of the office of *gaon* lasted only two years, and after two more years of conflict, he was officially relieved of his appointment. During the last ten years of his life, up to 942, he produced a steady stream of works, including his major philosophic book. Much that he wrote, both before and after his brief term as head of the academy of Sura, dealt with questions of Jewish law. Some of his legal treatises were abstract and theoretical; these show that he was well acquainted with Muslim legal theory and that it had influenced his thinking. In short, Saadia wrote on virtually every subject with which Jewish writers of his time busied themselves, and in every field his work achieved distinction. He was the outstanding Jewish intellectual figure of his age.

That age, as we have seen, was one in which the Muslim world in which Saadia lived was concerned with the rational and systematic understanding of its faith. The palmy days of Arab philosophy began but shortly before Saadia's own times. Furthermore, the school of Jewish thought that Saadia opposed, the Karaite sect, had made its own use of the rationalistic impulse that swept through the Middle East. Saadia could neither defend rabbanite Judaism nor attack Karaism successfully without facing the philosophic issues that were hotly debated all around him. To meet the challenge of Karaism and Islam, Saadia's rabbanite philosophy had to be presented in rational terms throughout; yet to be thoroughly successful as a polemic and acceptable to the rabbanites, the conclusions to which he came by the use of reason had to be completely in accord with the dogmas of faith. Nothing less than the confirmation of revealed truth by natural knowledge was Saadia's aim.

In his *Book of Beliefs and Opinions,* written to gain this difficult objective, Saadia followed the literary pattern of writings of the Mutazilite school. That is to say, he divided the whole body of questions to which he addressed himself into two groups, the first concerned with the Unity of God, the second with Divine justice and human morality. The *Book of Beliefs and Opinions* was not evenly divided into two sections. Saadia's emphasis fell on the ethical side by giving over more than half of the ten major sections of his book to such matters as the commandments, man's freedom to obey or disobey the will of God, the soul and immortality, rewards and punishments, the doctrine of resurrection, and the messianic age. At most, the theme of God's unity, which looms so large in many of the Muslim writers, may be said to be central to the first two sections of Saadia's work. This is to say that although Saadia followed a major tradition of his time, he was by no means a mere copyist or blind follower. It might be fairer to say that he was a reshaper of the Mutazilite tradition to adapt it better for use in the philosophic defense of rabbanite Judaism.

THE BOOK OF BELIEFS AND OPINIONS

The *Book of Beliefs and Opinions* begins with a preliminary treatise having to do with neither of the major themes of Unity and Justice. This introduction gives Saadia's views on the nature of philosophic doubt and of the search for truth. Here he justifies the use of philosophic reasoning in defense of faith. Every major section of the work opens with an invocation praising or thanking God for one of the blessings with which He endowed men. Saadia's praise of God in the preliminary treatise is bestowed in gratitude for God's conferring upon men the ability to perceive the truth.

God himself is the "Evident Truth," the absolute standard of truth, and He makes men certain of the existence of their souls. The souls of men supply a secondary or derivative standard of truth; men are able to judge the validity of what they perceive by reference to the standard of truth provided by their souls. "Uncertainties are thereby removed from them and doubts disappear, so that demonstrations become lucid for them and proofs become clear."

But why do men doubt? Why are they infected by uncertainties as they search for truth? Why, in some cases, are the doubts and uncertainties so dominant that men are led to embrace skepticism —"how some of these uncertainties so intrigue some men that in their fancy and belief they become established truths"? Saadia's answer to these questions begins by asserting that the ideas or concepts in our minds are based upon what our senses perceive. There are two sources of confusion in respect to those things that our senses perceive. One is that we may be insufficiently familiar with the object we seek, as in cases of mistaken identity; the other is that we may be superficial in our examination of an object. Two other sources of confusion occur in transforming what we perceive into what we think. The first of these is an unfamiliarity with the rules and standards of evidence; this leads us to reject valid proofs and to accept proofs that are invalid. The second, occurring even among men who do know the proper ways of reasoning, is impatience; this leads to jumping to conclusions without thorough consideration of the evidence and, of course, to error. A person who is both ignorant of correct reasoning and impatient would have virtually no chance of reaching truth. Finally, Saadia suggests that there may be those who don't even know what they are looking for, who are not even aware that they seek truth, so that if, by chance, they should happen to stumble on it, they would not recognize it. As Saadia saw the state of the Jewish people and of Judaism in his own time, both were infected by doubts arising from these sources. He wrote his book to help resolve these doubts.

Those who have complained because God allows such confusions to enter the minds of His creatures are not justified in making this complaint. Because men are creatures, their knowledge is a process that takes place in time. Only God Himself can have the power of instantaneous recognition of truth. For a created being to ask for such a power is equivalent to a demand for equality with God, the Creator, and is, therefore, absurd. Truth is the truth of statements; there are some statements whose truth or falsity is immediately apparent, even to men. These are "necessary" statements, like "The fire is hot," and "impossible" statements, like "The fire is cold." Statements of these two sorts may be used to help in the rational analysis of statements of a third sort, which Saadia calls "possible" statements, like "John is in Chicago."

Belief is a conviction that an idea is true; but beliefs may be true or false. A true belief means "believing a thing to be as it really is" while a false belief means "believing a thing to be the opposite of what it actually is." Ultimately, Saadia says, reality is the controlling element. A sensible man bases his beliefs upon reality; he conforms his beliefs (subjective truths) to things as they are (objective truth). A fool, on the other hand, is one who assumes that reality is controlled by his beliefs, that his inner and subjective certainty dictates the pattern of outer and objective reality. In Saadia's thoughtful view, sensible belief is entirely unlike blind and unreasoning faith. It is, rather, belief founded on the proper use of the three natural sources of human knowledge, accessible to all men: sensation, intuition, and inference. A fourth source of knowledge is accepted by "the community of monotheists," by which Saadia probably meant the Jews, Christians, and Muslims, namely, "authentic tradition," including Scriptural revelation.

Because Scriptural revelation and tradition support and corroborate the other three sources of knowledge, the oft-repeated charge that speculation leads to unbelief and heresy is a delusion of the uneducated, comparable with other mass delusions and superstitions. Speculation without a foundation in the tradition may very well lead to false belief and the absence of religious faith. With a basis in authentic tradition, inquiry leads to factual verification of what appears in religious literature in theoretical form. An additional use of speculation and research is as a means of refuting anyone who denies any principle of the religion. Reason, properly used, comes to the support of religion and revelation. That it should be so is God's will. "He has . . . informed us, however, that, if we would engage in speculation and diligent research, inquiry would produce for us in each instance the complete truth, tallying with His announcement to us by the speech of His prophets. Besides that He has given us the assurance that the godless will never be in a position to offer a proof against our religion, nor the skeptics an argument against our creed."

PROOFS OF CREATION

Saadia's introduction, then, offers a clear account of what he meant by philosophic speculation and how he thought philosophy and religion were related. His view was optimistic. Reason is the staunch supporter and ally of faith. By the correct use of reason's appropriate methods, men come to a reaffirmation on intellectual grounds of the truths taught by revelation. The first of these is that everything that exists, except the Creator Himself, was created out of nothing. This truth is revealed in Scripture. The object of the first treatise of the Book of Beliefs and Opinions is to confirm its truth by reason. Since no man was present at the origin of the world, the truth of the doctrine of creation out of nothing cannot be established by direct evidence of the senses, nor yet is it something that is intuitively known. Verification must come by the third method, that of logical inference. Saadia presents four rational proofs that the world must have been created.

The first of these arguments is that the earth is finite and so is the heaven. That each of these is finite is established by their being different, for if either were infinite, it would include the other. But an infinite force cannot occupy a finite body, and therefore the force residing in heaven and that residing in earth must be finite forces. Since each is maintained by a finite force, each must have a beginning and an end. Heaven and earth must necessarily be created things.

Saadia's second proof is based on inference from the observed fact that all bodies are composed of combinations of parts and connecting links between them. He deduces from these combinations the necessity of a Creator. His third proof is that all the objects of experience have characteristics that are not necessary and that are subject to change ("accidents"), and that, despite this, the object cannot be shown to have existed before its accidental characteristics. If this is so, then the object cannot have existed from eternity and must have been created. Fourth, Saadia argues that the finite nature of time proves the necessity of a beginning or creation.

The necessity for a beginning established by these arguments did not eliminate the possibility that the world created itself, nor did they prove creation out of nothing. Saadia developed three further proofs that a thing could not create itself, in order to clear away any possible confusion that could arise on this score, and then turned to the more difficult task of showing that there was no previously existing matter for God to mold and form in the creation, that, in the usual expression, the world was created out of nothing. The general character of Saadia's argument here is that unless we are willing to admit that one "thing" existed before any other, we cannot account for the existence of anything; that the thing preceding all else could not be finite, else it, too, must have a beginning, in which case something else must have preceded it; that, therefore, that which preceded all else must have been an infinite, eternal Creator. Any material that He might have used in creation must either have been created by Him out of nothing or must be co-eternal with Him. If it were co-eternal with Him, then it would be of equal power with Him and we could not say that it was formed "according to His desire." This line of consideration would nullify the whole idea of creation. Therefore the alternative view, that the world was created out of nothing, is established indirectly.

THE UNITY OF GOD

Saadia now claims to have verified three Scriptural principles speculatively: that all things were created in time, that they were not self-created, and that they were created out of nothing. After a long chapter in which he states and refutes twelve other theories that had been expressed by various schools of thought, he returns to the main theme of his book by presenting, in his second treatise, arguments for the belief that God is one. Besides the pure logical arguments, Saadia presents the case against the Parsi theory of two Divine forces and against the Christian doctrine of the Trinity. He is not concerned to any extent with polytheism; that was, presumably, not an issue in the parts of the world with which Saadia was familiar. The "live options," or possibly those choices that might have been attractive to the confused fellow Jews for whose enlightenment Saadia wrote, were Islam, Christianity, and some form of Parsism. It is interesting to note that, writing in the Muslim-dominated Middle East, Saadia made no bones about attacking dualism and Christianity but that he did not present any direct arguments against Islam. Some parenthetical remarks in the seventh chapter of the second treatise suggest, in guarded language, that some of Saadia's criticism of other sects is applicable to the followers of Mohammed.

In relation to the absolute unity of God, of course, there was no occasion for Saadia to debate the Muslim theologians. He and they were on the same side, battling for a strict interpretation of monotheism against trinitarianism. Nor, Saadia insists, is it the crude and coarse belief in the Trinity of the mass of Christians that he is concerned to refute. His intention, he says, is "to reply to their elite, who maintain that they adopted their belief in the trinity as a result of rational speculation and subtle understanding." The view he is combatting asserts that God's vitality and His omniscience are distinct from His essence; the Trinity is composed of these three aspects of the Divine personality. Saadia admits that there are these three attributes, and that they are discoverable by means of "logical speculation." But, he claims, they are not found separately, in three distinct exercises of reason, but simultaneously; that is, by a single examination of the implications of the fact that God created all things, it becomes apparent to our minds that He must be living, omnipotent, and omniscient. The limitations of language make it impossible for us to express as one term what we discover in one act of reason. We are led to use different expressions and tend to be misled into assuming a distinctness of being where there is only a distinction of language.

When Saadia turned this argument specifically against the Christians, he added that distinctness of being can only be true of a physical being. Either, then, the learned Christians who rationally defended the trinitarian doctrine believe in a physical God, a very crassly materialistic belief; or they are confused, believing in a spiritual, non-physical God, and yet using arguments that imply that God is a physical being. Further, Saadia asserts, defenders of the Trinity do not pursue the logic of their own position to its ultimate conclusion. If they did, they would realize that not only those attributes that they mention as the basis of the tri-personality of the Divine essence, but other attributes as well, would require different "persons" of the Godhead. Either the one statement that God exists includes all other statements that can be made about God, in which case we are brought back to strict monotheism, or for every statement that can be made about God there would have to be a separate "person" in the Godhead. The defense of the Trinity is merely rationalization. Its defenders "merely make up this artificial thesis in order to uphold what they have been told."

There is considerable sophistication in Saadia's recognition of the role that figures of speech play in the Scriptures. He has no hesitation about explaining every passage of the Bible that suggests a physical or anthropomorphic view of God as a metaphor. Expressions that refer to the "eye" or "ear" or "hand" of God, or any other physical organ or dimension are readily interpreted as figurative language, not to be taken literally, but rather as a way of suggesting what words cannot directly express. Saadia goes beyond this, too. He claims that not only physical terms themselves but also those terms of quantity, quality, relation, and the rest of the ten "categories" of the Aristotelian tradition which are used of God are used figuratively, in a way that they are not to be used in ordinary discourse. This is clear, for example, in that we can talk of degrees, of "more" and "less," of any of the categories when we use these terms in everyday speech; but when we use these terms of God, we cannot talk of degrees. Thus any of the categorical terms is used in an unusual and figurative way when it is used of God. Characteristically, however, in the course of the very same line of argument in which he claims for the Jewish tradition the right to have its figures of speech interpreted, he declines to grant the same right to his adversaries. He insists upon taking the metaphors of Christian thought literally.

DIVINE JUSTICE

The remainder of Saadia's *Book of Beliefs and Opinions*, from its third treatise to the end, is devoted to the discussion of themes related to God's moral government of the universe, the second traditional division of Mutazilite theology. In Muslim theology, an early debate had centered on the question of whether man had freedom of will or whether his actions were determined. The Mutazilites defended human free-will, on the ground that if men received rewards and punishments for actions that they had not chosen freely, but that were determined, then the justice of God could not be maintained. Saadia, too, maintained that Divine justice necessarily implies man's freedom of choice, because actions that are involuntary cannot be morally approved or blamed. Man's freedom is, however, not absolute; it is limited to the choice of obedience or disobedience to God's commandments.

God's first kindness to men was to bring them into being. He added to this by giving them the opportunity to achieve salvation. The commands and prohibitions of the Scriptural law (Torah) furnish the means for attaining bliss. That there should be such a law, Saadia asserts, is reasonable, in order that the proper way of thanking the Creator should be set forth, in order that there should be indications of conduct offensive to the Creator, and in order to define proper and improper relations among the creatures. Not only is the Torah in general rationally necessary, but, in Saadia's view, each particular command or prohibition is in accord with reason. The law, in its statement, may not suggest the reason that underlies it; the prophetic revelations supplement the codes by giving detailed reasons for the laws. The Torah, though it came to Israel by the hand of Moses, is not the law of Moses but the law of God. Since Moses was a vessel of prophetic revelation, the law can never be set aside. Here Saadia's argument is directed against Muslims as well as Christians, for both groups claimed a later revelation that annulled all or part of the Mosaic law.

Man's freedom of choice is implied by his position as the highest of God's creatures. Man alone has the capacity for good as well as evil, and the Divine gift of intelligence, which makes it possible for man to choose well or ill. To choose well is to choose to obey God's commandments; to choose ill is to choose disobedience. God, even though His foreknowledge of how each man will choose is absolute, in no way tries to compel any man either to obey or to disobey His law. Thus there is no conflict between God's knowledge and man's freedom. Any Biblical passage that seems to assert that God does interfere with man's choice is to be understood as a figurative use of language. Here Saadia runs afoul of the problem of evil in one of its many forms. Why, he inquires, was it necessary for God to issue commands and prohibitions to the virtuous who would serve the Lord in any case, with or without specific injunctions? Why, on the other hand, did God "send missions to the unbelievers" to tell them of the laws which, in any case, they would not obey? His answers to both questions stress the importance of man's exact knowledge of God's will if rewards and punishments are to be justly assigned.

Saadia's discussion of merits and demerits is thorough. The effects of man's choices on his soul may not be evident to other men, but they are to God, Who keeps an account of each man's deserts. We are to understand that man's rewards and punishments are, for the most part, assigned after his death. To serve as an example, however, and to some extent as a token of what is to be, some part of the Divine retribution for any man's conduct is carried out before his death. There are eleven classes into which men are divided, based upon the extent to which good or evil predominates in their conduct. What is rewarded or punished in this world differs from class to class. Thus the righteous man, in whose life good conduct far exceeds evil, may be punished in this world for his few sins while his rewards for his many virtues are reserved for the hereafter. The wicked man in whom vice predominates may be rewarded here for his few good deeds while his many evil deeds are punished in the afterworld. This accounts for the apparent prosperity of the wicked and the apparent adversities of the righteous. Saadia also discusses each of the other classes into which men are placed because of merit and demerit.

In his sixth treatise, Saadia spells out in detail his beliefs about the soul. This, he finds, is created simultaneously with the body; he rejects any doctrine of pre-existent souls. At death, the soul is separated temporarily from the body to which it was attached during life, but in the end of days, at the time of the final retribution, each soul will be reunited with the body it inhabited. The belief in transmigration of souls, so dear to some Eastern peoples, must, therefore, be rejected, for if each soul had resided in many bodies, the reunion of soul and body could not take place. That the soul and body should be reunited is important, for both share alike in the merits and demerits received during the joint life on earth, and both must share alike in retribution. Man's soul and his body together constitute a single moral agent. The soul's substance is like that of the heavenly spheres, pure and luminous; its bodily seat is in the heart. One interesting feature of Saadia's position is that since the soul is separated from the body at death but later reunited with it, he must indicate what storage facilities are provided for the unencumbered soul. Those which are pure, he says, are stored on high, while those which are sullied are kept down below.

Next Saadia discusses the resurrection of the dead, arguing that such a belief is traditional in both Biblical and rabbinical writings. He considers a wide variety of questions that had been raised concerning the belief in physical resurrection, finding to his own satisfaction rational answers to such questions as how decomposed portions of human bodies are restored at the time of the resurrection. Other questions deal with whether the resurrected will eat, drink, and marry or not. One very difficult question is, "In the case in which those to be resurrected were married while they were alive in this world, will each man's wife return to him because of the fact that she had formerly lived with him, or does death dissolve all marital ties?" Saadia shrewdly evaded the necessity of answering this question by saying, "Our minds are capable only of grasping our present state. As for what is forbidden or permitted in a situation that has no parallel at all in our earthly existence, such as whether or not marriage bonds will be abrogated for those who are resurrected, we need not concern ourselves therewith, since there will be available in the beyond prophets and prophetic inspiration and divine guidance." The resurrection of which Saadia speaks in this section is the resurrection of the nation of Israel to bodily life on this earth at the time of the messianic redemption; there is a second, heavenly resurrection at the end of days which encompasses all mankind. The redemption of Israel and the end of its long exile is promised in the Bible, and this promise must be believed. Christians believe that the prophecies bearing on the redemption of Israel were fulfilled at the time of the Second Temple; Saadia formulates fifteen arguments to refute the Christian belief that the Messiah has already come.

In the ninth treatise, Saadia considers the question of rewards and punishments in the hereafter. He argues that it is rationally impossible that all retribution should take place in this life; therefore it is necessary that there be a future life in which due rewards and punishments may be handed out. The form of retribution, according to Saadia, is very simple and efficient. At the time of the judgment, God will create "two very fine substances" which "will both consist of the same essence." The essence is that of "burning, luminous fire." The substance applied to the wicked will burn, but not shine; that applied to the virtuous will shine and not burn. It is conceivable that the shining light will not only give pleasure to the righteous but also nourish them; it is necessary, however, that some provision for preserving and sustaining the wicked be assumed. They cannot be nourished by the fire that burns them, yet they must be preserved to bear their punishment.

As a kind of afterthought added to Saadia's system of philosophical theology, a tenth treatise dealing with ethics appears in the book. This can hardly be called a part of his system, because, as we have already noted, man's obligations are set forth in the law of God and man's freedom is to choose obedience or disobedience. Within the system itself there is no room for a philosophic ethics. Yet Saadia felt the need to say something on this score. There is nothing very original in what he found to say; the time was not yet ripe for an original Jewish contribution to philosophical ethics. Saadia's treatise on how it is most proper for man to conduct himself in this world does no more than to assert the need for a sane and balanced blending of a wide variety of activities, none carried

to excess, and none omitted altogether. In this counsel of moderation, the authority of the Biblical book of Ecclesiastes is used
to support a program that is essentially derived from the Platonic
tradition, a psychology of morals based on the golden mean.

The intellectual activity stimulated among Jews by their contact with Muslim schools of philosophy came to a peak in the
work of Saadia. His work may have begun as an attempt to refute
the Karaite rationalism of such men as Anan and Benjamin. It
grew and developed far beyond its original intent and became the
first complete philosophic interpretation of Judaism. Saadia's ingenious use of reason to support Biblical and rabbinic traditionalism was the climax of Jewish life in the Muslim east.

CHAPTER SIX

Jewish Philosophy in Spain

AT THE HEIGHT of its expansion, in the wave of dynamic activity
that followed the birth of the religion of Islam, Muslim political
and cultural power threatened to overwhelm Europe. One of the
geographic areas in which Muslim advance came early was Spain,
where by the middle of the tenth century A.D. a strong and highly
cultivated Muslim kingdom flourished in Andalusia. The Umayyad
family of Caliphs who ruled Muslim Spain were men of liberal
spirit. They recognized and rewarded intellectual and cultural
activity regardless of whether it came from Muslim or non-Muslim
sources. In this atmosphere, Jewish intellectual life opened a
glorious period of flourishing creativity. The center of the Jewish
world shifted from the dying Talmudical academies of Sura and
Pumbeditha, in Babylonia, to the rising schools and scholars of
Andalusia. Jews carried on work in the medical sciences and astronomy, wrote poetry, began studies in the grammar of the Hebrew
language which had far-reaching effects on Bible study, and even
started a Talmudical academy in the city of Cordova. Some Jewish
leaders rose to positions of prominence and influence in court
circles and used their wealth to support learning among their co-
religionists. For nearly five centuries, until the expulsion of the
Jews from Spain in 1492, Spanish Jewry lived in a true Golden Age.

During this time of glorious development, Jewish scholars wrote
in the Arabic language as well as in their sacred tongue, Hebrew.

They read and studied books and treatises that were available to them in Arabic and translated many of these works into Hebrew. They were subject to all the intellectual influences that flowed from the Muslim world, and a major part of their intellectual effort was devoted to the attempt to reconcile this new world of ideas with the traditional heritage of the Bible and the works of rabbinical scholarship. A great many of the ideas to which the Jews were now introduced were preserved from the high point of ancient Greek speculations in science and in philosophy. Most of these works were unknown in the Christian world of Europe, and had been preserved through the devotion of Asiatic Christians in Syria and Persia. From these sources, the Greek works had been taken over by Muslims and had become the basis upon which their advanced thought was founded. In Spain, for the first time, these much traveled Greek ideas became part of the intellectual currency of Jewish thinkers.

We must remember that the Muslim conquerors did not dominate all of the Iberian Peninsula, not even all of Spain. Portugal and a good part of Spain were still in Christian hands. As a result, the cultural life of the peninsula, and, in particular, its religious life, revealed a crazy-quilt pattern, with Islam, Christianity, and Judaism, three sister religions developed out of the same Biblical tradition, competing for prestige and power. In the confrontation of these three cultural traditions, there was frequent occasion for controversy, and a consequent sharpening of the tools of intellectual argumentation. As far as argument from the Bible was concerned, the Jews of Spain were at no disadvantage; when, however, their opponents began to utilize the philosophic ideas that had passed from Greece into the Muslim world or into the Christian mind, it became necessary for the Jewish scholars to absorb the contents and the meanings of these into their own thought systems. If they had not done so, they would have been overwhelmed in debate.

Yet these ideas were Greek; they arose within the Greek pagan culture, and while it is unquestionable that they represent a trend to monotheism among the ablest speculative minds of Greece, the approach they illustrated was philosophic and rational. The Jewish tradition was of a different sort. It was not, as we have seen, without its philosophic themes, but the characteristic form in which these themes were developed was not rationalistic. Jewish defenders had not only to master a new set of ideas; they had also to acquire a new technique for the presentation of their modified versions of these ideas. Muslim scholars, and, to a lesser extent, Christian scholars, had already developed the techniques of rationalism. It is all the more to the credit of the Jewish philosophers who developed in Spain that they gained a rapid mastery over the tools of philosophic presentation.

In the first instance, they may have moved too rapidly. The first Jewish philosopher in Spain was also the first Spanish philosopher. Even the Muslims did not produce a philosopher born in Spain until half a century after the Jews had done so. Yet this first Spanish philosopher, who was also the first Jewish philosopher in Spain, expressed his ideas in so abstract and untraditional a fashion that he was not identified, until many years later, as a Jew.

SOLOMON IBN GABIROL

Solomon ibn Gabirol was a Spanish Jew, born in 1021, who died before reaching the age of fifty. He was one of the most highly regarded of Jewish poets. Some of his religious verses are still used as part of the religious services in synagogues that follow the liturgy of the Spanish and Portuguese (Sephardic) Jews. In addition, Gabirol wrote much love poetry, though it is uncertain whether he was celebrating a secular love or the love of God. There is a real possibility that Gabirol's theme was the likeness between the love of a man for a woman and the love of a man for God, because one of the central elements in his thinking was the importance of personal faith. He thought that the intuitions of individuals who were moved by a deep religious faith provided true insights into the nature of reality.

During the eight centuries in which Gabirol was known as a poet but not as a philosopher, there was a philosophic work, *The Fountain of Life* (*Fons Vitae*), that was widely studied by Arabic and Christian scholars. *The Fountain of Life* became a popular book because it expressed the widespread sense that religion could not be made a matter of the intellect alone. The core of the view expressed by the book was that feeling and faith are closely connected with truth. The author of this book, originally written in Arabic and then translated into Latin, was known as "Avicebron" or "Avicebrol." Some of the non-Jewish thinkers who studied and quoted *The Fountain of Life* considered its author a Muslim; others regarded him as a Christian. The possibility that he might be a Jew never seems to have crossed their minds. One reason for this is that the author, unlike virtually every Jewish writer, nowhere quoted from the Bible or the Talmud. Perhaps a more important reason is that he devoted himself to the discussion of the most abstract and theoretical questions with which the human mind has ever concerned itself, and carried on his discussion on a level appropriate to the themes he was concerned with, a level of pure speculative thought. At this level of generality, the differences between Judaism, Islam, and Christianity fade into the background and their family likeness shines forth clearly.

It was not generally known that a manuscript abridgment in Hebrew of *The Fountain of Life* had been made, toward the end of the thirteenth century. The Hebrew title was *Mekor Hayim*; the summarizer was Shem Tob ibn Falaquera (1225–90), a minor but careful writer of philosophic commentaries. Falaquera's digest was composed in full awareness that the author of *The Fountain of Life* was Solomon ibn Gabirol, the poet. But the abridged manuscript was not studied among Jews or Christians, nor did Falaquera know that Christian students had translated "Avicebron" into Latin a century earlier. He certainly could not have known that "Avicebron's" idea that there was one universal matter which was the underlying substance of all existence except God's had been accepted by those Christian philosophers who supported the Franciscans against the Dominicans! Not until 1845, when the French-Jewish scholar Salomon Munk found a manuscript copy of Falaquera's summary in the French national library and compared this with the Latin *Fons Vitae* was it known that "Avicebron" was a corruption of "Ibn Gabirol," that the brilliant Spanish-Jewish poet and the influential philosopher were one and the same person.

Like so many other philosophic works, *The Fountain of Life* is written as a dramatic sketch of the unfolding of a pattern of ideas, as a dialogue showing the interplay of minds, rather than as a systematic treatise. It is held together less by logical consistency than by psychological coherence. The two persons of the dialogue are a teacher and his student. Their discussion concerns the three basic concepts of matter, form, and will. Gabirol's view is that matter is not a low and recalcitrant stage of being, but an emanation, or flowing forth, of spiritual substance from the highest of beings, God Himself. Spiritual beings as well as the objects of our common experience are constituted of matter. Matter, then, is not crude physical substance; Gabirol regarded it as intellectual or spiritual. It is inaccurate to think of matter as the equivalent of body. Of course matter as it emerges from the essence of God is more spiritual than matter as we find it in physical objects. There is, for Gabirol, a "chain of being," a descending order of gradations of being from the purely spiritual being of God, in which there is no admixture of body, through the existences of the spiritual realm, such as Intelligence, Soul, and Nature, to the beings of our sublunar world. His theory of emanation, however, accounts for the presence of some spiritual remainder in even the beings farthest removed from the Divine Source. Even what our senses reveal to us in its ultimate coarseness and crudity has its origin in spirit and bears within it some traces of its beginnings. Man, the "little universe" or microcosm, shares the qualities of body with the beings of the sublunar world, yet he is not entirely of this world, since he also shares the qualities of soul with the beings of the intermediate range. Man's make-up is, therefore, a miniature model of the universe, the macrocosm.

MAN AS THE MICROCOSM

The philosophic importance of the conception of man as a microcosm cannot be exaggerated. For if man is a model in miniature of the larger universe, then it follows that we can learn the secrets of the universe by an exploration of the nature of man and his activities. The basic sciences are the human sciences, but through the study of the human sciences we can master the metaphysical and even, to some extent, the theological disciplines. When, in the tradition of the Middle Ages and of classical Greek philosophy, we examine the objects of ordinary experience, including man himself, we find them to be partakers in common of a material basis, but to differ in respect to their form. This leads to the assertion that all things of the sublunar world are composites of matter and form. Gabirol, applying the principle that "We must regard what we find in the lowest levels as the symbol or the analogy of that which exists in the upper realms, for that which is below is a faithful representation of that which is above," now maintains that spiritual beings, with the exception of God, are also composites of matter and form. Their matter is both like and unlike that of the objects of our senses. It is like in being substantial; it is unlike in being closer to the Divine Source.

Next to God, the highest type of existence is Intelligence. Intelligence, too, is composed of matter and form, but these are universal matter and universal form. Universal matter must be understood to include within itself all later, less universal matters;

universal form, similarly, must include within itself all subsequent forms. Everything is, therefore, contained in Intelligence. By means of knowledge of itself, Intelligence knows everything. Its knowledge is not our ordinary knowledge, which requires a process of inquiry. Intelligence has knowledge by immediate intuition of itself. There is no process of learning; there is no expenditure of effort; there is no struggle. In man, too, because he shares the qualities of the higher as well as those of the lower ranges of being, there is a power that corresponds to Intelligence. In addition to man's power of rational thought, moving from premises to conclusions, man is capable of immediate intuitions of the intellect. Below Intelligence in the order of spiritual being is Soul, which corresponds to the rational powers in man. Below Soul is Nature, the agent by means of which body, which, in Gabirol's system, is incapable of any activity, is moved. Man's body, like other bodies, is not capable of self-action; there is, however, a power in man, called "vegetative soul," which is the non-bodily agent causing man's growth, nourishment, and propagation. A further power in man, called "animal soul," underlies and causes man's movements in place or from place to place and his sense perceptions.

We are enabled to understand the higher existents by means of the lower; we move to the upper rungs by climbing the lower ones. When we reach the topmost rung, however, the analogy which has held before no longer holds. There is no specific power in man that enables him to reach out to the knowledge of God. Men can approximate this knowledge; their glimpses of the unity of all existence lead them toward God, the perfect Unity. Nevertheless, human will enables men to hold fast to the reality of God; thus by an act of will man can achieve what cannot be reached by reason. But man's will is a spark of the fire which is the Divine will, the force by means of which God creates His effects in the world. We must not think of the Divine will as something different from God Himself; since God is perfect Unity, His will and His essence must be the same. Yet Will is distinguishable in God's activity as the power that produces both matter and form and unites them into the world and all that is therein. God's will is the dynamic force that explains all creation. "The Will, which is the power of the Creator, extends through and penetrates all things. There can be nothing outside of it, for from it the existence and the continuation of all things is derived."

Gabirol even speaks of a mystical union with the Divine will, though he does not guarantee its final fruition. He refers to a work, now unfortunately lost, in which he treats this question in more detail. What we have in the *Fountain of Life* is the description of a process of spiritual abstraction and purification of the vision from all traces of sense objects, reaching, in the end, to a point from which the ultimate vision may be perceived. The teacher tells his student:

> If you wish to form a picture of these substances, you must raise your intellect to the last intelligible, you must purify it from all sordid sensibility, free it from the captivity of nature and approach with the force of your intelligence to the last limit of intelligible substance that it is possible for you to comprehend, until you are entirely divorced from sensible substance and lose all knowledge thereof. Then you will embrace, so to speak, the whole corporeal world in your being, and will place it in one corner of your soul. When you have done this you will understand the insignificance of the sensible in comparison with the greatness of the intelligible. Then the spiritual substances will be before your eyes, comprehending you and superior to you, and you will see your own being as though you were those substances. Sometimes it will seem to you that you are a part of them by reason of your connection with corporeal substance; and sometimes you will think you are all of them, and that there is no difference between you and them, on account of the union of your being with their being, and the attachment of your form to their forms. . . . When you have raised yourself to the first universal matter and illumined its shadow, you will

see there the wonder of wonders. Pursue this therefore diligently and with love, because this is the purpose of the existence of the human soul, and in this is great delight and extreme happiness.[n]

There are problems in Gabirol's philosophy to which his answers are not particularly satisfactory. One of these is how to deal with space, for spiritual beings are non-spatial, while physical beings exist in space. Yet if there is to be space in the lower world, there must be an analogous principle in the upper worlds. Gabirol does, in fact, say that "Space, as it is seen here below, is a representation of space as it is in the mysterious upper spheres." But what can it mean to say that there is a spiritual space? A similar question may be raised with regard to time. God is eternal, which means timeless; how, then, can He also be Will exerting itself in time? The answer that Gabirol offers maintains the paradox that the Divine will is both eternal and working in time, on the analogy of the spoken word, which in itself corresponds to the Divine will working on the hearer, and the meaning of the spoken word, which is timeless, like God Himself. This analogy does not clarify the problem, but rather obscures it further; we are left with the realization that Gabirol intended to deny the possibility of a knowledge of the Divine will by human reason. We can "know" will only by an act of will. "To reach knowledge of this power, which is not merged either with matter or with form, you must learn to bind your soul with this power." Precisely where a philosophic explanation would be most needed, Gabirol leaves philosophy behind and draws his readers on a mystical quest.

ETHICAL IDEAS OF IBN GABIROL

There are some suggestions, in *The Fountain of Life*, of what Gabirol considered to be the ultimate values and goals of a well-lived life. Man's duty in this world is to strive constantly to bring about the union of his soul with the upper world to which it properly belongs. In a small treatise called *The Improvement of the Moral Qualities,* written about the year 1045, the poet-philosopher tried to present a systematic account of ethical principles. There has been a great difference of opinion concerning his success in keeping religious dogmas or beliefs out of his account. There is no doubt that Gabirol quoted the Bible much more frequently in *The Improvement of the Moral Qualities* than he did in his longer and more fundamental book. Certainly it would be foolhardy to use the term "secular ethics" of any product of medieval Jewish thought. For all this, Gabirol's work seems to come as close as possible to that description. Saadia had attributed qualities leading to virtue to man's "higher soul," thus largely removing the possibility that man's voluntary effort could lead to the perfection of these qualities, and making man's moral life depend upon the indwelling of dynamic spiritual forces. Gabirol bases his exposition of the moral qualities upon the natural endowments of the human soul, those impulses of the "lower soul" that may be led, by training and discipline, to the living of a moral life, or that may, if undisciplined, lead to evil. He argues, in effect, that virtue can be taught, and he supports the view that the highest achievements possible to man were firmly grounded upon the very same impulses as his everyday activities. For example, Saadia considers "discernment" to be the balancing force of the higher soul, while Gabirol regarded it as the upper limit of the lower soul, "the line, so to speak, where the purely human and the divine meet in man," as Stephen S. Wise [n] said in his excellent study of Gabirol's ethics. Gabirol is concerned with *human* behavior and the way in which *human* character develops.

This does not mean that Gabirol's [n] *Improvement of the Moral Qualities* works out an ethical position completely in independence of the ideas of Jewish theology. Quite the contrary; the author assumes as an unquestioned background the conventional theology of his age. Like most other Jewish thinkers, he felt that it was unnecessary to prove the existence of God. God simply is, and is the Creator. Perhaps the point at which Gabirol may be said to differ most from the philosophies of his age is in his view of man. He is totally unsympathetic to any view that attributes low rank to man in the scale of being. Man, in his thought, is the chief work of God, and man's highest good was God's purpose in the whole creation. Physically man is the most wonderful of the animals; spiritually man is the equal of the angels. Indeed, by "the improvement of the moral qualities," man may become the superior of the angels. Man comes into existence by the emanation, or flowing forth, of Divine qualities, and his soul aspires to ultimate reunion with the Source of all being. The differences between men are the result of the degrees to which they discipline their impulses. To a considerable extent, men are free to choose higher, spiritual ideals as the guides of their lives and to shun baser, physical impulses. The limits of human freedom, Gabirol thinks, are fixed by the celestial bodies; like so many others in his time, he believed in astrology.

Still, he did not believe that astrology was an exact science or that we can foretell precisely what the destiny of each individual may be. Each man, while recognizing that there are limits to the extent to which the process of self-cultivation can be carried through to perfection, should remember also that we do not know what these limits are in any individual case, and should, therefore, strive for the highest development. "Help the celestial bodies with your souls, even as plowing and irrigating help the seed to grow." The first step in the process is self-knowledge, and the heart of man's self-knowledge is included in the idea that man is a microcosm. In the larger universe, or macrocosm, everything is made up of the "four elements," earth, air, fire, and water, in various combinations. Gabirol regards man's five senses as human powers which manifest themselves through the combining of the four elements in the human body; it is the senses which serve as the

164

connection between man's physical body and his spiritual element, his soul. There are non-physical powers in man; but Gabirol considers them to be unrelated to moral development. Once again, since the non-physical powers might be the subject of theological study, Gabirol displays his more secular interests. He maintains that man's moral qualities are judged by his actions, that is, by his relation to the outer world, rather than by the psychical processes going on within himself. But man's relation to the world outside himself depends upon his encounter with the world, and this takes place by means of the physical senses. Man's physical senses are, therefore, the foundation on which he may build a moral life.

To each of the senses, Gabirol assigns specific qualities of the soul; in this way he is able to suggest a pattern of training for each of the virtues. To sight, the most important of the senses, Gabirol attributes meekness and a sense of shame as appropriate virtues, and pride and impudence as their corresponding vices. The power of sight is within the control of the individual; he can decide what he is to see. The use of the eyes can be directed by the will; one can close or open his eyes consciously. The eye has vision only while a man is awake. Similarly, the virtues of the sense second in importance, hearing, are love and mercy; its vices, hatred and cruelty. Gabirol's position here is most at odds with that of Saadia, who considered love and hate among the spiritual or psychic powers which are independent of will and therefore impossible to train. Gabirol's insistence upon the ability to train men to practice the virtues of love and mercy rather than the vices of hatred and cruelty accounts for his placing them among the natural qualities of animal life, the qualities in respect to which men can improve by training. The third sense, smell, yields the virtues of good-will and alertness and the vices of wrath and jealousy. Touch, represented especially by its chief organ, the hand, reveals the virtues of liberality and courage and the corresponding vices of miserliness and cowardice. Taste, the lowest of the senses in Gabirol's scheme, is connected with the virtues of cheerfulness, tranquility, and

165

remorse, and their opposites, grief, apprehensiveness, and an un-repentant spirit. As may be imagined, Gabirol is forced to perform feats of great ingenuity in accounting for the connection between the qualities and the senses.

It is interesting to notice that the aim of the ethical life, the goal sought for by "the improvement of the moral qualities," is the reunion of the human soul with its Divine source. Although Gabirol's presentation is secular to a degree just short of naturalism, we must recognize that the underlying motive of his manual for the training of the senses toward the higher qualities is unques-tionably religious. More than this, as we have seen, the more speculative discussion in *The Fountain of Life* also points to the union of man's upward-reaching spirit with the Divine will, to a knowledge of God coming not through the ordinary channels of intellect but through an exertion of human will climaxed by mysti-cal intuition. The parallel between the two methods proposed is striking. Perhaps these two works suggest ways for two types of men to strive for union with God: for the man of questing and querying intellect, it is the way of *The Fountain of Life* that is proper. He must follow the promptings of intellectual analysis until they lead him beyond physical substances to the spiritual substances from which the physical draw their being; here he will stand at the threshold of union with God, a threshold that can be crossed only by an act of will. For the average, not particularly intellectual man, the way leads from the objects of the senses to the refinement of the qualities of soul that are associated with the senses; the discipline of the moral qualities can lead him, too, to the threshold, in a path suitable to his character and temperament. The final fulfillment, the crossing of the final barrier, is not dis-cussed in either of the two works by Gabirol that we have preserved to us. It may be that this ultimate step was the subject of another work, for all we know the lost work to which reference has been made. One thing that we can assert with confidence is that the last step could be neither a work of the mind, of philosophical character, nor a work of the will, of ethical character; mystical experience alone would be adequate to its consummation.

BAHYA IBN PAKUDA

One of the best-loved and most widely read of the classics of Spanish-Jewish philosophy was the *Duties of the Heart* (*Hoboth ha-Lebaboth*), of Bahya ben Joseph ibn Pakuda. So little is known of the life of this wise and sensitive, warm-hearted and pious writer that even the date of his book is in dispute. The most probable of the guesses is that Bahya's masterpiece was written during the first half of the twelfth century, and that the thought of its author was influenced by the ideas of the Arabic philosopher al-Gazzali (1059–1111) as well as by Gabirol and other earlier Jewish thinkers. We must also bear in mind the less likely possibility that Bahya worked a full century earlier and that the similarities between his ideas and those of Gabirol and Gazzali are owing to his influence on them, rather than the reverse.

The *Duties of the Heart* is typical of a class of philosophic books whose authors are less interested in pure speculative thought than in the application of speculation to the everyday business of living; it is a work of practical ethics, not one concerned with ethical theory. In large measure the practical tone that is maintained throughout Bahya's book must have been a major factor in establishing its popularity. It is not only in the twentieth century that most people are concerned with ideas for their bearing on daily life and for their practical consequences, rather than for their internal consistency or their absolute truth. Among the Muslim theologians, particularly those whose ideas had an ascetic tendency, there was an established contrast between external conformity with the ceremonial and ritual requirements of religion and the inner attitudes of the believer, the index to his true religious feelings. The original source of this distinction may have been the great Prophets of the Hebrew Bible, for they, too, emphasized the central importance of inner religion, manifested externally in ethical relations with one's fellow men. They, too, suggested that one might conform to all the ritual requirements without a spirit of religious concern. Bahya was certainly familiar with the message of the Prophets; but he knew also what the Muslim writers had said. His title was borrowed from the Muslims, for they referred to outward observance as "the duties of the limbs" and to inward spirituality as "the duties of the heart."

Bahya's most characteristic and possibly most original idea is a modification of both the prophetic and the ascetic views. For he saw that the same distinction between outer practice and inner intention could be made with respect to ethical practice itself. There are men whose lives are marked by incessant preoccupation with the most minute of ethical distinctions, but who are not moved to this ethical concern by an inner spirit of piety. Ethics, too, can be transformed into a matter of ritual. There is an ethics of "the limbs" as well as an ethics of "the heart." Bahya's intent was to persuade his readers that true piety demands a joyous and loving performance of the ethical "duties of the heart." He acknowledges the force of a distinction made by Saadia between those of the Biblical commandments that are in complete accord with the dictates of reason and those with regard to which reason has nothing decisive to say and which, therefore, are obligatory only because they are revealed or traditional. Saadia had made this distinction apply to all the commandments of the Bible; Bahya considered it to apply only to the "duties of the limbs." All of the "duties of the heart," he was convinced, are in accord with reason, the positive commandments of the Bible being directions to act in a way which reason approves as right, and the negative commandments being injunctions against acting in a way which reason condemns as wrong. Yet Bahya went on to insist that even the most minor of the traditional commandments, if observed out of

168

love of God and loyal devotion to His commandments, could be transformed into a profound spiritual experience.

Before entering into the ten major sections of the *Duties of the Heart*, Bahya explained and justified the work in an introductory section. Wisdom, he says, is, next to the creation of men with mature faculties of perception and comprehension, the noblest gift of God to men. Wisdom, which "constitutes the life of their spirit," is of three sorts: physics, mathematics, and theology. Although these three divisions are all "gates" which God Himself has opened as ways in which men can gain an understanding of religion and of the world, they differ in their areas of usefulness. The physical sciences are needed in particular for our knowledge of secular affairs; mathematical sciences, too, are additional ways of learning about the world in which men live. Because these sciences are concerned chiefly with man's physical well-being, they hold a lower rank than theology, the source of man's knowledge of religion, which men have an obligation to study. "To study it, however, for the sake of worldly advantages is forbidden." The three avenues to knowledge of theology are a sound intellect, or Reason, the revealed Scripture, and the Tradition of the sages of the past.

THE INWARD DUTIES

Bahya explains that he has studied the works of other writers and found the study rewarding, but that he has not found any of them to have written specifically of the "Inward Duties." To supply the need for such a treatise on "the science of the Duties of the Heart," presenting the principles and divisions of this "science" systematically, he composed his book. He expresses the interesting thought that the division of duties into the visible and the invisible, the outward and the inward, rationally flows from the division of man into body and soul. Body and soul are equally indications of God's goodness to men. Body is visible; human gratitude to God for the gift of body should be manifested by visible service, the outward duties. Soul is invisible; human gratitude to God for the gift of soul should be manifested by invisible service, the duties of the heart. These duties are:

> that we should acknowledge the Unity of God in our hearts; believe in Him and in His Laws and accept His service; revere Him, be humble and abashed before Him; love Him, trust in Him, and surrender our very lives to Him; abstain from what He hates, dedicate our activities to His name; meditate on the benefits He bestows, and similar duties that are fulfilled in thought and by the exercise of inward faculties, but do not call for the activity of the bodily organs.

One thing that should be evident from this list is that the inwardness of Bahya's spirituality is not of a mystical character. There are those who have found in Bahya a similarity to the Sufi mystics of Islam, whose aim was the absorption of their own individuality into the being of God. At no point does Bahya share such an aim. The highest stage of human life, in his thought, is marked by an intense love of God, achieved by the complete triumph of reason over desire. The love of God which is the goal of human striving should have in it no admixture of other motives. God is to be loved solely for His own sake, not for any reward that He may give.

Bahya's reflections lead him to the belief that the entire structure of inward duties rests upon the "whole-hearted acceptance of the Unity of God." He begins his treatment of the subject, accordingly, with a section on Unity in which his arguments follow closely those advanced by Saadia in the *Book of Beliefs and Opinions,* and of course those of the Mutazilite philosophers to whom, as we have seen, Saadia was indebted. Necessarily, as Bahya himself points out, his discussion of the Unity of God has to be presented in a technical style instead of the direct and easy manner of the remainder of the book. The argument for God's Unity is both too subtle and too frequently presented by the philosophers of Bahya's time to be restated without the use of logical and even mathematical proofs.

Perhaps the clearest instance of the need that Bahya feels for a more careful and precise presentation comes in the eighth chapter of the first part of the *Duties of the Heart.* Here his problem is one that Saadia had also faced. We use the word "one" constantly in talking of weights and measures or of objects of our day-to-day experience; even in such a use, the word must bear some relation to the idea of unity. When we use the word "one" in speaking of God, again it is derived from the conception of unity. There must surely be some way in which we can distinguish between God's Unity and other senses of "unity," for if there is no such distinction, then God is like other things in respect to unity; this, to a pious medieval student, is intolerable. Bahya makes the distinction, first, as one between absolute or true Unity and relative or conventional Unity. Relative Unity is the unity ascribed to those things that in another context might equally well be spoken of as plural. We may speak, for example, of one species when we wish to call attention to the classification of a number of individuals under one general name; if, however, we wish to call attention to the similarity of this species and others, we must speak of a plurality of species, a number of which are grouped together in one genus. In such a case, the unity that we assign to the species is an accidental product of the context, not an essential property of the species. A similar but not identical case, to Bahya's way of thinking, is the ascription of unity to an individual person; here the plurality is that of a composite being, made up of body and soul or of matter and form, which are two, not one.

In addition to this sort of relative Unity, there is a Unity which is essential, not accidental. This is of two types: numerical, and concrete. Numerical Unity is the number one, which is essentially an instance of Unity, but Unity of a subjective or mental kind; it is a Unity which must be grasped in thought and cannot be experienced. It is true Unity, but differs from the second type of absolute Unity, the absolute Unity of God, which is concrete and existent. Now God's Unity has been so described as to be unique and incomparable; it is an essential Unity, which can be called plural in no possible context; it cannot be subject to change or to transformation or to any form of movement. Since Unity (mathematically conceived) is the cause of plurality, the true concrete Unity, the Divine Unity, is the root and cause of all that is. In Bahya's era, it would have been impossible for him to have discussed his subject without using such an argument.

THE DIVINE ATTRIBUTES

At the end of his first part, Bahya divides the attributes of God into two groups. The first group is of God's "essential" attributes. These are the attributes that belonged to God before the creation of the world and will continue to belong to Him after the world has been destroyed. They are not, in any sense, accidental, for we cannot conceive of God as not possessing these attributes. God *is;* for from that which is non-existent, no action and no result can come; His works are manifest; therefore, He *is.* God is *One;* we have sketched above the reasoning on which this assertion is based. God is *Eternal;* the world must have a beginning which is not preceded by any other beginning; God must, therefore, be the absolute beginning and hence be eternal. These are stated as three essential attributes, but they are not three, because each of them necessarily implies the other two. That we must express them in three statements is a limitation of our language, not an indication of any plurality in God.

The second group of Divine attributes is composed of those terms that we apply to God because of His actions or their effects. Bahya calls these "active" attributes. To this group belong all those references in the Bible which speak of God in terms of form and bodily likeness or which refer to bodily movements. The older rabbis and the translators of the Bible into Aramaic, Bahya observes, paraphrased expressions of this sort by referring them to God's Glory, not to God Himself. The reason for the Bible's using these bodily terms is not to give a description of God but only to provide some conception by means of which the thought of God's existence can be firmly fixed in men's minds. If the Scriptures had used a precise philosophical language instead of these pictorial and picturesque terms, the majority of mankind would have remained without any knowledge of God.

Bahya went one step further by saying that even the essential attributes should not be understood as making positive statements about God's nature, which is beyond human ken. He anticipated Moses Maimonides in suggesting that the purpose of asserting the essential attributes was not to affirm anything of God, but to deny the opposite of what was asserted. Thus to say "God is One" must mean "God is not plural"; "God exists" means "God is not non-existent"; "God is Eternal" means "God is not subject to destruction." And so the upshot of Bahya's argument is that there are two and only two kinds of attributes of God: negative and active.

THE PIOUS LIFE

From the end of the first part, Bahya is able to avoid the subtleties of philosophic reasoning and to present his case for a life of pious inwardness simply and forthrightly. The second part speaks of created things and the goodness of God to His creatures. If the majority of men do not recognize God's superabundant goodness, the reasons are that they are too preoccupied with secular affairs and with the pleasure of the world, too concerned with what they would like to get but have not yet gained, to think of the benefits that they have received. They take the many benefits that He has bestowed upon them for granted and consider the losses and misfortunes that no life is without as evidence of evil. Men are unable to understand that God's intention in causing them to suffer in person or property is that they may come through these mishaps to beneficial results. In this part, what Bahya means by the "examination" of created things is meditation on the marks of Divine wisdom that can be discovered in God's creation. The obligation to study created things rests upon this further reflection. It is not enough merely to study the elements and what results from their combination; one must use this study as a way of leading his thoughts to God.

> The wise and intelligent man will choose from the world for study its fine and spiritual elements; use them as a ladder by which to obtain proofs of the existence of the Creator, to Whose service he will then devote himself with zeal according to his heart-felt recognition of the exalted greatness of the Creator, and his realization of the Almighty's goodness to all creatures and special favor He has shown to the observer who had done nothing special nor acquired any moral quality that would entitle him to divine reward.

The true student embarked upon this course will shun luxuries because of their tendency to distract his heart from the contemplation of God. He will be sparing in attention to his comfort and material well-being; but Bahya does not suggest any extreme form of asceticism.

Although there are marks of the Divine wisdom to be found all about us, and although Bahya classifies these marks in seven groups, yet it is to the study of mankind that men should most ardently devote themselves. "The evidence of Divine wisdom which is nearest and clearest is that manifested in the human species, a world on a small scale, the ultimate purpose of the existence of the larger world." Bahya passes man's constitution and his powers in brief review and shows in how many ways he is the beneficiary of the Divine love and wisdom. It is interesting that under this head Bahya considers the question of human government and argues the virtues of monarchy. The argument for Divine design in the universe is sometimes pursued to absurd lengths; Bahya's economic views, for example, appear in the following quotation.

A subject that you should also examine, and derive from it evidences of the divine wisdom and beneficence, is the agreement of human beings to buy and sell goods for gold and silver which, through God's mercy, they endeavor to accumulate and thus improve their positions, though their actual needs are not thereby satisfied. For when any one is afflicted with hunger and thirst through want of food or lack of water, an abundance of gold and silver will not avail him or supply his wants. And if any one suffers pain in any of his limbs, he will not be cured by silver and gold; for while other minerals are largely used for medicinal purposes, this is less so in the case of gold or silver.

A wondrous evidence of wisdom it also is that, while a few individuals possess large amounts of these precious metals, the majority of mankind have but little of them. If all human beings possessed them in abundance, they could not use them as a medium for obtaining what they desire. Some people have much and others have little. They are precious from one point of view and of little account from another, because intrinsically they are useless. This too is within the plan of the Creator's supreme wisdom.

Surely it is surprisingly naïve to ascribe the shortage of precious metals and the inequality of their distribution among men to the providential wisdom of God.

In the third part of *Duties of the Heart,* Bahya explains the grounds that lead to the obligation of men to devote themselves to the service of God. Part Four develops the most indispensable of man's duties to God: to trust in Him. Tranquility of soul is the reward of those who place their trust firmly in God; a man who does not do so inevitably places his trust in someone or something other than God, and "God withdraws His providential care from that individual and leaves him in the power of the one in whom he trusted." The man who trusts in God becomes, as it were, an alchemist of the spirit. He learns how to turn the baser content of his life into the true gold of the spirit. Next Bahya turns to the obligation to carry on all affairs in a spirit of wholehearted devotion to God and a warning against the hypocrisy of an external pretense of wholehearted devotion when the spirit of devotion is not present. Wholehearted devotion to God means "that in every act, public and private, the aim and purpose should be service of God for His name's sake, to please Him only, without thought of winning the favor of human creatures." Anything less than this is inadequate to the superabundance of God's goodness to men. Parts Six and Seven deal with specific virtues, Humility and Repentance.

SPIRITUAL ACCOUNTING

In the eighth part, however, Bahya moves to the question of Spiritual Accounting, that is, "striving with the aid of one's understanding to consider his religious and secular concerns, so that he may know what he possesses and what is due from him." The duty of spiritual accounting falls on all men alike, but the extent to which each man can carry out this obligation varies with his intelligence and the clarity of his understanding. There are many ways of spiritual accounting; Bahya enumerates thirty of them as illustrations of the methods by which the accounting process can be made the basis for reorganizing and redirecting one's spiritual life. The process is not completed by a knowledge of the methods of spiritual accounting, even though this knowledge itself demands far more than a surface understanding. The completion of the process is the changed life; "Strive by means of these instructions to improve yourself, and improve others; so you will attain the great recompense bestowed by God."

One of the methods of spiritual accounting that Bahya mentions and discusses briefly in the eighth part is abstinence from worldly interests. Part Nine is devoted to a fuller discussion of the theme. This is the section of the *Duties of the Heart* that has led some critics to associate Bahya with the ascetic Muslim thinkers and mystics. Abstinence, as Bahya uses the term, is, however, not as extreme as asceticism. Generally speaking, abstinence means having the power to do something and voluntarily refraining from doing so. It is, says Bahya, "bridling the inner lust." Abstinence is of two sorts; there is a general abstinence that is practiced by men and by other living creatures for the sake of health or of proper management of one's affairs. This includes government under laws and rules prescribed by physicians. In addition, there is a special abstinence to which beings possessed of reason and of the Bible are obligated. This way of abstaining is the particular subject which concerns Bahya here. The aim of the Bible is "to make the understanding predominate and prevail over the soul's longings." When the longings overwhelm the understanding, the result is sin. The aim of the Bible is, accordingly, to teach men to avoid sin. Of all the definitions of special abstinence given by various writers, Bahya considers the one most in accord with the Bible to be "denying oneself all relaxation and physical pleasure, limiting oneself to mere satisfaction of natural needs without which one could not exist, and excluding everything else from the mind."

We should note that among the other definitions of special abstinence which Bahya repeats but does not accept is "holding this world in abhorrence and curtailing desires." This is more nearly the position of those who advocate asceticism; Bahya, true to the Jewish tradition which holds that, since the world was created by God, it cannot be evil, never suggests abhorrence for the world. He never demands that the abstainer deny his natural needs, only that he keep his indulgence of these natural needs to a minimum. Indeed, Bahya describes the true ascetics in the following words:

> They renounce everything that distracts them from the thought of God. They flee from inhabited places to the deserts or high mountains, where there is no company, no society. They eat whatever they find—grass growing on the soil and leaves of the trees. They dress in worn garments and raw wool. They take shelter in the rocks; their fear of God drives away fear of creatures. The love of God delights them so much that they do not think of the love of human beings.

He follows this description by saying that "Of all classes, this class is furthest removed from the 'golden mean' which our religion teaches, because they renounce worldly interests completely, and our religion does not bid us to give up social life altogether."

A type of abstinence that is nearer to the Biblical demand is a middle way. It is a control of life in the midst of life. Those who follow the middle way renounce the superfluous only, not the needful. They improve both their bodies and their souls and thus earn a double reward, happiness in this world and bliss in the world to come. But those who are nearest to the Bible and, therefore, most in tune with the spirit of the Jewish religion are "those who walk on the lowest level of abstinence." These men do not withdraw even from the physical occupations of other men; their separation from the world is a separation of hearts and minds, never a separation of bodies. They are not eager for death, though they yearn for the world to come. "They prepare provisions (good deeds) for the time of their departure, and before they are taken hence they give thought to what will await them in their abode of rest. . . . This class in its conduct is nearer the correct balance and nearer the right road . . . than the classes previously mentioned." Piety, Bahya believes, is shown by abstinence, but he rejects all forms of extreme asceticism, as contrary to the Bible.

The final section of Bahya's book is concerned with the love of God. Abstinence frees the heart from attachment to the things of the flesh so that men can give their full love to God. "This is the final aim of all noble qualities and the highest degree which men serving God can attain." All that has gone before is but preparation for this last step in moral development. Not until the love of the world has been ousted from the heart by rigorous self-discipline can love of God find room there. Love of God is "the soul's yearning for the Creator . . . the ultimate manifestation of pure love." There are other ways of loving God; we may love Him for His goodness to us or for His mercy in over-looking and forgiving our sins. Pure love of God, however, goes beyond these lesser loves to a love of God for Himself. It is reached only as the climax of the process of understanding and self-development described in the *Duties of the Heart*.

The early phase of medieval Jewish philosophy in Europe culminates in the books of Solomon ibn Gabirol and Bahya ibn Pakuda. They strove valiantly to lead the understanding and the reason of their fellow Jews, sharpened by contact with the Arabic versions of classical Greek philosophy, to a recognition of the inward piety and poetry of the Jewish religion. It would have been inconceivable to them that reason might destroy faith. True reason, they thought, was in accord with their faith. Indeed, they might well have said that faith was needed not to support but to soften and humanize the cold light of reason.

LESSER LIGHTS OF SPANISH-JEWISH
PHILOSOPHY: PSEUDO-BAHYA

In addition to the masterly works of Gabirol and Bahya, there were a number of lesser philosophic writings that arose in the same cultural and social context. One of these, a treatise on the soul, written in Arabic, was incorrectly ascribed to Bahya on the title page of the surviving manuscript. There are major differences in view between Bahya and the anonymous author of this treatise, *Reflections on the Soul*. The author, unlike Bahya, believes in the doctrine, which we have spoken of earlier, that the spiritual and material aspects of the created world form a graded descending series of emanations. Like the Kabbalists, our author thinks that there were ten such emanations. In other respects, however, the anonymous author follows a pattern of thought more usually associated with the tradition deriving from Aristotle. If, therefore, we try to establish a source for his ideas, we should look for an Arabic school of philosophy which combined a doctrine of emanations, derived from the neo-Platonic tradition, with other teachings coming through the Aristotelian tradition. Such a source is to be found in the Brothers of Purity, a secret Muslim order of the tenth century. In the encyclopedic work, composed of fifty-one treatises, that was compiled by this secret order, these two traditions are coupled in precisely the fashion of the anonymous author of *Reflections on the Soul*.

Our author conceives of the soul as an altogether spiritual substance that existed before the body to which it is attached and that will continue to exist after the body has decayed. He had no sympathy with any view that eliminated, even in part, the complete independence of the soul, especially any attempt to account for the soul as an "accident" of physical substance. It was his contention that spiritual substance behaved in ways that were out of the question for physical substances; that the soul, in these respects, behaved like spiritual substance; and, therefore, that the soul could not be, in any sense, physical or accidental to the physical. For example, every physical substance has a saturation point; there is a point at which it can absorb no more of any attribute. But knowledge is an attribute to the soul, and there is no saturation point with respect to knowledge; indeed, quite the reverse is the case—

the more knowledge a person has, the more capable he is of absorbing more knowledge.

To account for the nature of the human soul, we must look at this author's theory of emanations. The first of these pure and simple essences, nearest to God, is that which the Bible refers to as the Glory or Name of God (or the *Shekhinah*); other Hebrew writings call it Wisdom, but the Greek philosophers call it the Active Intellect. The second emanation is called "the Glory of the God of Israel" (Ezekiel viii, 9); the philosophers refer to it as Universal Soul. The third emanation is Nature conceived as the principle of life and motion, that is, an angelic or spiritual principle, not a physical nature. Since these are emanations from God, they are to be conceived more as a continuity than as separate entities. Universal Soul, intermediate between Intellect and Nature, shares in the qualities and characters of both.

Fourth in order of emanation, but differing from these three in having no powers of activity or life or motion in itself, is the matter out of which the world and all that is in it are made. The power of matter is limited to its capacity to accept whatever accidental form is impressed upon it. Matter is the primeval darkness of which the creation story in the book of Genesis speaks. Fifth comes the celestial Sphere; sixth the stars which are moved by the Sphere; seventh, fire; eighth, air; ninth, water; and tenth, earth. In a broad sense, the term "creation" may be used of the emergence or emanation of these ten primary essences; more strictly, creation would be used only of the first three, for they are the product of the will of God, and come out of nothing else.

After we have passed the ten emanations to which by extension the term "creation" may be applied, the appropriate word is "formation," because all subsequent beings are formed by the combination of the elements. Man was the last creature to be formed. In man's being there are traces of all that came into existence before him. The order of emanation is, however, reversed in man, so that the first emanations, Intellect and Soul, appear last in man. Man's soul is, then, related to the Universal Soul as well as to Intellect and to Nature. The individual differences that distinguish one man from another result from the fact that the soul of each man stays a longer or shorter time in the spheres through which it passes on the way to being incorporated in him. How long its stay is to be, God determines. Thus God's decision is responsible for the temperamental differences between man and man and for the differences in capacity to which these varieties of temperament give rise. Man's soul, despite this degree of Divine predetermination, has freedom of choice in this world; it is individuation, not destiny, that God intends by varying the qualities of the souls of men.

Our author's proof of the immortality of the soul is, if his theory of its origin be accepted, an easy one. Those things which are composed of the elements, we know, return in decay to the elements of which they are composed. Like them, the soul returns to its own source, which is indestructible. Again, God, Who has a purpose in all that He has instituted, has decreed death for men. If death meant the destruction of the soul as well as the body, then death would be purposeless, and we may not assume that God would decree anything purposeless. The destruction of the body in death must, therefore, be for the purpose of liberating the soul to a form of existence like that of the angels. There are rewards and punishments attached to this return to pure spirit, indeed, if a soul has permitted itself to be completely sullied during its stay in the body, it may even be destroyed. Other souls, those that have retained their moral purity and the intellectual integrity with which they left the angelic state, will return to that state immediately on the dissolution of the body. Those souls that have fallen into patterns intermediate between the perfection of the unsullied and the wickedness of the doomed will be treated in various intermediate ways, according to the degrees of virtue and knowledge which they have retained.

ABRAHAM BAR HIYYA

In the first half of the twelfth century, Abraham bar Hiyya was one of the learned intermediaries who made much of the scientific thought of the Orient available to Europe. He was particularly important in transmitting mathematical, astronomical, and calendric science to the Jews of France and Germany, who utilized what they learned from him in their rabbinical studies. Abraham was only very incidentally concerned with philosophic matters, and here, too, it is less for his originality than for his scholarship that he is remembered. In but one work he introduced philosophic themes, a small treatise called *Meditation of the Soul*. Like the major work of Bahya, this is primarily a work of practical ethics. Abraham was chiefly concerned to preach the necessity of repentance. The philosophic ideas are secondary and subordinate to this purpose. They are, like the ideas in the anonymous treatise on the soul, derived from the remnants of Greek psychology that were current in the learned world of the time. The doctrine of emanations, however, which was central in the work of pseudo-Bahya, is not to be found in Abraham bar Hiyya's *Meditation of the Soul*.

To replace the emanations as a method of accounting for the celestial origin of the human soul, Abraham introduces the Aristotelian idea of pure form. Matter and form combine to make up everything that exists, except God. God is outside of these elements, a principle that makes their combination possible. Indeed, both matter and form were present potentially in God's wisdom. Form most completely free from mixture with matter, pure form, is to be known in the beings of the upper world, including souls as well as angels. The closest visible parallel to pure form, which Abraham uses as a symbol of pure form, is light. Just as light illuminates objects, making them visible, so pure form enters into combination with unformed matter and transforms it into particular visible things. This analogy may be carried even further, for just as light is invisible in itself, so pure form cannot be seen. Only in combination are the possibilities of both matter and form to be realized. They are dependent upon one another.

Abraham bar Hiyya classified pure form into four types, one of which never unites with matter and therefore remains always unseen. A second type joins firmly and permanently with matter to make the everlasting beings, the heavens and the stars. Third, there is a kind of form that unites temporarily with matter to make earthly beings of all sorts except for man. The fourth kind of form, represented by the human soul, can exist either united with matter or independent of it. This type can join with a particular body for a time and then leave it and return to a bodiless existence. By means of this special classification of the human soul, Abraham was able to argue for the immortality of the soul without any difficulty. We should, however, point out that on this view of the soul it would be equally easy to argue in favor of the doctrine of reincarnation. There is no reason why each soul should be limited to one act of combination with a particular body. If the soul can exist either in bodily shape or as pure form, then a restless soul might alternate between embodiment and spiritual existence throughout eternity. Abraham himself suggests this rational possibility, in discussing the views of those thinkers who argue from reason alone, since they do not accept Divine revelation. But he limits the possibility of reincarnation to the souls of pious men who have not gained enough wisdom during their lives.

Rewards and punishments, then, depend upon the extent to which during life each embodied soul has developed in piety and wisdom. Piety is expressed in moral terms as well as religiously; it includes both right conduct and the fear of God. Wisdom may be purely speculative, but such a philosophic theory of the nature of wisdom would not tell precisely and specifically what a man must know. The one source that is able to tell men what they must know and what they must do to be saved is Divine revelation, the *Torah*, the sacred Law. The Jews, to whom the Law was given and for whom the study of the Law is a cardinal obligation, have an advantage in the search for salvation; this is what the doctrine of the Chosen People means to Abraham bar Hiyya. He is not convinced, however, that others are unable to reach the same perfection of character and wisdom as Jews can; these others start with a certain handicap, but they can make it up through repentance.

JOSEPH IBN ZADDIK

A rather more substantial attempt to develop a systematic philosophic position was made by the scholar and poet Joseph ben Jacob ibn Zaddik (died, 1149), of Cordova. Ibn Zaddik's philosophic work was called *The Microcosm* (*Olam Katon*). Generally, this word suggests a treatise in which man, the microcosm or "small universe," is used as a means of understanding the macrocosm or "large universe." That is to say, a microcosmic philosophy bases itself upon the theory that there is a point-for-point correspondence between the nature of man and the nature of the universe. Human self-knowledge, on such a theory, furnishes us with a digest of all knowledge. There is no need for the seeker after wisdom to go through the lengthy process of studying each of the special sciences. The study of human nature will get him much more rapidly and more simply to the same destination.

In fulfilling his program of showing that this is a proper approach, Joseph ibn Zaddik wrote what is, in effect, a small encyclopedia. His work discusses science in its first part; man and human nature in the second part; Divine unity in the third part; and questions of God's justice in its final section. The latter two sections, on Unity and Justice, constitute a philosophical theology on the pattern of the Mutazilite works of the Arab philosophers and of some of the earlier works of Jewish philosophy that we have discussed. In the first two parts, Ibn Zaddik establishes the central point in his philosophical outlook, the detailed correspondence between the universe and man, the macrocosm and the microcosm.

By way of prelude, before coming to the subject of physics or the nature of the physical world, Joseph introduces his readers to his theory of knowledge. Before one can speak of *what* one knows, it is important to describe *how* one knows. Man, he says, knows through perception, but perceiving means more than the mere physical act of using the sense organs. There is a second type of perception through the intellect. What men perceive by the use of the organs of sense is merely the outer shell of things. Intellectual perception, or reason, is necessary to get beyond the outer shell to the inner reality of things. He associates this distinction with the classical philosophic distinction between particulars, which are available to sense perception, and essences or universals, which can be reached only by reason. True knowledge, then, cannot be achieved by sense perception alone, for true knowledge is knowledge of essences. Ibn Zaddik also accounts for the distinction in terms of the mixture of the body and soul and man's make-up. The sense organs are of the body, and share with the body a certain grossness and materiality. This coarseness prevents sense perception from getting below the surface of the objects of knowledge. Reason participates in the nature of the soul, which is nonmaterial and fine; reason can, therefore, penetrate beneath the surface of objects to their very essence.

Ibn Zaddik also divides knowledge on another basis. Some knowledge, he says, is necessary; if a man is sane and normal, he cannot reject necessary knowledge. Other knowledge is based upon proof or demonstration and logical inference. The evidence for demonstrated knowledge is, however, necessary knowledge, so this is the basis and foundation of all that men know or can know. Now necessary knowledge is of four sorts, which can be reduced to two. Sense perception gives men accurate information, as far as it goes.

Traditional truths, as they come down to us from wise men of the past or as part of the anonymous tradition of a community, constitute a second kind of necessary knowledge, because they are not dependent upon the evidence of our senses. Ultimately, however, they are based upon the sense perceptions of our predecessors, so that this class of necessary truths may be included with the first kind. The third class is composed of statements that carry their own evidence with them, for which no sensible man would ever ask for further proof. These are called self-evident truths. Finally, there are those statements which are called axioms or first principles; ultimately, our philosopher says, these are but a special group of self-evident truths. We have, therefore, two sorts of necessary truths on which to build demonstrations: the evidence of the senses, and self-evident statements. Of these two, man and the lower animals both have physical senses, so that the evidence of the senses is common to man and the animals; for this reason, Ibn Zaddik regards self-evident statement as a higher kind of knowledge.

What, granted this account of knowledge, do we know about the physical world? We know, Joseph says, that it is a combination of matter and form. Of these, it is form that is the decisive element, for it is by means of form that we can differentiate objects. But matter and form are not absolute beings; they are, rather, relative to each other, so that what is matter on one level of analysis is form on another. If we are talking about a wooden chair, for example, wood is the matter of the chair and the form is the particular type of chair intended by the maker or designer. But if we are talking about wood in general, as distinct from metal, then the matter is the four classical elements, earth, air, fire, and water, and the form is wood. In this discussion, Ibn Zaddik does not move far from Aristotle in his general outlook, although he does differ from the Greek philosopher on some matters of detail. Thus Aristotle had said that, of the four elements, earth and water are heavy, because their tendency is to move toward the center of the world, whereas air and fire are light, because their tendency is to move upward, away from the center of the earth. Ibn Zaddik speaks of light and heavy as relative terms, suggesting that a body is light when it is in its natural place and heavy when it is away from its natural place. This is, it is fair to say, a minor difference of interpretation and does not touch the basic structure of the universe as understood by both philosophers. Joseph ibn Zaddik's physics may, then, be described as Aristotelian.

When Ibn Zaddik turns to psychology, the doctrine of correspondence becomes central to his view. Point for point, man's nature corresponds to the physics of the universe. Man is a conbination of the four elements; he is born in their combination. Like other composite things, man is also subject to decay; generation and corruption is the story of man, as it is the story of all physical beings. Some powers, Ibn Zaddik holds, man has in common with plants, some with animals. Even some of man's qualities of character and temperament can be compared with the corresponding qualities of certain animals. Over and above these similarities, however, there is one distinguishing mark in man which differentiates between him and the animals. In man there is a rational soul which survives the destruction and corruption of his body. In the animals, life is the result of a lower type of soul, which man, too, possesses: the animal soul. The animal soul does not survive death. Man's life is the result of the rational soul; death separates the rational soul from its attachment to a body, so that the rational soul survives death and is not subject to decay. Man's rational soul cannot, therefore, be a material or bodily thing, for if it were, it could not give life to the body nor could it survive the body. The rational soul is, therefore, a spiritual substance.

By virtue of his rational soul, man is a being who is obligated to a constant and unremitting search for knowledge and understanding. The ultimate destination of the rational soul is the spiritual world; only those rational souls that fulfill themselves by seeking for knowledge will attain that goal. A man who fails to carry out the purpose of his existence by his refusal to study, so to speak, reduces his rational soul to the level of an animal soul. He eliminates the difference between himself and the animal; indeed, he falls to a level below that of the animals, because they never fail to use their capacities while he does fail to use his. This distinction provides one of the bases on which Ibn Zaddik rests his case for rewards and punishments after death. Of course, he realizes that knowledge alone does not bring eternal rewards; to knowledge, he adds the virtues of righteousness, hope, and humility. Knowledge comes first, however, and is by far the most important, for the other virtues are imitations of the Divine character; and imitation must be based upon previous knowledge. It may be that some men who do not seek knowledge will, nevertheless, seem to manifest the other virtues; Ibn Zaddik argues that, when this is the case, the appearance of virtue is the result of some weakness in, perhaps, the animal soul rather than strength of the rational soul. Thus a man may seem merciful because he is lacking in the fiery qualities of the animal soul. This would not be to his credit. If, on the other hand, he had these fiery animal qualities, but controlled them by the force of his rational soul, he would not merely *seem* merciful; he would *be* merciful, as God is merciful, and his soul would then receive its reward on his death. Once again in Joseph ibn Zaddik, as in so many other Jewish philosophers of the Middle Ages, knowledge and virtue, reason and ethics, are tied together in an unbreakable unity.

ABRAHAM IBN DAUD

If we conceive of the philosophy of medieval times as an attempt to explore the relative merits of faith and reason as avenues to secure knowledge, we should have to say of all the philosophers that we have thus far examined that they regarded faith as the primary highway to truth. They sought in reason a way to clarify the doctrines of faith. Reason was an auxiliary method; its results had to harmonize with the teachings of the Law and the rabbis. With the advent of Abraham ibn Daud of Toledo (born about 1110; died about 1180), a new interpretation was put upon the task of the philosophers. For Ibn Daud regarded reason, the method of philosophy, as primary, and thought that the beliefs and doctrines of Judaism had to be studied to see how they could be made to conform to the teachings of philosophy. He remained convinced that this study would show the harmony of faith and reason; certainly he did not believe that it would be necessary to jettison any of the beliefs of Judaism. He was sure, however, that a study of the Jewish religion that did not begin with a study of scientific philosophy, by which he meant the philosophy of Aristotle as it was known in his time, would end in confusion, contradiction, and even false interpretations of the nature of God.

Abraham ibn Daud was, then, not a poetic or mystical thinker. He was most unsympathetic to the philosophic work of Solomon ibn Gabirol. Gabirol's poetic style Ibn Daud described as diffuse. Ibn Daud's goal was to reach a precision and economy of statement, wholly systematic and scientific. His philosophic method, expressed in his book *The Exalted Faith* (*Emunah Ramah*), was technical and analytic, not speculative, evocative, or suggestive. His knowledge of the work of previous philosophers, and of the Arabic followers of Aristotle in particular, seems far greater than that of any of his Jewish predecessors. In part, this may merely be the result of the fact that more of the writings of Aristotle had become available for study by his time. But it is also, in part, the fruit of a greater temperamental inclination to an analytic approach to ideas.

The starting-point of Ibn Daud's *Exalted Faith* is the question of free-will. Passages in the Bible that can be used for evidence to resolve the dilemma of free-will are contradictory, so that the Bible can be used on either side of the case. The dilemma, put most simply, is that either man's will is free or it is determined by God. If man's will is free, then there is something that God does not control, and God is not all-powerful. On the other hand, if man's will is determined by God, then God's punishment of man is unjust, for man is being made to pay for deeds resulting from choices that he did not make. On one alternative, we give up the absoluteness of God's power; on the other, we give up the absoluteness of God's justice. To resolve this dilemma, to emerge with a solution that satisfies both the demands of justice and those of power, Ibn Daud argues, requires a study that includes both science and philosophy. Ultimately, the search will lead to the affirmation of human freedom; this is in accord with Ibn Daud's expressed belief that the purpose of philosophy is to lead to right conduct. He does not maintain this belief consistently; there are times at which he presents theoretical knowledge as a higher goal. But, on the balance, he retains the ethical emphasis that is characteristic of Jewish philosophy.

Man is distinguished from other beings in the world by his possession of a rational soul. When this rational soul turns its attention to spiritual matters, it gains theoretical knowledge from the angels. When it turns its attention to worldly matters, it learns, by making critical judgments on the activities of the world, a practical or ethical wisdom. Both are proper functions of the rational soul. Exclusive devotion to one and neglect of the other is undesirable. The ultimate purpose of both theoretical and practical knowledge is the knowledge of God. This knowledge, the crowning glory of man's life, cannot be achieved directly by human effort. It is, rather, a gift of Divine grace to the man who has prepared his rational soul to receive it by the study of science, leading to intellectual enlightenment, and by conscientious self-examination and purification, leading to moral perfection. In true Aristotelian fashion, Ibn Daud spoke of knowledge of God as a "form" bestowed by God on the "matter" of the prepared soul.

We need not be concerned here with the detailed exposition of Ibn Daud's philosophy, since its most important themes will recur, in more satisfactory form, in the philosophy of Moses Maimonides, which will be discussed in our next chapter. The chief value of Ibn Daud's work in the story of Jewish philosophy lies in its stress on reason and its insistence that faith must be harmonized with reason, instead of reason with faith. This shift represents a turning-point which gradually leads to limitations and restrictions on the practice of philosophy as an antagonist of religion. Even though Ibn Daud himself never had quite the consistency that would have been needed to abandon the idea of revealed or traditional belief entirely, even though he felt, in the end, that the irrational aspects of tradition might be spiritually of more importance than the full pursuit of rationality, others who followed him carried the germs of a new attitude forward and developed major new formulations of Jewish thought.

CHAPTER SEVEN

Peaks of Spanish-Jewish Philosophy

BOTH TENDENCIES of Spanish-Jewish philosophy that have been discussed came to fullest maturity of statement during the twelfth century. The romantic and somewhat mystical philosophy that we have seen in the work of Solomon ibn Gabirol reached fulfillment about A.D. 1140 in the masterly work of Jehudah Halevi, the *Book of the Kuzari*. Half a century later, in 1190, Moses ben Maimon (Maimonides) wrote his *Guide for the Perplexed* (*Moreh Nebukhim*), the one work that, above all others, has come to stand as representative of the highest achievement of medieval Jewish rationalism. Each of these works is a masterpiece of its kind. Neither can be declared, in an absolute sense, to be the better of the two. The books of Halevi and Maimonides stand as twin peaks towering over the many lesser productions of their time.

Yet we should not over-emphasize the differences of method and literary form to the point of overlooking that which is common to their objectives. Both Halevi and Maimonides had as their chief purpose the defense of the separateness and integrity of the Jewish people and the Jewish faith in a world where, as we have seen, the Jewish minority was pressed between the two expanding world religions of Christianity and Islam. The challenge to both Halevi and Maimonides, as it was the challenge to all Jews of their time, was to justify the right of the Jews to remain Jews.

Jewish philosophy, whether romantic or rational, did not arise out of a pure love of speculative ideas for their own sake. Always it arose as a response to an environmental challenge to Judaism. Temperamental differences among philosophers may have been the chief factor in determining what form the response would take. There may indeed be, as William James suggested, tender-minded and tough-minded temperaments, inclining philosophers to one form or other of philosophic activity. Behind these differences, however, lies the common incentive of the defense of Judaism in a hostile world.

Once this shared motivation has been stated and noted as central to the philosophic enterprise within medieval Judaism, the differences between Halevi and Maimonides can become the focus of attention. Here the most significant of these differences is that Halevi centered his defense of Judaism on the unique quality of the Jewish people, while Maimonides made a more direct attempt to formulate a rational statement of Judaism itself. Maimonides reacted to the metaphysical challenge to Judaism by creating a metaphysical interpretation of Judaism. Halevi took, in our modern terms, a more existential approach; he began not from ideas but from the living reality of people. This difference may, perhaps, explain why the work of Maimonides has been studied and respected, but the work of Halevi has been read and loved. There is a concreteness about Halevi's *Book of the Kuzari* that is lacking in the more abstract and theoretical speculations of Maimonides' *Guide for the Perplexed*.

THE CONVERSION OF THE KHAZARS

The historical peg on which Halevi hung his philosophical dialogue was the conversion, reputed to have occurred some time about A.D. 740, of Bulan, king of the Khazars (*Kuzari*), to Judaism, an event that was followed by the mass conversion of the entire people to the "despised faith." The Khazars, about whom very little is known, were one of the many Asiatic tribes, possibly of Tatar or of Mongolian stock, who emerge occasionally out of the general darkness that encompasses the migration of peoples in the early Middle Ages. It has been suggested that they were a people related to the Turks, for there are customs they maintained which are similar to those of the Turks. One such is that the occupant of the throne of the Khazar kingdom is a purely ceremonial figure, without power, while a secondary figure, a vice-king, holds the actual reins of government. Another is that a new king, before being invested with the office, was forced to declare the number of years that he intended to occupy the throne. If he survived until the appointed time, he was put to death.

The Khazar kingdom was located on the Eurasian border in the region of the Caucasus. Its conquests extended into Europe; during the Middle Ages, the Khazars were masters of the Crimea. Thus they were in a precarious position between the Eastern Roman Empire (Byzantine) to their west and the Persian Empire, and later the Arabs, to the south and east. There was a considerable Jewish population in the Khazar territory; some may have been settled there from antiquity, while others arrived later, after expulsion from the Byzantine Empire or, in the middle of the seventh century, from Arabia. Muslims and Christians also lived side by side with the Jews and with the pagan Khazars; every inhabitant of the kingdom had complete freedom of religion. Indeed, it is reported that the authorities demolished the mosque in the capital city of Khazaria (Itil, at the mouth of the Volga River) in reprisal for Muslim destruction of Christian churches.

In the tenth century, news reached the Jews in Spain of the conversion of the Khazar kings to Judaism, supposedly about two centuries earlier. Hasdai ibn Shaprut, one of the most highly placed Jews in Spain, after much difficulty succeeded in getting an answer to a letter of inquiry addressed to the king of the Khazars. This answer reported that at one time there was a Khazar king named Bulan. This king dreamed of an angel who advised him to pray, for God had been watching over him and was pleased with his actions. Bulan did this and he was rewarded by such great military and governmental success that the rulers of the Byzantine Empire and those of the Arabs sent envoys, bringing substantial gifts, to try to induce this powerful king to become a convert to their respective faiths. To the representatives of Christianity and Islam, Bulan added a third sage, speaking for the Jewish faith. The three engaged in a disputation, each advocating his own religion. None of them succeeded in persuading the king, however, though each seemed to him to have considerable success in overthrowing the arguments of the others. So the king tried another method of getting the information he sought. After several days had passed, he sent for the Christian and asked him which of the two remaining faiths, Judaism or Islam, was superior. The answer was that the Jewish religion was the better, for the Jews were the people chosen by God as the vehicle of the Biblical miracles and revelation. Then the king sent separately for the Muslim spokesman, and asked him whether Judaism or Christianity was the superior faith. The Muslim also preferred the Jewish faith to its major rival, because the Jewish religion preserved in its integrity the law of God. As both agreed on this superiority of Judaism, the king announced his intention to convert to the faith of Israel. "Henceforth Almighty God strengthened him. He and his servants became circumcised. Then he sent for a Jewish sage who explained the Torah to him with all its commandments. Up to this day we observe this honored and true religion."

The story of the confrontation of the spokesmen for the three faiths is the framework which Jehudah Halevi adopted for his *Book of the Kuzari.* He made minor changes in the story to suit his purposes, but he kept the major outlines intact. Indeed, the *Book of the Kuzari* might be described as an imaginative and philosophic attempt to supply the dialogues between the Khazar king and the rabbi who was the spokesman for Judaism—dialogues at which the letter to Hasdai ibn Shaprut hints, but of whose contents there is no indication. This form of presentation, a dramatic reconstruction of a historical event, may have been the most politic for Halevi to adopt, for it enabled him to criticize and question both Christianity and Islam, the dominant religions of Spain, without giving the appearance of criticism. Alternatively, it may be that this historical event had served as a stimulant to Halevi's imagination, leading him to develop his own ideas of what might have taken place.

JEHUDAH BEN SAMUEL HALEVI

For it must be remembered that Jehudah Halevi was a distinguished poet, whose writings were on secular as well as religious themes. Most especially, he was known as the poet of Jewish nationalism. His sense of the relationship between the Jewish soul and the Land of Israel was most intense. It was in fulfillment of his almost mystical love of Zion that he left Spain late in his life to journey to the Holy Land, there to end his days. Whether Halevi ever achieved his goal we do not know. He vanished from sight some time during his journey, and any attempt to fill in the details of his last days is mythical. Legend has it that he died, pierced by the spear of an Arab horseman, at the very gates of the Holy City, while singing his Ode to Zion. This is, however, too pat to be true.

Halevi was born about A.D. 1080 in the city of Toledo in Spain. In the shifting of political power taking place about this time, Toledo was one of the cities that the Christian forces, under Alphonso VI, recaptured from the Muslims. But, although the city of Toledo now became part of the Christian kingdom in Spain, many years were still to pass before the traces of Arabic culture were eradicated. In particular, it should be noted that Arabic remained the language of Toledo during the lifetime of Halevi, so that there was nothing strange in his writing his major philosophic work in that language. He studied the Talmud in the rabbinical academy in Lucena. His teacher was Isaac Alfasi, a noted authority, and among his fellow students was Joseph ibn Migash, who was to become Alfasi's successor as head of this academy. In addition to his rabbinic studies, Halevi, like so many other leading intellectual lights of Jewry in the Spanish period, became a physician. He practiced in the Muslim city of Cordova, where his medical reputation gained him entry to the royal court. During this time, he wrote a great deal of poetry which was as highly regarded as the poetry of Gabirol.

There is no indication that Halevi himself ever suffered any discrimination or affront because he was a Jew. Toledo, in his time, was a very tolerant place, and Cordova, though no longer the haven it had been in earlier times, was kind to him. It was not, then, his personal misfortunes, but those of his co-religionists that affected him and led him to the longing for Zion that was expressed in his greatest poems, and that became part of the structure of his philosophy. There is no doubt that he was concerned; this is eminently clear from his letters as well as from his poems. One manuscript of the *Book of the Kuzari* bears the interesting subtitle "The Book of Argument and Demonstration in Aid of the Despised Faith." The very first sentence of the book indicates its scope: "I was asked to state what arguments and replies I could bring to bear against the attacks of philosophers and followers of other religions, and also against sectarians who attacked the rest of Israel." Halevi's work, written toward the end of his life, was designed to give his fellow Jews spiritual courage to face religious and philosophic attacks, whether from the Christians and Muslims or from the Jewish sectarians, the Karaites.

The central principle by means of which Halevi attempted to bolster up the courage of the members of the despised faith was his defense of revelation against reason. This principle was applied to matters of religion; Halevi did not deny the importance of reason in such fields as mathematics and physics. But in these fields, he asserted, the materials which men study are available to them and may be known completely. This is not the case with knowledge of God and of the truths of religion. As God cannot be completely known by reason, reason is not an adequate guide in matters of faith. Furthermore, as only God can possibly know how far man's obligations to Him extend and what forms of worship satisfy and fulfill these obligations, reason is incompetent to serve as an instrument of discovery in religious practice. God and the Jewish religion are not data of science. God must be confronted, loved, adored; then He will reveal His will to His servants.

Jehudah Halevi, in reconstructing imaginatively the discussion leading to the conversion of King Bulan of the Khazars, tells of a philosopher who was consulted by the king to explain his dream. The king had dreamt that "his way of thinking was agreeable to God, but not his way of acting." The philosopher's interpretation of this dream did not satisfy the king, for it asserted that only belief and purity of heart were important, not the details of religious practice. God, the philosopher insists, cannot like or dislike, favor or disfavor, for liking and disliking both indicate a need or desire in God's nature and to desire anything is to be incomplete. God's perfection itself makes it impossible for Him to be concerned with the details of the individual life. "He . . . does not know thee, much less thy thoughts and actions, nor does He listen to thy prayers, or see thy movements." God is a philosophic abstraction, to the philosopher, not a personal Divine being. The conclusion to which the philosopher comes is most distasteful to Halevi: "Be not concerned about the forms of thy humility or religion or worship, or the word or language or actions thou employest. Thou mayest even choose a religion . . . for the management of thy temperament, thy house and country, if they agree to it. Or fashion thy religion according to the laws of reason set up by philosophers, and strive after purity of soul."

It is interesting to observe that this part of the story makes a very significant change in the original letter to Hasdai ibn Shaprut. In that letter, we are told that the wording of the angelic message in the king's dream was, "I have seen thy ways and am pleased with thy actions." Halevi's version has the king report the angel to have said that his "way of thinking was agreeable to God but not his way of acting." Halevi is suggesting, by means of this change, that the ways of acting—that is, the actual modes of worship—have far more importance than is given to them in a philosophical account of religion. Ultimately it may even be the case that ways of thinking are universal; but not so with regard to ways of worshiping. Knowledge of the proper ways of worship must come from God Himself. Thus it is that the king of the Khazars replies to the philosopher that there must be a way of coming to know that is not the road of science or reason.

After all, the king continues, if philosophy is the correct mode of approach to God, "one might expect the gift of prophecy to be quite common among philosophers," whereas, in fact, it is not to philosophers that "true visions" necessarily are given. Now, if we eliminate the extreme claim for philosophy as the source of religious knowledge, we are left with the conflicting claims of the various religions. Christianity, Islam, and Judaism all claim to have exclusive knowledge, through revelation, of the correct and proper way of worshiping God. Each religion asserts that its forms of practice are pleasing in the sight of God. An evaluation of these conflicting claims is, then, the next step the king takes in his effort to find out the meaning of his dream. First he inquires of a "Christian scholastic," but finds himself unable to accept the logic of the Christian position. Then he calls in one of the "Doctors of Islam," and rejects his position, too, on the ground that the miracles called upon by the Muslim to testify to the truth of Islam are Jewish miracles. Finally, although he had not originally intended to consult with a representative of the Jewish faith, because "they are of low status, few in number, and generally despised," and because he is "aware of their reduced condition and

narrowminded views," the king finds himself "compelled to ask
the Jews, because they are the relic of the Children of Israel. For
I see that they constitute in themselves the evidence for the
divine law on earth."

HALEVI'S NATIONALISM

The king of the Khazars is thus led to the threshold of a view
that is central to the thought of Jehudah Halevi. There is a special
national character or national inheritance by virtue of which the
Jewish people are peculiarly the vehicle of revelation and prophecy.
The validity of the original revelation to the Children of Israel is
acknowledged by both Christians and Muslims. This is the revelation upon which the Jewish religion still rests; the rabbi replies to
the king's question about his beliefs by saying, "I believe in the
God of Abraham, Isaac and Israel, who led the children of Israel
out of Egypt with signs and miracles; who fed them in the desert
and gave them the land, after having made them traverse the sea
and the Jordan in a miraculous way; who sent Moses with His
law, and subsequently thousands of prophets, who confirmed His
law by promises to the observant, and threats to the disobedient."
The king challenges this answer by suggesting that the rabbi should
have replied in a more universal fashion. The rabbi defends his
mode of answer: "I answered thee as was fitting, and is fitting for
the whole of Israel, who knew these things, first from personal
experience, and afterwards *through uninterrupted* tradition." It
is possible, the rabbi adds, for a convert to Judaism to partake of
this special relation to the original revelation, but never to be
completely on a par with the born Jew.

Of course, both Christians and Muslims, while allowing that
the Children of Israel were the original vessels of revelation, add
that because God became angry with Israel He withdrew the gift
of prophecy from them. But the rabbi argues that though the

prophetic spirit in Judaism may have diminished, it was never lost, that, we might say, the revelation to the Jews was continuous. Thus not only the Bible, but also all later works in the Jewish religious tradition are divinely inspired. Even the slightest of local ordinances in any Jewish community is instituted in the light of the total tradition. There is no place for individualism in religious matters. "Those who judge according to their own tastes and reasoning may arrive . . . at an opposite conclusion. . . . It is only necessary to examine the roots of the traditional and written laws with the inferences codified for practice, in order to trace the branches back to the roots. Where they lead thee, there put thy faith, though thy mind and feeling shrink from it." Tradition, not speculation or reasoning, is the basis for the assertion of a special Jewish gift for religious inspiration.

Jehudah Halevi echoed the Arabic philosopher al-Gazzali in his distrust of rational proofs. But Halevi never carried philosophic skepticism about rational method to the extreme that Gazzali did. In its proper place, reason was acceptable; only in its application to religion did he distrust its leadings. This distrust is especially evident in Halevi's distinction, one that has often been repeated, between the God of philosophers and the God of religion. The God of philosophers can be *proved* to be; the God of religion must be *experienced* as being. The rabbi asserts that "the meaning of *Elohim* [here used to mean the God proved by reason] can be grasped by way of speculation, because a Guide and Manager of the world is a postulate of Reason. . . . The meaning of *Adonai* [here used to mean the Living God of faith], however, cannot be grasped by speculation, but only by that intuition and prophetic vision which separates man, so to speak, from his kind, and brings him in contact with angelic beings." To this statement the king of the Khazars responds, "I see how far the God of Abraham is different from that of Aristotle." If reason, which is universal among men, cannot lead to the true God, Who is attainable only by intuitive vision, and if that special kind of intuitive vision is the unique heritage of the Jewish people, then surely the superiority of the Jewish religion must be acknowledged.

Potentially, Halevi claims, every Jew is capable of prophecy, and if the conditions were right, many of them might actually achieve this height. In exile, however, conditions are seldom right. In the Holy Land, prophecy is more common. Here Halevi's special pleading for the Jewish people and the Jewish religion enlarges to embrace the case for the Jewish national homeland. "No other place would share the distinction of the divine influence, just as no other mountain might be able to produce good wine." It should, therefore, be the goal of every Jew, the Khazar king suggests, to return to the Land of Israel. Those Jews who dwell abroad may be compared with the sick, rather than the dead, replies the rabbi. "We are not like dead, but rather like a sick and attenuated person who has been given up by the physicians, and yet hopes for a miracle or an extraordinary recovery." The Hebrew language, too, shares in the general exaltation of all things Jewish. Hebrew is superior to all other languages. "According to tradition it is the language in which God spoke to Adam and Eve, and in which the latter conversed." It is the original language, from which all other tongues diverged. It is, above all, the ideal language for poetic expression and for the communication of religious ideas. Hebrew can communicate without the need of aids such as expression and gesture. "In the remnant of our language which was created and instituted by God, are implanted subtle elements calculated to promote understanding, and to take the place of the above aids to speech." People, religion, land, and language are bound together in the romantic web of Halevi's Jewish nationalism.

THE NATURE OF GOD

We have seen, now, that Jehudah Halevi expressed what may best be called a psychological or experiential view of the way in which man comes to know God. Not by the exercise of reason but by meeting the living reality of God in our lives do we discover Him. God's existence does not have to be proved by elaborately constructed arguments, leading to inadequate conclusions. His existence is attested by the miraculous history of the Jewish people and by the continuing revelation through the Jewish people. Philosophy reduces God to an operative force in the universe; God is a condition for the understanding of nature. Religious insight reveals God as the Divine will behind all of the phenomena that we call natural; our understanding, we might say, moves through nature to God. But that which has will is a person, so that in realizing in our lives the will of God, we realize His personality.

One of the philosophic "dangers" to which the Muslim and earlier Jewish thinkers had pointed was that the use of personal and human terms in speaking about God (anthropomorphism) would lead to a false and harmful conception of God as merely an enlarged human being. As we have already seen, much attention was devoted to a careful attempt to explain away, or to rationalize, the anthropomorphic expressions in the Bible. The reason for this stress is that, to the philosopher, knowledge is the central value. To the religious man, however, not knowledge but conviction and regeneration are central. For these purposes, it is more important that our doctrine of God be effectively stated than that it be rationally precise and consistent. For this reason, Jehudah Halevi, although he was in perfect accord with other philosophers in the recognition that human qualities could not be asserted literally of God, still thought it indispensable to speak of God imaginatively and metaphorically in this fashion.

The earliest question the Khazar king puts to his rabbinical master after his decision to convert to Judaism concerns "the names and attributes ascribed to God and their anthropomorphistic forms, which are unmistakably objectionable alike both to reason and to law." In reply to this question, Halevi's rabbi speaks precisely as a philosopher might. The names of God, he says, are not descriptions of God but "attributive descriptions"—that is, they are descriptions of the various ways in which men and other creatures of God are affected by Him. When we say that God is merciful, we are not asserting that there is a quality of mercy that God possesses, but that He has bettered the lot of all or some men. There are three types of attributes: creative, relative, and negative. The creative attributes describe ways in which men are affected by God's actions through natural agencies; attributes falling into this class are such as "merciful," "compassionate," "jealous," and the like. The relative attributes, like "blessed, praised, glorified, holy, exalted, and extolled," are derived not from God but from man's reverence for God. The multiplicity and plurality of these attributes, therefore, do not in any way indicate a plurality in God; His unity is untouched by their number, for they do not proceed from Him. The third class of attributes, negative attributes, are those such as "Living, Only, First, and Last," which appear on superficial glance to refer directly to God Himself. These, however, Halevi says, "are given to Him in order to negative their contrasts, but not to establish them in the sense we understand them." We call God Living; by this we do not mean that He possesses a quality of Life, but that He is not-dead. But in reality Life and Death are applicable to bodies that are subject to birth and decay. "The divine essence is as much exempt from both as it is highly extolled above them."

Clearly, in such a discussion as this, Halevi puts himself in the company of those who reject the naïve and simple literal view of the descriptions of God in the Bible. Yet in a later passage in the *Book of the Kuzari* Halevi defended, on grounds of religious utility, those images in which God is metaphorically compared to man. Whatever the prophets wrote down was endowed with attributes "as if they had seen them in corporeal form. These attributes are *true* as far as regards what is sought by inspiration, imagination, and feeling; they are *untrue* as regards the reality which is sought by reason. . . . Do not find it out of place that man should be compared to God." Halevi even uses the theory of man as the microcosm to justify his position that anthropomorphism is permissible. Some philosophers, even some among the Jews, as we have seen, "compared the world to a great man, and man to a small world. If this be so, God being the spirit, soul, intellect and life of the world—as He is called: the eternally Living, then rational comparison is plausible." When the Bible says that God created man "in our image," it suggests that man approaches in his make-up the Divine. This, so to speak, legitimates the comparison of God and man. The purpose of all such comparisons is to implant reverence for God in the human mind and heart.

An interesting detail of Halevi's argument for this imaginative road to God as opposed to the philosophic avenue of speculation is that the way of prophetic insight is instantaneous. When the prophet sees, in one flash, the glorious figure that imaginatively represents God, all the attributes of God stand simultaneously revealed to him. On the instant, the seer is struck by the fear and love of God, and in so impressive a form that the effect remains with him throughout his entire life. When the philosopher tries to achieve a knowledge of God through thought, he engages in a process that occupies time. "Thinking," says the Khazar king, "is like narrating, but one cannot recount two things at the same time." While one aspect of God is in the forefront of thought, other aspects fade into the background. No one engaged in such a process can absorb all aspects simultaneously, as the prophet can. No philosopher can achieve as clear an idea of God as the prophet can, although clarity is the aim and ideal of all philosophy.

FREEDOM, DIVINE AND HUMAN

Unlike many other medieval Jewish philosophers, Jehudah Halevi felt himself under no intellectual necessity to prove the existence of God. Yet, in answer to a request of the Khazar king, the rabbi of the dialogue does summarize a number of the current arguments. In the very moment of presenting these arguments, however, the rabbi declares them to be useless and idle. But the characteristic form of the arguments for the existence of God, as we have seen in our discussion of Saadia, was closely related to the argument that the world was created, that it had a beginning in time. In declaring the current set of arguments useless, Halevi, in effect, declines to prove that the world was created. Nevertheless he believed that it had come into being, and must therefore consider (if only to reject) other ways besides creation in which it might have done so. If God created the world, He must have done so of His own free will or out of some necessity in His own nature. If God did not create the world, then we may allow the possibility that it came into existence by chance. Thus, there are three conceivable alternatives: Divine freedom, Divine necessity, or chance. If the world came into being by virtue of some necessity in the Divine nature, then it follows that it could not have come into being in time. For to have come into being in time when it had previously not existed, there must have been an alteration in God's nature, and this cannot be admitted. If the world is a necessary consequence of God's nature, then it must have existed from eternity.

The alternatives to be considered for a world that began in time are, therefore, limited to chance and Divine freedom. Halevi is never explicit in his presentation of the alternatives. Implicitly, however, it is clear that he rejected the eternity of the world and also a world that came into being by chance, in favor of the belief that the world was created by the freely acting will of God. But this belief, coupled with the view that God is the cause of all that happens in the world, and that God has knowledge of all that is to be—all of which are held by Halevi—seems to dispose of the possibility that men can act of their own free wills, voluntarily. He seems to be faced with a dilemma; for only if man has free will can it be just for him to receive rewards or suffer penalties for his acts; yet, if man has free will, then not every event that occurs in the world can be determined by the will of God. To escape this dilemma, Halevi is forced to defend, with respect to human free will, the very position that he rejected in considering God's free will.

In the first instance, Halevi argues that the causes that seem to our investigations to operate in the world, the secondary causes, are merely agents of the Primary Cause, the will of God. The secondary causes have no share in bringing about the consequences that we see follow from their apparent operation. Yet to give men freedom and the ethical responsibility that derives from their freedom, he must now shift his ground and argue that secondary causes do have the power to influence results. To achieve this result without overmuch inconsistency, Halevi classifies all events into four groups: Divine, natural, accidental, and voluntary. Divine acts are those that require no intermediate or secondary cause, but are directly brought about by the power of God. Natural events represent the regular operation of the will of God through secondary causes; an example would be the growth of a tree. This is a particularly apt example, because it brings out one most important distinction between a Divine event and a natural event. There is no way in which a Divine event can be avoided or its consequences averted, but it is clear that there are a number of ways in which the growth of a tree, or any similar natural event, may be prevented from coming to fulfillment. Accidental events are also the consequences of secondary causes, but they do not occur regularly and they are not in fulfillment of any purpose. A man may fall from a rooftop, but it would be false to say that the rooftop was there just so that particular man might fall at that particular time.

Voluntary acts are those in which the operative secondary cause is man's will. Like other secondary causes, Halevi must admit, man's will is connected to the Divine will, or Primary Cause. There may be a number of links, or stages, in establishing this connection. Ultimately, however, God's will is the remote cause of men's choices. But, says Halevi, this causal chain is made up of links whose connection is not *necessary*. Therefore the freedom that man feels he has, since he feels that he is making voluntary choices, is truly freedom. Praise and blame here, reward and punishment hereafter, are justifiable, because man has a choice among alternatives. Nevertheless, since there is a chain of causes, man is not completely removed from either Divine Providence or Divine Omniscience. Men's actions "are completely outside the control of Providence, but are indirectly linked to it." As for Divine Omniscience, or foreknowledge, we may still say that since knowledge is not the cause of an event's occurrence, God may know how a man is going to choose and man may still be said to have chosen of his own free will.

Inadequate and unsatisfactory as this resolution of the dilemma of maintaining both Divine and human freedom may seem, it enabled Jehudah Halevi, in concluding his *Book of the Kuzari*, to assert both the possibility that a man by repentance and a change in his ways may change his eternal destiny, and a principle of uncertainty, returning all to the decision of God. Thus the end of the dialogue is a call to complete dependence and faith, to an ethical life, to true worship, and to the return to the Holy Land.

MOSES MAIMONIDES

If Jehudah Halevi's *Book of the Kuzari* is taken as the high point of romantic philosophy in the Jewish Middle Ages, then the great work of Moses ben Maimon, the *Guide for the Perplexed* (*Moreh Nebukhim*), must stand by its side as incomparably the finest presentation of rationalistic philosophy in the same period. Maimonides was born in Cordova, Spain, in the year A.D. 1135, a few years before Jehudah Halevi's book was written. He lived into the beginning of the thirteenth century, dying in 1204. Early in his life, when he was but a boy, he and his family were forced to flee from Spain in the face of an invasion by Muslim fanatics. For at least five years this family lived to the outside world as Muslims before they were finally able to return to the open practice of Judaism.

Throughout his youth, even during the period when he had to conceal his Jewishness, Moses Maimonides must have been continuously studying the literature of his people and many other subjects besides. It is idle to debate the question of whether he had the greatest mind of his time; what cannot be doubted or debated is that he had the most thorough and comprehensive intellectual preparation of any Jewish figure of his age. He wrote important works on every branch of Jewish study, was accepted by his co-religionists throughout the Muslim-Jewish world as the leading authority, and, in addition, achieved signal distinction as a practicing physician and writer on medical subjects. He was also familiar with the other sciences of his time, but did not write significantly in these fields. No man of the Middle Ages came closer to realizing in one person the highest virtues of the Greek tradition of rationality and of the Hebrew tradition of rabbinic piety.

We might say that it was the central object of his entire career to make a perfect and complete synthesis of these two traditions. He hoped to achieve this object without sacrificing any essential element in either tradition. Maimonides did not want to justify by reason some of the principles of Judaism and then assert the remainder on faith, as did some of his predecessors, nor did he wish to eliminate or alter those principles of Judaism which could not be made to accord with reason, as did some of his successors. He thought that all of Judaism could be presented as a rational system, completely in accord with rational, Aristotelian philosophy. On the surface, there were many modes of presentation of Jewish principles that seemed to conflict with reason. Thus, for example, a considerable body of Jewish literature is composed of materials of a sermonic type, explaining Biblical passages by myth and allegory. Despite this superficial appearance of irrationality, Maimonides was convinced that behind each of these tales and homilies there lay a point that could be presented in an acceptably rational manner. He set himself the task of discovering the rational kernel within each irrational husk.

A philosophic concern in the life work of Maimonides appears very early; from his late teens we have preserved a short work in which he presented his understanding of logic as that discipline was worked out in his time. Logic is the handmaiden of a rational and analytic approach to the problems of thought; it did not appear, therefore, among the Jews until the Middle Ages; Maimonides' short *Exposition of Logical Terms* (*Beur Millot Ha-Higgayon*) is the first work on logic written by a Jew. We may speak, by an extension of the term, of the techniques of interpretation used by the rabbis as a "logic." This would, however, be an undue extension. There are slight literary traces of reading in classical and Arabic logical theory in the work of Saadia and Bahya. But there is no Jewish work exclusively devoted to logic until the little treatise written in Arabic by Maimonides. The *Exposition of Logical Terms* is not, as its title suggests, a comprehensive book on logical theory, and it is in no sense an original treatment of the subject. It attempted to explain, in slightly expanded fashion, the Arabic terms used to represent the Greek of Aristotle's logical writings. The later Hebrew translation of Maimonides' book, by Moses ibn Tibbon, fixed the terminology adopted by all succeeding writers of philosophical literature in Hebrew.

THE GUIDE FOR THE PERPLEXED

The chief philosophic work of Maimonides was written toward the end of his life; the Arabic original seems to have been completed about A.D. 1190 and the Hebrew translation, made by Samuel ibn Tibbon," was started almost immediately, so that it had the benefit of the author's oversight. The *Guide for the Perplexed* can hardly have been written for the common reader. It was designed primarily for those of the contemporaries of Maimonides who had a sufficient acquaintance with science and philosophy to be concerned about the inconsistencies between this literature and the rabbinical and Biblical documents (with which, as Jews, they would of course have been thoroughly familiar). This is the meaning of the title. In the Middle Ages, only the extraordinary person was familiar with enough philosophic and scientific literature, whether by Jews or by Muslims, to be perplexed. Most Jews then limited their studies to the writings that fell within the tradition.

Because of the character of the audience he sought, Maimonides assumed a basic knowledge of philosophy. He did not so much present philosophic principles as utilize them for the purposes of theological argument. The unprepared reader may, as a result, find himself quickly beyond his depth in the reading of the *Guide for the Perplexed*. In an Introductory Letter prefaced to the book, Maimonides addresses the work to a pupil, Joseph ibn Aknin. Here he details the previous preparation that Joseph had: a course in astronomy, after completion of preliminary studies necessary for the understanding of that science; advanced work in mathematics; a course in logic; study of some metaphysical problems; some study of the Arabic philosophers. When Joseph had asked for this last, Maimonides said, "I perceived that you had acquired some knowledge in those matters from others, and that you were perplexed and bewildered; yet you sought to find out a solution to your difficulty." He advised Joseph to continue his systematic studies, rather than jumping from theme to theme or trying too soon for advanced mastery. Then Joseph left his teacher, and "Our discussions aroused in me a resolution which had long been dormant. Your absence has prompted me to compose this treatise for you and for those who are like you, however few they may be."

It is clear from this letter that Maimonides was consciously writing for fairly advanced students, and that the nature of the perplexity he sought to overcome was the inconsistency between the principles of Judaism and those of reason.

Again, in continuing the Introduction to the *Guide*, after the letter to Joseph ibn Aknin, Maimonides stated the primary purpose of his work:

> The object of this treatise is to enlighten a religious man who has been trained to believe in the truth of our holy Law, who conscientiously fulfils his moral and religious duties, and at the same time has been successful in his philosophical studies. Human reason has attracted him to abide within its sphere; and he finds it difficult to accept as correct the teaching based on the literal interpretation of the Law, and especially that which he himself or others derived from . . . homonymous, metaphorical or hybrid expressions. Hence he is lost in perplexity and anxiety. If he be guided solely by reason, and renounce his previous views which are based on those expressions, he would consider that he had rejected the fundamental principles of the Law; and even if he retains the opinions which were derived from those expressions, and if, instead of following his reason, he abandon its guidance altogether, it would still appear that his religious convictions had suffered loss and injury. For he would then be left with those errors which give rise to fear and anxiety, constant grief and great perplexity.

The chief cause of "perplexity," then, is the conflict between a literal understanding of the language of the Bible and the demands of trained reason. Maimonides suggests that knowing when to read the Bible figuratively will relieve the problem in most cases.

Furthermore, Maimonides was not fanatically convinced that reason always throws a brilliantly clear light on every difficulty.

There is no one, he says, who understands thoroughly all the perplexities and problems. "At times the truth shines so brightly that we perceive it as clear as day. Our nature and habit then draw a veil over our perception, and we return to a darkness almost as dense as before." Intellectual insight comes and goes like lightning flashes. The height of prophetic insight, as in Moses, is a series of flashes so frequent in occurrence that the light seems continuous. At the other extreme are those who never see the light at all; "They are the multitude of men; there is no need to notice them in this treatise." Human perfection is measured by the degree of illumination that a man experiences at any time in his life. Men fall into place on a scale whose unattainable high point is arbitrarily assigned to Moses for sole occupancy, and whose low point is shared by the masses, who "walk in continual darkness." Between these extremes, men attain to varying degrees of perfection and characteristically try to teach others to reach the same degree. Yet in teaching there is a limit as there is in studying; one has the same difficulties in explaining to others what he has learned that he had in the learning. While we are learning, some subjects seem at some times clear, at others obscure. When scholars try to teach, their explanations of these thorny questions are at some times clear, and at others obscure. "For this reason, great theological scholars gave instruction in all such matters only by means of metaphors and allegories."

We have come, with this comment, to the heart of the method proposed by Maimonides. In order to account for the Biblical and rabbinical passages that seem to come into conflict with reason, he is going to translate these from the language of metaphor and allegory, broadly speaking from figurative language, into the language of reason. He will claim that every instance of an expression in the literature of Judaism that repels reason is, in fact, a figure of speech. "The key to the understanding and to the full comprehension of all that the Prophets have said is found in the knowledge of the figures, their general ideas, and the meaning of each word they contain." It must be remembered, however, that when an interpretation is given to figurative expressions, it is the ideas of the interpreter, rather than those of the author of the figures of speech, that we are sure to have presented. Since Maimonides' purpose was to show the agreement between Judaism and the philosophy of Aristotle, we may expect that his interpretation of the figurative language of the Bible will discover Aristotle, where another interpreter, with a different purpose, would discover Plato or any other philosopher he set out to discover. A figure of speech is a work of art, and, like other works of art, means different things to different interpreters.

MAIMONIDES ON GOD

Maimonides considered the most important object of study to be theology, or metaphysics; man's primary intellectual obligation is "to form a conception of the Existence of the Creator according to our capabilities." In the *Guide for the Perplexed*, the author's stress falls on the problems of understanding, on the philosophical side of theology. In the short preface to his Commentary on the Mishnaic tractate Aboth, often separately printed as *Eight Chapters on Ethics*, though their chief concern is psychology rather than ethics, Maimonides suggests a broader obligation than this. All the activities of man, not merely his intellectual activities, should concentrate on achieving a knowledge of God. Whatever the immediate end of any activity, it should also have a further goal, connected with the knowledge of God. Nothing should be done for its own sake; everything should be engaged in as contributory to man's central purpose in living.

This emphasis on the centrality of the knowledge of God led Maimonides so far as to assert that even the development of the moral qualities has as its ultimate goal the achievement of a higher degree of intellectual perfection, in order to heighten the possi-

215

bility of knowledge of God. Taking this position, he went further and devalued the study of the rabbinic literature, which had traditionally been regarded as the chief repository of wisdom. Of course, Maimonides did not say that the rabbinic literature had no value. He limited its usefulness, however, to the secondary task of supplying guides for the life of the pious Jew. To the extent that such guide lines led to ethical development, they were preliminary to intellectual striving. The study of the Talmud could not be the highest of human studies, because the Talmud carefully skirted metaphysical questions. One of the major enterprises in which Maimonides engaged was the production of a comprehensive *Code of Jewish Law* (*Mishneh Torah* or *Yad Hahazakah*) designed to simplify the task of mastering the entire body of rabbinic interpretation. If, he thought, this mastery could be won by means of a simplified codification, the time and energy of the students thus saved could be devoted to the higher study of theology.

The "proper study of mankind," then, is God, but to know God, within the limits of our capacities, we must know the world of created things. Physics is the necessary preparation for metaphysics. There are many ideas that must be discussed in the study of God that can be understood only by first studying nature—like, for example, the ideas of potentiality and actuality. All existence is of two kinds: the existence of God and the existence of His creation. In order to learn what is properly assigned to God's existence, we must first study creation. We must move from that which can be observed to that which cannot be observed. Maimonides did not, however, accept the widely current proof of God's existence from the existence of a created universe. He recognized, as many other thinkers of his time did not, that a theory of the eternity of the universe would invalidate this proof. He did not himself believe in the eternity of the universe. But he felt that a proof of God's existence was not solid and firm unless it took account of this theory. When, in his "Introduction" to the Second Part of the *Guide for the Perplexed*, Maimonides reviewed twenty-five propositions that Aristotelian philosophers used in proving the existence of God, he prefaced his list by saying, "There is, however, one proposition which we do not accept—namely, the proposition which affirms the Eternity of the Universe, but we will admit it for the present, because by doing so we shall be enabled clearly to demonstrate our own theory."

Assuming, then, for the sake of the argument, that the universe is eternal, Maimonides declares that we must find an explanation for an endless process of motion and change. For the observed events of life include birth and death, generation and decay, yet if the universe is eternal, these observed beginnings and endings clearly cannot themselves be its eternity; there must be some being or force that persists through all and that starts the process of change and motion. Aristotle had assumed a *body* as the cause of the observable movements and changes in the universe, and was forced, therefore, to say that "the heavens are not subject to genesis or destruction." Maimonides substituted an *incorporeal* God for the *corporeal* heaven of Aristotle and thus developed a proof of the existence of God that he found satisfactory from the very assumption of the eternity of the universe which he could not accept. He made the change from a corporeal to an incorporeal cause of movement because all bodily things are composed of a number of different elements, and composition implies a coming together of the elements, which is itself a kind of movement, understandable only in terms of a prior cause of their joining.

There are other conclusions besides the bodiless, or spiritual, character of God that follow, for Maimonides, from the line of argument that he takes to prove the Divine existence. One, most important, conclusion is that there can be no more than one God. For, if there were more than one, then each would have to be made up of at least two elements. There would have to be an element by virtue of which He was a God; but if there were more than one God, then there would be a number of beings, each of whom possessed this God-making element. The various Gods could not be distinguished from one another by the element that they all possessed in common; they would, therefore, require another element at the very least, an element of difference or of individuality. If, however, each of the plural Gods was made up, composed, of two or more elements, then, as we have seen, a prior cause would be required to bring the elements together. We are driven to the conclusion that there can be no more than one God. In this fashion, Maimonides gave an argument in accordance with reason for the traditionally accepted Jewish belief in the Unity of God.

Again if, as Maimonides' argument proves, God is the cause of movement in the universe, then God Himself cannot be in any way dependent upon any force or being outside Himself. For, if we were to argue that God was, in any sense, acted upon by forces outside Himself, then these forces would have to be regarded as causes of God's acts. God would then be subject to these forces, and that would mean that He was inferior to them, and this would be an absurdity, for God as the cause of all cannot Himself be an effect without contradiction. That God is without bodily attributes, that He cannot be plural, and that He must be conceived as independent are the major consequences, for Maimonides, of the proof of the existence of God from the necessity of a First Mover. We must notice, however, that each of these statements is a denial rather than an affirmation; Maimonides tells us that God is *not* bodily, *not* plural, *not* dependent. He does not tell us what God *is*.

THE WAY OF NEGATION

Maimonides reserves his severest expressions of disapproval for those who take the figurative language of the Bible literally, and therefore think of God as a being like ourselves, with physical organs and senses. "Therefore bear in mind," he says, "that by the belief in the corporeality or in anything connected with corporeality, you would provoke God to jealousy and wrath, kindle His fire and anger, become His foe, His enemy and His adversary in a higher degree than by the worship of idols." In effect, Maimonides is saying that a false belief in the true God is more seriously in error than is belief in a false god. Yet the foundation of this false belief lies in the Bible itself, for it is the language of the Bible that leads the ignorant astray. It is the Bible that speaks of God as having physical organs and attributes.

The Bible was written in this fashion in order to convey some impression of the reality of God to the common people. God had to be described in a way that would show even the most unlearned that He exists. But it is clear that every organ and every sense perception and every power in man is his way of satisfying his needs; every way of satisfying needs is an evidence of something that man lacks, of an imperfection in man. To assert that God has physical attributes like those of man is equivalent to saying that God has needs and lacks, and is therefore imperfect, which is obviously incorrect. "I do not believe that any man can doubt the correctness of the assertion that the Creator is not in need of anything for the continuance of His existence, or for the improvement of His condition. Therefore, God has no organs, or, what is the same, He is not corporeal." A naïve and literal reading of the Bible leads to a false notion of God.

In addition to its crude physical anthropomorphisms, the Bible also uses expressions of a more subtly misleading kind. These are the expressions that assert various non-physical qualities or attributes of God, like justice and mercy. In the technical language of Maimonides' time, this involves the assertion that an attribute is an "accident" (a quality that a substance may or may not possess) added to the "essence" (what the substance is in itself), or else that the attribute is the definition (and therefore the cause) of the thing. The second of these possibilities must be immediately dismissed, for, as we have seen, God has no cause and therefore cannot be defined. The first possibility conflicts with the conclusion that God is not a composite being, for if we assert that He has attributes, we are saying at least that God is made up of an essence and some accidents, and that He is, therefore, a composite being. We cannot avoid falling into error by saying that an attribute is an indicator of relations, because relations can exist only between things of the same sort. We might go through the different types of relationship in detail and show, in each case, that this relationship cannot be asserted of God. What this line of argument would show is that for God to be in relation with anything whatsoever, He would have to possess the "accident" of relation, and we have already seen that God, as a unitary being, can have no accidents.

There is one type of attribution that can be applied to God in the strict way that Maimonides insists upon. This is that a thing may be described by its actions. Maimonides' intent in permitting this usage is most limited; he is unwilling to permit attribution of this sort in terms of capacity for a certain type of action, or what might be called potentiality. When we call a man a carpenter, for example, we mean that he has the capacity to perform the kinds of actions ordinarily expected of a carpenter; this is to describe him in terms of potentiality, and we must not describe God in these terms. But we might say of a particular carpenter that he made this specific piece of furniture; that is, we might attribute to him work that he had already performed. This is the only way in which it is legitimate to make an attribution to God; that is, we may refer to Him as, for example, the Creator of heaven and earth, since this refers to an action that He has already performed. Even this must be done with caution, so as not to suggest that God's creation of heaven and earth is in any sense separable from His being. There must be no hint of plurality or "accident" in the way we speak of God. We must remember that "all the actions of God emanate from His essence, not from any extraneous thing superadded to His essence."

Some philosophers had spoken of what they called "essential attributes" without which it is impossible even to have a conception of the being of whom we are talking. The four essential attributes are existence, power, will, and wisdom. These attributes, as applied to men and other living things, involve some form of alteration or change. Even though we must conceive of God as existent, powerful, willing, and wise, we must do so within the range of His infinite perfection, rather than in terms of change. The essential attributes, then, must apply to God in some fashion that corresponds to the way in which they apply to men, yet sufficiently different from the way in which they are used of men so that their use will not lead to confusion. This requirement led Maimonides to the formulation that "God exists, without possessing the attribute of existence. Similarly He lives, without possessing the attribute of life; knows, without possessing the attribute of knowledge; is omnipotent, without possessing the attribute of omnipotence; is wise, without possessing the attribute of wisdom; all this reduces itself to one and the same entity; there is no plurality in Him." But, of course, even unity is an "accident," so Maimonides is forced to add that "God's unity is not an element superadded, but He is One without possessing the attribute of unity."

These difficult, even paradoxical expressions are forced upon us by the limitations of language and by the limitations of our human intellects. They reduce, as Maimonides himself points out, to negative assertions which are themselves denials of negations. To say that God exists, Maimonides claims, is not to affirm existence of God, but to deny that God does not exist. We cannot speak of God affirmatively without being led, in some subtle form, into anthropomorphic or polytheistic expressions. All that we can do is to follow the way of negation, to try to come to some knowledge of God by an understanding and appreciation of what He is not. Maimonides realized that in proposing that negations about God be substituted for affirmations, he was suggesting something most difficult. Yet he said, "Know that the negative attributes of God are the true attributes; they do not include any incorrect notions or any deficiency whatever in regard to God, while positive attributes imply polytheism, and are inadequate." Both positive and negative atributes are, in a certain sense, limits. But whereas positive attributes impose their limitations directly, by describing something that we wish to know, and therefore require an affirmation of something about the essence of the object to be known, negative attributes make their limitation indirectly, circumscribing the object without claiming any knowledge of its essence.

We are left, then, with two classes of statements that we may properly make about God. One of these is the class of statements telling what God has done, attributing to Him the actions in the world, the effects of His being, that we can observe. The other class of proper statements is the class of negative attributions. In these statements we deny false statements about God without claiming a kind of knowledge that is impossible to us. We can grow in our knowledge of God by learning more about what He is not. As our thinking matures, there is more and more that we understand not to be applicable to God. "In the same way as by each additional attribute an object is more specified, and is brought nearer to the true apprehension of the observer, so by each additional negative attribute you advance toward the knowledge of God, and you are nearer to it than he who does not negative, in reference to God, those qualities which you are convinced by proof must be negatived." Ultimately, it may well be the case that the sincere student will join with the generations past in affirming, "None but Himself comprehends what He is, and . . . our knowledge consists in knowing that we are unable truly to comprehend Him." Maimonides' discussion of the Divine attributes certainly shows how rigorous and uncompromising was his attachment to the rationalistic mode of philosophizing.

CREATEDNESS

We have taken note of the peculiar and striking extent to which Maimonides carried his intellectual integrity—that although he did not believe in the eternity of the world, a doctrine attributed in his time to Aristotle, nevertheless he insisted upon proving the existence of God on the assumption of eternity, since this made the problem of proof most difficult. That is to say, he took what was at his time regarded as the hardest conditions to overcome, feeling, we may guess, that if he could make his proof stand up under those conditions, it was beyond criticism. But even in the moment of making the assumption of the eternity of the world, Maimonides left no doubt that he did not, for himself, accept this assumption. At some time in his work, therefore, he had to show why he did not believe in the eternity of the world, and why he favored the view that it was created.

In opening his discussion of this question, Maimonides summarized three theories that were current. The first was the Biblical theory of creation out of nothing. God existed alone; all else, even time itself, He produced from nothing "by His will and desire." When the word "time" is implied by speaking of God's prior existence, or when God is spoken of as having "existed an infinite space of time before the Universe was created," the word is used in a special sense, but only to mean something similar to time. This is an important consideration for Maimonides' argument, for unless time is considered as created, it is impossible to refute the theory of the eternity of the universe. "For time is an accident and requires a substratum. You will therefore have to assume that something [besides God] existed before this Universe was created."

The second theory that Maimonides presents is associated with Plato and various schools of followers of Plato. This theory asserts that it is impossible for God (or of course any other being) to produce *from nothing*. For every object is a combination of matter and form, and it is impossible that such an object can be made in the absence of an existing matter or destroyed in such a way that its matter goes out of existence. It is no disrespect to God to say of Him that He cannot do the impossible, nor does it argue any imperfection in Him that He cannot do what cannot be done. If, therefore, it is an impossibility to produce without matter, there must have been matter eternally co-existing with God in order for God to be able to form this matter into the universe. Though matter co-exists with God, it is not, in any sense, equal in rank. God can do with this eternal matter whatsoever He desires to do. He can form whatever He wants to form out of it; He can destroy whatever He wants to destroy, and reuse the matter in other forms. The power of God over matter extends to the matter of the heavens. "The process of genesis and destruction is, in the case of the heavens, the same as in that of earthly beings." This is a theory of creation, and in this respect, it agrees with the Biblical theory; but it is not a theory of creation out of nothing.

The third theory is that of "Aristotle, his followers, and commentators." It is in accord with the Platonic theory insofar as it holds that a corporeal object cannot be produced without some sort of body or matter out of which it is formed. Where the Aristotelian theory differs from the Platonic is in its insistence that the heavens are not subject to the process of genesis and dissolution. The heavens constitute the permanent and eternal element in the universe. Time and motion, which are products of the heavens, are also eternal. Since the heavens are the cause of all that is, there is no real change in the universe. "The sublunary world, which includes the transient elements, has always been the same, because the prime matter is itself eternal, and merely combines successively with different forms; when one form is removed, another is assumed. This whole arrangement, therefore, both above and here below, is never disturbed or interrupted, and nothing is produced contrary to the laws or the ordinary course of Nature." To this physical assertion of design and necessity, says Maimonides, Aristotle added a metaphysical principle that God cannot change His will, because this would imply a change in His essence, which is impossible. For this reason, in addition to the consistency of Nature, the universe must be today what it has always been and what it will continue to be.

There are other theories of the universe, but Maimonides sees no need to consider them, since they do not accept the existence of God, which he regards as proved. Nor does he think it necessary to take special account of what he has described as the Platonic theory; even though this differs in detail from the Aristotelian, it agrees with that theory in what Maimonides considers to be the critical point, that there is something eternal besides God. It is to the disproof of the Aristotelian theory that Maimonides devotes his attention. There are four major and three minor Aristotelian arguments that Maimonides presents. (1) Motion must have been eternal, for otherwise motion itself must have come into being, and coming into being is a form of motion; since time is related to motion, time, too, is eternal. (2) The prime matter or First Substance common to the four elements must be eternal, for if it were not, it would have had to come into existence from another substance. In coming thus into existence, it would have been endowed with a form, for coming into existence means receiving a form. But First Substance means formless matter; therefore it cannot have come into existence from another substance, and must be eternal. (3) The substance of the spheres can contain no "opposite elements," because their motion is circular. But whatever is destroyed owes its destruction to its containing elements that are in opposition to each other. Containing no such elements, the spheres are indestructible, and must as a result be thought of as without beginning. (4) If we assume the universe to have been non-existent at any time, then at that time its existence must have been either necessary, or possible, or impossible. If it was necessary, then it could never have been non-existent; if it was impossible, then it could never have come into existence. There is but one remaining alternative; the universe must have been possible. But to assert a possibility always means that there must be something of which that possibility is asserted. That of which the possibility of becoming actual as the universe is asserted must itself have been in existence. Maimonides says of this argument, "This is a forcible argument in favor of the Eternity of the Universe." The three minor arguments were: (5) If God produced the universe out of nothing, then God must have been a potential agent before he was an actual agent, and thus must have passed from a state of potentiality to one of actuality; this transition is neither necessary nor impossible, but merely possible, and therefore requires an agent to bring it about. (6) To speak of God as a potential agent before He was an actual agent involves the view that God was active at one time and inactive at another. This would require a change of God's will; but God is not subject to accidents which can bring about a change. He must, therefore, be always active. (7) The Divine actions are always perfect; the existing universe, if it is regarded as the result of a Divine action, must be perfect and unimprovable, and must, therefore, be permanent, for "it is the result of God's wisdom."

Surely to one who was as much the rationalist as we have seen Maimonides to be, these are powerful arguments. They are plausible and may have seemed to many to be beyond refutation. Maimonides claimed, however, that their plausibility was merely apparent, and that Aristotle himself, who was, after all, the greatest of logicians, must have realized that they were not conclusive. Maimonides contends that Aristotle was not convinced by his own arguments, but that his followers, less able men, were persuaded. He says that all the Aristotelian arguments rest on one supposition, namely, that the laws which apply to nature and the universe after it has come into being applied before there was a universe. Every one of the Aristotelian arguments assumes these natural laws. But if we make the contrary assumption that when God created the world, there were no such laws, but that the laws themselves were a product of His creative activity, then the counter-arguments are of no avail. This, of course, merely minimizes the effect of the Aristotelian arguments; it does not prove the theory of creation out of nothing. Either theory, Maimonides says, is admissible; he accepts the creation theory "on the authority of Prophecy." Having done so, he then proceeds to argue philosophically for its superior acceptability, in terms of the substitution of an intelligent cause, God, operating in the universe with will and purpose, for the Aristotelian theory of the necessity of the laws of Nature and a mechanistic operation of cause and effect. In a theological work, such as the *Guide for the Perplexed* designedly is, we cannot be too sharp in criticizing the author for resorting to the principle of authority at a critical point.

PROPHECY

Yet surely, from what we have seen of Maimonides, he would not have turned to "the authority of Prophecy" if he had not had a theory of the nature of prophecy and prophetic inspiration that justified to his mind a reliance upon the words of the prophets. Unlike Halevi, Maimonides regarded prophecy as an aspect of rational understanding of the universe. Prophecy was not an instance of arbitrary Divine intervention in the affairs of the universe. Maimonides did not agree with the romantics among his predecessors in the belief that the mantle of prophecy fell most often upon those who were intellectually unprepared. He viewed it, rather, as a continuation and supplement to the development of human powers of rational knowledge. His opinion was as little magical as any theory of prophecy could possibly be.

Where the opinion of most people was that the prophet served merely as a vehicle, a vessel into which God poured his inspiration, Maimonides interpreted prophecy as the fruit of a co-operative activity carried on by God and man together. Man's part in this work is to develop his reason to its utmost by study and self-discipline. God's part is to stimulate the man who has prepared himself by an illumination that goes beyond the scope of human reason but does not contradict it. Thus prophecy becomes, in a certain sense, the limiting case of knowledge. Even in normal study, understanding comes as if by illumination after mastery has been gained by disciplined work. To the prophet, illumination comes much more intensely and powerfully, but it does not come unless man has gone as far toward knowledge as he can by the power of his reason. Of course, not every person who refined his knowledge would receive the gift of prophecy. God was not compelled to award the gift as, for example, a school might be compelled to award a diploma to a student who had satisfactorily completed a course of study. But no one, in the opinion of Maimonides, ever reached any degree of prophetic inspiration without previously preparing himself.

Maimonides distinguished eleven classes of true prophets, and beyond them a still higher degree of prophetic inspiration that was limited to a unique example, Moses. Theoretically, prophets of one degree or another should be able to appear in any generation, yet it was a commonplace in Jewish thought at the time of Maimonides that there had been no true prophets in Israel since the completion of the Bible. Maimonides explained this apparent inconsistency of theory and fact by claiming that not only did prophecy require the highest perfection of man's senses, imagination and intellect, but also that the physical conditions by which the potential prophet was environed should be such as to bestow upon him a serene spirit. "Prophets are deprived of the faculty of prophesying when they mourn, are angry, or are similarly affected." In exile, this serenity of spirit is denied to the Jew, for his life is a perpetual mourning. In exile, therefore, there is no prophecy, but in the days of the Messiah, when there is a return to the Holy Land, "prophecy will . . . again be in our midst, as has been promised by God."

As Moses was unique among the prophets, and as all prophets since his time urged the people to follow the law of Moses, Maimonides felt justified in asserting the perfection and the unchanging character of the Mosaic law. This perfect law could be supplemented by interpretation, prophetic or rabbinic, which did not distort it or come into any conflict with it. Even, temporarily, the authority of a prophet or a rabbinical court might take account of special conditions to suspend the operation of the Mosaic law. This, he thought, was permitted only when, by temporarily suspending a part of the law, it became possible to insure the survival of the whole law. To place so high a valuation on the Mosaic law, as a rationalist, Maimonides had to be able to satisfy himself that every commandment, whether positive or negative, in the law has a rational justification. In some cases, this rationalization of the laws is relatively easy; some of the laws rest upon fundamental truths like those which Maimonides has already proved. Other laws, especially those bearing upon ceremonials and rituals, are not so readily justifiable by reason. In matters of this sort, Maimonides used a psychological justification; "No opinions retain their vitality except those which are confirmed, published, and by certain actions constantly revived among the people." Ritual commandments are methods of fixing ideas in the popular mind. By means of this shift from rational to psychological argument in support of the commandments, Maimonides was able to maintain the integrity of his philosophic system and at the same time to retain in every detail the religious regulations whose observance had bound the Jewish community together through the centuries of exile.

CHAPTER EIGHT

Five Centuries of Criticism and Defense

THE THIRTEENTH century ended the period of glory in the life of the Jews in Spain. The increasingly bitter struggle of the Christian forces to regain possession of the entire Iberian Peninsula led to a decline in the favored position that the Jewish people had held for several hundred years. There were intense persecutions of the Spanish Jews, and as a result many of them left Spain and migrated to other European countries. The center of European Jewish studies was reconstituted in the southern part of France, but this center was not fated to enjoy the brilliance of philosophical development that the Spanish center had seen. Maimonides, because of the splendor of his reputation, had to be reckoned with; all of Jewry was divided into two warring camps—those who bitterly attacked the thought of Maimonides and held him responsible for the distracting of Jewish scholars from the traditional paths of legal studies, and those who felt, as Maimonides had, that the philosophic challenge to Judaism had to be met with a philosophic answer. Each group hurled bitter denunciations at the other; each declared the other to be the scourge of Judaism.

For an entire century, then, the philosophic soil so ably cultivated by the geniuses of Spanish Jewry was tilled only by inferior husbandmen. It must be added that the decline of the Spanish cultural center and the substitution of a center in the south of

France made a difference in the language patterns of Jewish scholarship. We have already noted that the Jewish men of learning in Spain used the Arabic language for their philosophic writings. Now knowledge of Arabic became less common among Jews in Europe. We enter upon an age of translation, in which the writings of all the Spanish Jewish philosophers had to be worked into a Hebrew language that lacked an adequate philosophical vocabulary. Not only works by Jewish authors had to be translated; scientific and mathematical works by Arabic thinkers and the works of Aristotle himself were known only in Arabic and had therefore to be turned into Hebrew before their usefulness could be maintained. The thirteenth century was, thus, an age of secondary studies rather than one of original creativity.

LEVI BEN GERSON (GERSONIDES)

The first philosopher of stature to emerge after the death of Maimonides was Levi ben Gerson (1288–1344), known as Gersonides. Like Maimonides, Gersonides was a scholar in many branches. He was widely known as a mathematician and an astronomer, but he was equally well known as an interpreter of the Bible. He wrote commentaries on various parts of the Bible; his Commentary on the book of Job is a minor philosophic masterpiece as well as a distinguished work of Biblical scholarship. But he also wrote commentaries on the work of such Muslim philosophers as Averroes (Ibn Roshd). His chief philosophic book was called The Wars of the Lord (Milhamot Adonai), and was written a century and a half after Maimonides' Guide for the Perplexed. Now, Gersonides was a resident of the south of France, and the son of a distinguished scholar. Unlike Maimonides, therefore, his works were written in Hebrew rather than in Arabic. His reputation extended beyond the limits of the Jewish group. Many of his scientific and some of his philosophic works were translated into Latin; indeed, one of his astronomical treatises was thus translated by express order of the Pope, Clement VI.

The philosophic attitude of Gersonides was like that of Maimonides, perhaps carried to even more of an extreme. Maimonides had felt that, in general, there could be no conflict between the truths of (Aristotelian) philosophy and those of religion. If he found an apparent conflict, he exercised great ingenuity in resolving it in such a way as to retain both philosophic and religious traditions. Gersonides, although he agreed that there should be no conflict, was ready, when a conflict appeared, to resolve the contradiction in favor of Aristotle. He covered himself against possible charges of heterodoxy, however, by saying that wherever the traditional religious views of Judaism are sufficiently precise and forthright, even though a conflict may exist between faith and reason, man should not insist upon his rational position. Probably the best way of explaining Gersonides' position is to say that he left to the human mind complete freedom of theoretical exploration, but urged humility on man in putting the conclusions of reason into practice.

Gersonides believed that both philosophy and religion existed for the same purpose, to lead to the happiness and the moral improvement of men. Because he held this belief, he felt that God, Who is both the Revealer of religious truth and the Grantor of man's reason, would not have led men in two different directions by His two gifts. In the Introduction to *The Wars of the Lord,* Gersonides presents in briefest form the optimistic basis of his thought: "The Bible," he says, "is not a law that compels us to accept untruths; its purpose is rather, to lead us to the attainment of truth, as far as this is possible." Even more than Maimonides, as a result, he wove clever and ingenious interpretations of Biblical passages to transform its text into a consistent philosophic system. This he did at the cost of a literal view, of course. Sometimes he slipped in an additional assumption, as in his account of creation. At other times he used the same technique as had Maimonides, declaring Biblical expressions to be figures of speech. At still other times, he interpreted a Biblical narrative as a dream or fantasy.

The explicitly legal sections of the Bible, particularly the Pentateuch, Gersonides accepted in much the same sense as the rabbinical literature did. He regarded this material, however, as preparatory to the Biblical exposition of social and ethical principles. The Bible was not nearly as precise in its formulation of these principles as in its expression of the legal matters; ethical ideals are presented in the form of parables. Biblical narratives show how certain character types behave and what results their behavior leads to. This is meant to stir men to imitate the worthy and to avoid the unworthy. He gives a very unusual explanation of the Bible's lack of precision in these matters. It is very hard for men to become perfect in moral and social matters; if the Bible did lay down the law in such matters in the same precise fashion as it did in connection with belief and religious practice, men could not easily live up to its injunctions. They would come to despair of living up to these commandments and would disobey them. Disobedience in one regard would lead to disobedience in others, and the commandments of the Pentateuch would also be neglected. In addition to the legal and moral matters found in the Bible, Gersonides suggests that there is a third type of teaching, concerning matters of science and philosophy. This the Bible could not present directly, but did reveal in an indirect way, as in the story of creation.

The philosophic account of creation is, in fact, one theme of Gersonides' work in which he comes to a conclusion different from that of Maimonides. The earlier (and greater) sage, it will be recalled, had summarized several different theories of creation and had, in the end, favored the Biblical view of a creation out of nothing, in time, over against an "Aristotelian" view of the eternity of the world and a "Platonic" view that the world was created, in time, but out of an eternally existing formless matter, rather than out of nothing. After reviewing the various arguments,

233

as they had been presented by Maimonides and others, Gersonides accepts the Platonic theory that God created the world, in time, out of an eternally existing formless matter. To square this position with the Biblical story, Gersonides says that there is not one account of a miracle in the entire Bible in which something comes out of nothing. It is therefore improbable that the story of creation would make a claim that is to be found nowhere else in the Bible. With this insight as a starting-point, he examined the story of creation in Genesis and discovered that a formless matter was assumed by the writer of the creation story. He based this deduction upon the words "without form" (*tohu*) and "void" (*bohu*) in the second verse of the first chapter of Genesis. These two words bear, for him, the weight of Greek, Muslim, and Jewish speculation about form and matter! He reads a great deal more into the story of creation, too. But since the details of his argument are far too technical to be presented, we had better let the one instance serve as an example of the way in which Gersonides twisted the Bible narrative to his purpose.

Gersonides used an argument based upon the nature of miracles, as we have seen, to support his view of creation. For the occurrence of miracles, he accepted the Biblical accounts as evidence. The value of this evidence he considered to be as great as the value of the evidence of our senses in matters of science and common sense. The miracles of the Bible are of two sorts; there are some recorded miracles in which one substance is changed into another, and there are others in which no such change occurs, but in which there is an alteration of quality or an increase or decrease of quantity. All the miracles of the Bible occur in a situation in which they will lead to good results; they seem to fulfill the purposes of a beneficent being. Finally, either miracles are performed through the agency of prophets, or they are performed in some direct relation to the activities of prophets. These pieces of information concerning the nature of miracles and their occurrence serve as the foundation for a conclusion concerning the author of miracles.

Because miracles are purposive, they cannot have occurred by mere chance. They involve an understanding of the regularities of the universe, especially of the order of the world, and must therefore have been caused by some being who knows this order. In Gersonides' mind, this means that the maker of miracles must be either God, man, or that Aristotelian conception which Gersonides transformed into the guiding and controlling spirit of the world of men, the Active Intellect. If the miracle-maker is any man, it is the prophet; but prophetic inspiration, he says, comes to the prophet by way of the Active Intellect, and it is by prophetic inspiration that the prophet comes to know about the miracles. If the prophet were himself responsible for the miracles that take place, he would not have to learn about them from the Active Intellect. The author of miracles is not man. Nor can the author of miracles be God, for miracles do not take place all the time, but only occasionally; the implication is that if God were responsible for miracles, their occurring sometimes and not occurring others would be incredible, for it would mean that God changed His mind. The upshot of this argument, which is presented here in greatly condensed form, is that the Active Intellect is both the inspirer of prophets and the maker of miracles.

This discussion makes it obvious that the rationalism of Gersonides was extreme. In his time, it would have been unthinkable to have denied the miracles of the Bible. Instead, what Gersonides did was to reduce the significance of miracles by making them the work of a lower and subordinate being in the scale of things, so that they were not regarded as the work of the Supreme Being. This left him free to consider God as essentially a rational Governor of the universe, operating strictly according to the natural laws that He had Himself set forth. Because this ultimate constitution of the universe is God-given, even the miracle cannot violate its basic principles. Miracle cannot change the past; miracle cannot change mathematical principles; miracle cannot make a thing black and white at the same time. These are principles so basic that to argue for the possibility of their violation would be to assert that there was something at fault in the underlying laws by which God had ordained the operations of the universe. The God of Gersonides is the ideal type of the logical thinker.

HASDAI BEN ABRAHAM CRESCAS

The over-intellectualization of religion manifest in Gersonides and present, though to a lesser extent, in Maimonides was exceedingly distasteful to Hasdai ben Abraham Crescas (1340–1410). Crescas made the chief work of his life the recapture of Judaism from rationalism. He was not himself a man of poetic capabilities; indeed, his native talent seems to have been intensely logical. His logic, however, led him to the wish to reinstate the spiritual, affective, and emotional aspects of Jewish religion and thus to end the domination of Aristotle. The book in which Crescas represented his intellectual defense of anti-intellectual religion is called *Light of the Lord (Or Adonai)*.

Aristotle, and after him the Jewish Aristotelians, had based much of their argument on the denial of the possibility of an infinite. Crescas maintained that there could indeed be an infinite, that such an infinite actually exists. By this acknowledgment, he took the force away from practically all the Aristotelian proofs for the existence of God. He also supplied a rational proof, not very different from one that was common in the literature, but the weight of his position was that the proof of the existence of God is the Biblical assertion that there is a God. Similarly, he used essentially Biblical arguments for belief in the Unity of God, although he supplemented these by other arguments of a rational sort. One of the points at which his difference from Maimonides is most noticeable is in his readiness to accept positive attributes of God. He argued that there was an arrogance to the philosophic limitations on the definition of God. The most simple man of faith might come closer to the truth than the philosopher with his logical distinctions.

If God is truly unknown, then, surely, it is folly for philosophers to specify his unknown character in terms of negative attributes. Besides, we may be led into the error of denying, by means of our negations, an attribute that God actually has, and this is equivalent to a repudiation of the divinity of God. The limitations imposed by philosophic rationalism may lead, he insists, to a spiritual emptiness that is more displeasing to God than anthropomorphic overstatement. True, reason cannot grasp the essence of God; yet it is not necessary for us to succumb to total skepticism. We can deduce some facets of God's nature from his actions. Thus we know that God must delight in bringing things into being, for He does create under no necessity. As a consequence of this we know that, in addition to His creativity, God must feel something akin to joy.

Crescas knows that the philosophers, too, had allowed joy to God, but it was the ideal form of the joy that philosophers themselves might feel, joy in the activity of thought. For this intellectual delight Crescas substitutes an emotional delight, suggesting that God feels joy in the activity of love. He manifests His love constantly by bestowing His goodness upon men. Man's joy, then, and man's "likeness to God" comes from the love he directs to God. The ideal expression of man's total love of God, and therefore man's greatest good, is a complete turning to God in prayer. Not by *taking* thought, but by *giving* love does man come nearer to God. The devotion of the saintly man, the pious servant of God, is a better preparation for perfection than the intellectual discipline of the philosopher.

True to the Jewish tradition, Crescas thinks of the prophet as the highest type of man, the man nearest to God. Unlike Maimonides, who argued for philosophy as the avenue to prophetic inspiration, though Divine grace was necessary as a supplement, Crescas says that it is the saintly men from whom God chooses those on whom the mantle of prophecy will rest. "He only is ready for prophetic perfection who cleaves fast unto Him, removing himself from human society for the sake of concentration upon the Divine service." God's choice is based upon man's character; it is not completely arbitrary. Men must prepare themselves by increasing their sensitivity, developing their powers of intuition. Then they will be ready to receive the revelation, whether it comes directly from God or from such an intermediary as Gersonides had suggested.

One major novelty in the thought of Crescas is his way of dealing with human freedom of will. This is one theme on which both the rational and the romantic philosophers of Judaism had agreed; man is free, even though to our human comprehension it may seem that to grant man freedom is to impose a boundary to God's knowledge and power. In truth, these philosophers were caught up in the toils of one of the most difficult of traditional philosophic and religious problems, the problem of evil. For on the one hand, if God knows all and is all-powerful, then He is responsible for the evil in the world and for men's evil actions; it is, in this case, unjust that men should be rewarded or punished in the after-life for actions for which God, not they, bore the responsibility. On the other hand, if human evil and wickedness can really be laid to the charge of men, then either God does not know what is taking place and is, therefore, not all-knowing, or He knows but cannot prevent its taking place, and in this case He is not all-powerful. The problem of evil is a serious dilemma for religious thought. Most philosophers, Jewish or non-Jewish, have evaded the issue rather than solved it.

Maimonides took refuge in the evasion that the whole dilemma of the problem of evil depends upon the assumption that God's knowledge is like human knowledge, and that, since we do not really know what God's knowledge is, there is no problem; Gersonides argued that God's knowledge is knowledge of universal and necessary matters, not of particulars, whereas men's actions are based upon particular decisions of the will, and therefore not matters of Divine foreknowledge. Unlike both of these rationalists, Crescas comes out flatly for the view that God, as the Cause of all that is, must know all that there is about His own effects; he will not compromise the absoluteness of God's foreknowledge. In spite of this, Crescas has to find some way of leaving a shred of freedom to man, so that the justice of rewards and punishments may be maintained. The tortured argument by means of which he does so is not convincing. He distinguishes, in effect, between determination of the will and fatalism. It is fatalistic, he says, to assert that anyone is predestined to carry out a certain course of action, under any and all circumstances. Determination of the will makes the lesser claim that there is no event without a cause, and that an act of will, since it is an event, also has a cause, which is the latest of a chain of causes reaching ultimately back to God, the First Cause of all. But man feels himself free in his choices and thinks that he is making choices even though they may rest on a chain of linked causes reaching back to the very beginning of things. Thinking himself free, man makes his choices for motives that are praiseworthy or blameworthy. The righteousness or wickedness of these motives, their basis in obedience or disobedience to God's law, determines the justice of rewards and punishments. This solution, too, it is clear, is evasive of the problem of evil, but it is an unusual form of evasion within the Jewish tradition.

CREEDAL FORMULAS

Judaism, in its classical rabbinic form, provided elaborate directions for the living of a moral and religious life. Its prescriptions for action were detailed and entered into many aspects of life that most people of modern times would consider private affairs exclusively. For all this precision of commandment and prohibition with respect to the actions of the Jews, there was nothing that one could call a formal or explicit creed of Judaism. One of the intellectual sports of the rabbis seems to have been the attempt at the briefest statement of a rock-bottom minimum of belief that constituted Judaism. Nevertheless, in the medieval situation in which Judaism directly confronted two major faiths derived from the same Biblical background, Maimonides had found it desirable to produce a formal creed of Judaism, consisting of thirteen articles of the Jewish faith. The passage of the Mishnah in commentary on which Maimonides drew up this thirteen-articled creed refers to only three beliefs as decisive: belief in revelation, belief in resurrection, and belief in God's moral government of the world. Maimonides' expansion of this number had, as its chief purpose, to present the Jewish alternatives to Christian and Muslim creeds.

One of the features of the work of Maimonides that came under attack after his death was this precise schematic presentation of a creed for Judaism. Two motives may be seen in the attack: some of those who protested were moved by the realization that a formulated creed, rigidly used as a touchstone, would lead to a kind of "orthodoxy" with respect to belief that Judaism had up till then avoided by stressing the "orthodoxy" of practice; others made protest because Maimonides' formulation was based upon a too highly refined philosophical conception of God and thus dismissed the popular anthropomorphic notions. After a time, Maimonides' thirteen articles were included in the liturgy of the Jewish synagogues and the controversy on this point was stilled.

We have seen that one of the chief impulses that led Crescas to the composition of his philosophic book, *Light of the Lord,* was his desire to refute the emphasis that Maimonides (and others) had placed upon theoretical, intellectual speculation and knowledge as the highest avenue of human approach to God. Religious worship and moral conduct, as expressions of love of God, are, for Crescas, the high road to communion with God. From this starting point, Crescas criticizes Maimonides' articles of the Jewish faith for making no mention of the love of God and for failing to differentiate between truly basic and necessary beliefs and those of lesser authority. He replaces the Maimonidean listing with a division of the beliefs of Judaism into three classes: (1) Fundamental principles, of which there are six; (2) True beliefs, which are authoritative, but a denial of them does not automatically take a person outside the Jewish fold; (3) Opinions, which form a proper part of the traditions of Judaism, but which are in no sense required beliefs and are left to individual decision.

Behind all of these lie those principles of the existence and the nature of God that are not specific to Judaism but common to all religion. The fundamental principles of Crescas include God's absolute and total knowledge (of both universals and particulars); God's Providence, both in general matters and in the special oversight of individuals—a distinct variety of Providence is God's special concern for the Jews; God's omnipotence, enabling Him to do anything except the self-contradictory (even God cannot make an object simultaneously black and white in the same respect); prophecy; freedom; and purpose. Crescas suggests that even if one chose to list the existence of God and His revelation as two additional fundamental principles, the whole list would come to but eight, not thirteen, as in Maimonides.

Crescas adds eight true beliefs; this intermediate classification is somewhat puzzling, for a denial of these beliefs does constitute heresy, and yet the one who denies them does not exclude himself from the community of Israel. The link in Crescas' mind is, it seems, that a denial of the fundamental principles would destroy the idea of a Divine Law, whereas denial of the true beliefs would not. The true beliefs that he discusses in *Light of the Lord* are: Creation, Immortality, Rewards and Punishments, Resurrection, the Eternity of the Law, the superiority of Moses to other prophets, the priests' ability to predict the future by the casting of lots, and the belief in the Messiah. Finally, Crescas' list of opinions, which have traditional but not compelling authority, includes some philosophical opinions, such as the unknowable character of the essence of God, and some popular superstitions, such as the belief in the power of charms and amulets.

JOSEPH ALBO

The discussion of a Jewish creed was carried on in the very popular but not very distinguished philosophic compilation of Joseph Albo (1380–1444), *The Book of Roots* (*Sefer Ikkarim*). This, rather than philosophy, was Albo's chief interest. A considerable part of *The Book of Roots* is taken up with the presentation of some philosophic ideas, but Albo merely compiled these materials from his predecessors. His distinctiveness is partly stylistic; he wrote in a way that was far more readable than any of the Jewish philosophers since Jehudah Halevi. Chiefly, however, what sets Albo apart from the rest of the medieval Jewish philosophers is that he was defending the Jewish faith against a different kind of threat. The problem faced by the others had been truly the intellectual defense of the Jewish faith. Albo lived later, in a period when forced conversions to Christianity had become commonplace and when rabbis and other Jewish scholars were forced by the Christian authorities to take part in public debates, or disputations, against Christian theologians and preachers. Albo himself, while still comparatively young, was one of the eight Jewish spokesmen at just such a conference, at Tortosa and San Mateo, in 1413 and 1414. It is amazing to think of the apparatus and preparation that must have gone into the scheduling of sixty-nine sessions between February 1413 and November 1414, when not only all the participants, but also everyone in the audience knew that the final decision had been made before the first session was held! The disputation, after all, was presided over by no less a person than the Antipope Benedict XIII (Peter de Luna), who held his fragment of the divided papal authority from 1394 to 1428.

Quite conceivably the experience of participation in the Disputation of Tortosa may have led Joseph Albo to see that what the Jews of his times needed was a straightforward exposition of the doctrines of Judaism to help them hold to the conviction that theirs was the true religion. For Maimonides, the central task was philosophy; creedal formulation was so far a secondary matter that he did not deign to refer, in his *Guide for the Perplexed,* to his list of articles of the Jewish faith. Crescas did make his doctrinal scheme a major feature of his *Light of the Lord,* but his focus was still on philosophic argument directed chiefly against the Jewish Aristotelians. But when we come to *The Book of Roots,* we find that Albo makes the establishment of doctrinal positions his chief concern and introduces philosophic material only to the extent that he feels necessary in order to carry out this central intention. This way of using philosophic material does not involve him in the omission of many of the matters that had been discussed by Jewish philosophers before him. Virtually every question they had included in their works comes into *The Book of Roots* at one point or another. But the systematic presentation of a philosophic point of view is apparently not Albo's intention.

The "Roots" of Albo's title are the fundamental principles, in the same sense as this expression was used by Crescas. They are bases upon which other beliefs rest, and without which those other beliefs would have no standing. After criticizing various previous attempts to make lists of fundamental principles, Albo sets forth his own view that there are three Roots: the Existence of God, Revelation, and Providence, including Rewards and Punishments. Now, these are not specifically principles of Judaism; at a minimum, it is clear that they are shared by Christianity and Islam. Albo's

Roots are, then, the basic beliefs, one might say, of any religion worthy of the name. In fact, Albo goes so far, in the twenty-fifth chapter of the first book of *The Book of Roots*, as to argue that "there may be two divine laws existing at the same time among different nations," each giving expression to the fundamental principles and the derived principles in a manner suitable to the conditions of each nation. There can, of course, be no difference in the principles, because all Divine law comes from the same source, the unchanging One. The differences among the various forms of Divine law are for the benefit of those who receive it, not because of any diversity or plurality in the One who gives it.

Because the derived principles (*Shorashim*) are logically necessary consequences of fundamental principles (*Ikkarim*), mere belief in the fundamental principles is not enough to make one a believer. We must follow through on our beliefs and accept their consequences. To deny a logical consequence of a fundamental belief is equivalent to a denial of the belief itself. Each of the three fundamental beliefs carries with it one or more derivative beliefs. The Existence of God has four derivatives: God is One; He is not in any sense corporeal; He is not subject to time; He is free from all defects. Revelation implies three derivatives: God's knowledge of what takes place on earth; Prophecy; and the genuineness of the Divine messenger. From the third fundamental principle, Rewards and Punishments, Albo derives only one secondary principle, the Doctrine of Special Providence. It should be noted that there is some confusion about the treatment of Providence in Albo; on the one hand, he seems to say that Providence is more fundamental than Rewards and Punishments, whereas but a few paragraphs later he refers to Providence as "based upon" the principle of Rewards and Punishments. Since God's knowledge of what takes place on earth, a belief that is essential both to Rewards and Punishments and to Special Providence, has already been presented as a derivative of the belief in Revelation, the confusion is still more difficult to resolve.

If the eleven primary and secondary principles that have been mentioned are to be found in any real religion, then it is clear that Albo follows (as indeed he quotes) the rabbinic saying, "The pious men of other nations have a share in the world-to-come." For his age, and for most periods of the Western world, this was a remarkably liberal attitude, found only among the most advanced thinkers. Lesser men believed that their own religion had exclusive possession of the avenues to salvation, to the world-to-come. Even Dante, the greatest of medieval Italian poets, had difficulty with this question; he resolved it less liberally than Albo by providing especially comfortable accommodations outside Paradise for the "pious men of other nations." But if this is the case, in what way is Albo to defend the particular beliefs of Judaism? If every genuine religion has its own version of Divine law, and if the righteous followers of each of these religions will be saved, why should Jews undergo torment, torture, and even martyrdom for the sake of their own traditional brand of Divine law?

Albo answers this critical question in two chief ways. First, he suggests that the particular commandments (*mitzwoth*) of the Jewish tradition were specifically intended by God to make the road to salvation easily achievable by the ordinary person; second, there can be doubts about the genuineness of every other religion, but not about Judaism. In addition, Albo argues that the superiority of the Jewish version of Divine law is proved by the superiority of Moses to all other prophets, since "The divinity of a law may be proved in two ways, from the law itself and from the lawgiver." The first of these arguments, from the relative ease by which the average follower of the Jewish faith can attain salvation, is a sharp descent from the high level of Albo's previous universalism. Now he speaks as an interpreter of the "Chosen people" tradition; by fulfilling even one of the many commandments of the Jewish law a man may be saved. The second argument, that everyone (that is to say, Christians and Muslims, as well as Jews) acknowledges the authenticity of Jewish law, while there are doubts possible about every other law, is essentially the same argument that proved so effective in Jehudah Halevi's *Book of the Kuzari.*

THE DOGMAS OF JUDAISM

We are led, now, to consider briefly the six dogmas "which every one professing the law of Moses is obliged to believe," that is, the specific doctrines of Judaism. These are neither fundamental principles nor derivative principles, yet Albo asserts that "they are connected with the three fundamental principles that we laid down." Precisely how they are connected, never becomes clear. They are not even, in all cases, unique to Judaism, nor can they all be considered as essential to Judaism. Albo himself, in his discussions of them, cites many Jewish sources that are in disagreement with his dogmas or his way of interpreting particular dogmas. They have none of the compelling quality of the fundamental and derivative principles.

The first dogma of Judaism proposed by Albo is creation of the world in time, out of nothing. This is certainly not held by Jews only. Albo says, "It is a dogma common to divine law generally," and adds that "we can conceive a divine law in general and the Law of Moses in particular without the idea" of creation out of nothing. We have seen in previous discussions that there were Jewish thinkers who rejected this traditional view. Albo's very first "branch," or specifically Jewish dogma, is, most peculiarly, one that is neither specific to Judaism nor universally accepted by Jews.

The second dogma in the scheme is the superiority of Moses to all other prophets. Here Albo's intent is clear; neither Jesus nor Mohammed is to be compared with Moses as a prophet. When the Bible says (Deut. xxxiv, 10), "And there hath not arisen a prophet since in Israel like unto Moses," Albo interprets this statement to mean, not only that Moses' equal had not appeared, but also that his equal would never appear. The evidence for this extension of the Biblical words he draws from "the high value of the law that was given through him." We have already noted that Albo's defense of the superiority of the Jewish law rests upon the superiority of Moses as a prophet; now we find that the superiority of Moses as a prophet is established by the superiority of the Jewish law—an argument remarkably circular and unconvincing. There is further discussion of the dogma of the superiority of Moses (in Albo's Third book); here he argues that "Moses asked of God that Israel and himself should be raised above all other nations in respect to prophetic inspiration," and that "God granted his request that no prophet should be equal to him in prophetic power, and that the gift of prophecy should not be given to the Gentiles."

Maimonides, too, had claimed that no prophet equal to Moses would ever arise. Yet, Albo points out, Maimonides had asserted as a dogma of equal rank that the Law of Moses is unchangeable and unrepealable. "From this it would seem that he thought that if not for the latter dogma, we might have to obey a prophet who desired to abolish the laws of Moses." To avoid this implication which he drew (without warrant) from the words of Maimonides, Albo avers that it is not necessary to regard the immutability of the Law of Moses as a dogma. He calls the principle that "the Law of Moses will not be repealed nor changed nor exchanged for another by any prophet" a "true belief," rather than an independent dogma. Yet he lists it as the third of his six specifically Jewish dogmas. Again, Albo makes difficulties for himself by trying to hold, at one and the same time, that the Law of Moses is unchangeable and that circumstances may, and probably will, arise in which this unchangeable law will, in fact, change. His reasoning is that that which is unchangeable is the essential core of religious significance that lies behind the Mosaic laws; the particular form that any legal precept is given in any age may change, since it necessarily is involved with the specific historical and cultural circumstances of the age in which it was first formulated. Albo's examples of changes that had taken place are drawn from both Bible and Talmud. He points out that in the days before Noah, human beings were not supposed to eat meat, whereas after the time of Noah the eating of meat was permitted. Again, the rules for proper sacrifice have changed in the course of time; the degrees of relationship within which marriage is prohibited have also altered. In short, "If we investigate the divine laws of the world, we find that they changed from time to time, forbidding what was originally permitted, and then again permitting what had been forbidden."

Albo's general conservatism was considerably modified by this conviction that the religion of Judaism had changed by Divine decree at various times in the past. He was willing to concede, in addition, the possibility that there might be future changes as great as any that the past had witnessed. Even such long-established statutes as the dietary laws might change; God originally instituted them because of their connection with the false worship of the Egyptians, the worship of demons and evil spirits. "But when this form of worship has been forgotten, . . . it may be that God will again permit it." Thus within Jewish law there are both eternal and unchangeable principles and temporary, local, changing expressions. When rabbinical ordinances seemed to modify the Biblical law, it was only the husk of the expression that they changed; the eternal underlying, Divine principle remained unmodified. "Though divine laws are not completely repealed, they may change in their permissions and prohibitions, as the character of the recipients changes."

Albo's fourth dogma has already been mentioned; it is that "Human perfection may be attained by fulfilling even a single one of the commandments in the Law of Moses." The argument for this dogma is a very complicated one, and it had been a bone of contention among the rabbis from early times. A more strict and rigorous approach demanded that Jews fulfill the entire law in order to achieve salvation. Yet, if this were the proper interpretation, Albo suggests, it would be more difficult for a Jew to attain perfection than any other person, for, as we have already seen, one who does not accept the Law of Moses can gain salvation by maintaining merely the eleven fundamental and derivative principles. Then we would have an unusual situation in which the Law, given to the people of Israel as an act of Divine grace, "so as to bring them all to eternal life, would be the very thing which would prevent them from attaining this happy privilege." The alternative, then, is to hold that God gave the Law of Moses to Israel to make it easier for Jews to achieve salvation, and, therefore, that fulfillment of even a single commandment is adequate and acceptable.

Fifth among the dogmas of Judaism, according to Albo, is the belief in resurrection. Once more, this is neither limited to Judaism nor a necessary principle of the Law of Moses. Nevertheless, because it comes with the authority of tradition, it is incumbent upon the Jews to accept it, as their ancestors did. Finally, the sixth dogma in Albo's structure of Jewish beliefs is that of the coming of the Messiah. Here, he points out, we have the same situation as we have with regard to resurrection. The belief is neither a fundamental nor a derived principle of the Law of Moses, yet every professing Jew is obligated to believe in it.

Albo's *Book of Roots*, like Bahya's *Duties of the Heart* and Halevi's *Book of the Kuzari*, despite its limitations, and perhaps because it accepted popular superstitious beliefs, has retained a strong hold on the heart of many Jews to the present. Its author was far less competent as a speculative philosopher or theologian than most of the writers whose works we have examined. Yet (or perhaps therefore) he has had an influence on the minds of Jews during several centuries which has been denied, for example, to his master, Crescas.

CRITICAL MINDS OF THE RENAISSANCE

The medievalism of Joseph Albo is so apparent that it is something of a shock to realize that his life span overlapped the beginning of that crucial transitional period in Western life that is often called the Renaissance—the rebirth—even though there is some doubt in the minds of many scholars as to just what was reborn. At the very same time during which Albo reacted to the conversionist movement in the Christian Church with a rebirth of the dogmatic spirit, Jews in Italy were reacting to the birth of the modern world of science and technology and to a spirit of cultural openness and intellectual adventure.

It must be remembered that the years of the Renaissance coincided generally with the period in which the compulsory ghetto was instituted in many parts of Europe. Voluntary ghettos there had always been, for the narrow limitations on permissible activities on Sabbaths and days of religious obligation made it impossible for Jews to live widely separated from each other and still practice the Jewish religion faithfully. There may also have been an element of mutual protection in ghetto living for a people who never knew when the words of an over-zealous missionary monk or the financial needs of an impecunious noble might incite a mob to anti-Jewish action. Then, too, the intricate web of Jewish philanthropic activities made a close-knit community desirable. Over and above all these reasons for the voluntary living together of Jews, the breakdown of the medieval world led to the enactment of compulsory measures forcing the Jews of urban Europe to live in restricted areas. Whatever the Jews developed in openness of spirit was not the result of a tearing-down of ghetto walls.

Nevertheless, first in Italy and then in Holland, Jews began to play a role in the intellectual community of their time in a way they had never done before in Christian Europe. We learn of one

Jew after another who was an intimate of intellectual leaders of the times—even of highly placed Churchmen. We find Jews assuming a role in the arts, especially the theatrical arts, which they have continued to play in Europe and in the United States. A composer like Salomone de' Rossi, in the late sixteenth century, wrote a large amount of music that was well appreciated by the nobility and the aristocracy of Italy, in all the favorite forms of the age; he also wrote liturgical music for synagogue use that imported into divine service the musical spirit of the Renaissance. De' Rossi was not the only Italian-Jewish musician; he was, however, outstanding.

In philosophy, by the end of the fifteenth century there had already begun, faintly and mildly, among the Jews of Italy, a wave of criticism of the Talmudic tradition in Judaism. The earliest contributor to this critical trend of whom we have record was a brilliant young man from Crete, Elijah del Medigo (1460–97). He came of a family of physicians, and his moving to Italy as a young man was probably for the purpose of carrying on his own preparation to follow in the family tradition. This young man, barely twenty, is reputed to have been called to the University of Padua as referee in a philosophical dispute that had arisen there. He was peculiarly well fitted to do so because, in addition to his natural abilities in philosophy, he knew Hebrew and Greek as well as Latin, and could therefore make use of sources in all three languages. There is no official record of Elijah's appointment to a teaching position at the University of Padua, yet there are many sources of the period that speak of him as an academic lecturer in philosophy there. The sources are clear enough to justify the claim that Elijah del Medigo was the first Jew to teach a subject other than Hebrew in any university in the Christian world.

Del Medigo composed several philosophic treatises in Latin that earned him considerable reputation and the friendship of another distinguished young man, Giovanni Pico, Count of Mirandola. Pico was a remarkable student and one of the most significant figures in bringing a knowledge of Jewish thought to the Christian world. This he did, in part, by subsidizing Jewish scholars to make translations, especially of Kabbalistic works, and in part by learning Hebrew himself and introducing ideas gained from his reading into his own productions. Del Medigo was one of the Jewish scholars paid by Pico to translate, from the Hebrew, the works of Arabic and even of Greek writers who could not be read in their original tongues.

In addition to these original compositions in secular philosophy and to his translations of philosophic works, Elijah del Medigo wrote, in Hebrew, a philosophic critique of rabbinic Judaism, entitled *Examination of Religion* (*Behinat ha-Dat*). The work is not particularly unorthodox; its criticisms of traditional Jewish practices are mild. Del Medigo does, however, examine critically the way in which the rabbis interpreted the Bible, and he reaches the conclusion that their interpretations are philosophically invalid. A philosopher, he says, can accept an interpretation of the Bible only if it accords with the teachings of philosophy. This criticism may have been enough to anger the rabbinic authorities in Padua. Though there are no positive evidences, it is widely held that a rabbinical court headed by Judah Minz, of Padua, placed Del Medigo under the ban. Whether this is an accurate story or not, by 1490 young Del Medigo had returned to Crete, where he lived out his few remaining years of life.

Soon after Del Medigo had left Italy to return to Crete, in the year 1492, a long series of anti-Jewish acts in Spain culminated in the expulsion of the Jews of that country. Among those who left and took up residence in Italy was the physician Judah Abrabanel (1470–1535), son of the distinguished Spanish-Jewish statesman Don Isaac Abrabanel. Early in the sixteenth century, Judah Abrabanel taught medicine, and perhaps astrology, in the University of Naples. He is of interest to our story of Jewish philosophy because in 1501 or 1502 he completed one of the most important works of Renaissance Platonic philosophy, *The Dialogues of Love* (*Dialoghi di amori*). This masterpiece of its type remained unpublished until 1535, after the death of its author, who was thus denied knowledge of the phenomenal success and popular acclaim that his work achieved. Within twenty years, at least five editions were published in Italian, and three Spanish translations and two French translations were made. Later *The Dialogues of Love* was translated into Hebrew. Professor Cecil Roth [n] has speculated that the language in which Abrabanel originally wrote his book may have been Ladino, the vernacular language of the Jews of Spain. Be this as it may, the language of the first publication was Italian, and the author was billed on the title page as "Leone Ebreo," Leo the Jew.

Properly speaking, *The Dialogues of Love* is but a minor phase of our theme, for it is not part of the story of Jewish philosophy. Its author leaves no doubt that he is a Jew; he is not, in any sense, concealing his background. He does use some Kabbalistic ideas—which were fairly common coinage among the Florentine Humanists of this time. But basically Judah Abrabanel was writing a secular work in a secular context. This type of philosophic literature was one of the conventional forms of Renaissance literature. So, while we take note of this work in passing, it need not detain us.

If we speak of Abrabanel's work as one in which the Jewish mind influenced the non-Jewish Renaissance, we find its counterpart, the work showing a considerable effect of the new scholarship of the times, in *The Light of the Eyes* (*Meor Einayim*), by Azariah de' Rossi (1514–78). What is of interest to us here in De' Rossi's work is not its content but its method. The author utilizes the techniques of free study that had been developed in connection with the examination of classical texts by the humanist scholars, but he applies these methods to the study of such sacred texts as those of the Bible and the Talmud. He quotes, in his study, more than a hundred classical authors, both Latin and Greek, and uses the materials he derives from these authors to criticize as well

253

as to clarify the Talmudic and Biblical works. His criticisms of the traditional Jewish theory of revelation are especially extreme. Because of them, his work was banned by the leaders of orthodoxy.

LEON DA MODENA

Some Jews of Venice were especially responsive to the liberalizing currents of the Renaissance. In minor matters this tendency was expressed by the failure to observe some of the ordinances of Judaism consistently; thus, for example, the rigorous harshness of Sabbath observance was considerably eased by some of the Venetians, even to the extent of playing tennis on that day. One of the leaders of Venetian Jewry, Simone Luzzatto, tried to make it acceptable for Jews to use gondolas on the Sabbath; prominent laymen and rabbis opposed and defeated this suggestion, but not on strictly legal grounds. In Venice, many Jews of the upper classes partially abandoned the traditional practice of keeping the head covered, removing their hats when they were in company with non-Jews. There was much laxness in the observance of dietary laws, notably in respect to eating and drinking the food and wine of non-Jews. Other Venetian Jews, perhaps in counter-reaction to this liberalizing trend, insisted upon precise observance of every detail of the regulations. Thus the Jewish community of Venice was far from harmonious, except on the need for destroying heretical views.

Leon da Modena (1571–1648), son of a prominent and wealthy Jewish family, gave expression in his many writings to the diversity of interests and viewpoints in the Venetian community. It was, perhaps, unfortunate for his development as a scholar and thinker that his father's later business ventures were unsuccessful, and that Leon himself failed in an attempt to restore the family fortunes. As a result, although he had been brought up to wealth, he lived under the constant threat of poverty, which led him to busy himself constantly with money-making occupations and diverted him from careful study. Thus he never fulfilled his promise as a thinker. He seems, rather, in many respects a hack writer, generally working on subjects and in ways that would reach the largest possible public.

The position that Leon da Modena developed has been characterized by a leading recent scholar as "enlightened Rabbinism." That is to say, he sought in all his works a pattern for establishing a lenient interpretation of the Jewish tradition. So, for example, he approved of the uncovering of the head, on the democratic ground that "the majority of the congregation do not observe this prohibition." He was particularly liberal in his views concerning the non-legal parts of rabbinic literature; these materials, he said, were not meant to be taken literally. The task of the student was to penetrate the figurative language of the rabbis and to discover the meanings intended. In the course of this interpretation of the rabbis, Leon was able to find ways of justifying the attitudes and practices of more liberal Jews of his own time and place.

One of the peculiarities of Leon da Modena's literary style was that in his works of controversy he quoted large sections from the works that he was presumably criticizing. As a result of this practice, his works preserve many of the arguments of heretical writings that are otherwise lost, but also he has been regarded as a heretic himself. Professor Ellis Rivkin's[n] recent studies defend very successfully the view that Leon da Modena was, indeed, attacking real heresies of his time and that he was genuinely and sincerely devoted to the Jewish tradition, in its laxer form. In the light of this suggestion, it is likely that one of the heretics attacked by Leon da Modena was Uriel da Costa.

Da Costa (1585–1640) came of a family that had converted, under pressure, to Christianity, but had continued secretly to observe the Jewish faith. There were many such families, especially in Spain and Portugal. They are referred to as Marranos, or

"Crypto-Jews." Uriel da Costa was actually reared in Portugal by the Jesuits. Later, on reaching manhood, he emigrated from Portugal to Holland, then a most tolerant land, where he professed his Judaism openly. He illustrates, however, the difficulty of one who was both Jewish and Christian, and therefore, in a sense, was neither Christian nor Jewish. Although he had acknowledged himself a Jew and rejected his Christian upbringing, Uriel retained enough of the criticism he had imbibed in the course of his Christian education to be dissatisfied with his Jewish co-religionists. He declared the ritualism of the Jews to be "pharisaical," echoing the long-standing Christian interpretation of Pharisaism. He deliberately violated the ritual laws, especially the dietary laws, of Judaism. Then he wrote an attack on the doctrines of immortality and of rewards and punishments. In his tract on this subject, he drew a contrast between the Bible, in which these doctrines are not taught, and the work of the rabbis, where they are to be found.

The position that Uriel took was as offensive to Christians as to Jews, for, after all, the doctrine of immortality and that of retribution were as much elements of the "Biblical" faith of Christianity as they were of Judaism. As a result, Uriel da Costa was fined and his book burned. He was excommunicated by the Jews of Amsterdam and left the country. Later, he returned and made a token submission to the rabbinical authorities. At this time, Da Costa's beliefs seem to be those of a minimum religion; he had abandoned the idea of revelation, and even the idea of a personal God, substituting a religion of nature, in which God was considered as an impersonal creative force. Again, he was led to publish his views and, in consequence, once more was excommunicated. After seven years he offered to submit. This time the rabbinical leaders insisted upon making a public spectacle of Uriel's renunciation of his heresies; the disgrace of this so affected him that he committed suicide. First, however, he wrote, in Latin, an autobiography entitled *An Example of Human Life* (*Exemplar Humanae Vitae*).

BENEDICT SPINOZA

By far the greatest philosopher to come out of the Jewish background was Baruch Spinoza (1632–77), often called by the Latin form of his name, Benedict. To so great an extent did he pursue the rational criticism of religion, however, that it is as a matter of courtesy and pride that he can be included within the heritage of Jewish philosophy. His father was a relatively successful man of commerce, who was well respected in the Jewish community of Amsterdam. Young Baruch studied rabbinic and Jewish philosophic literature as well as the secular branches of learning. Among the works he studied were Maimonides' *Guide for the Perplexed* and Gersonides' *The Wars of the Lord*. His reading led him to severe questioning of the traditional practical and ritual emphases of Judaism. His independent mind insisted upon following through its own thoughts. He relaxed his observance of rabbinic regulations and associated more and more with non-Jews.

Spinoza's attitudes and actions led to his arraignment before the rabbinic court in 1656. Still smarting from the bad publicity resulting from their dealings with Uriel da Costa, the rabbis offered Spinoza a bribe to keep silent and conform outwardly, whatever his inner convictions. Spinoza indignantly refused, and was forthwith excommunicated. From this time forward, he lived in spiritual isolation from the Jewish world. For Western philosophy, this has proved a great benefit, for Spinoza has come to be accepted as one of its outstanding contributors. For Jewish life, however, the excommunication of Spinoza has been a bane. Many young intellectuals who might have become leaders of their people have been drawn away from Judaism by the sense that what had happened to Spinoza might happen to them. In recent years, Jews from many lands, including the Israeli leader, David ben Gurion, have asked the rabbis of Amsterdam to rescind the decree of excommunication imposed against Baruch Spinoza more than three hundred years ago. As yet the leaders of Amsterdam Jewry have not done so.

The most sympathetic comment that can be made on the action of the rabbis in excommunicating Spinoza would point to the variety of heresies that had developed during the years of the Renaissance and to their justifiable hope of restoring the solidarity and integrity of the Jewish community. They saw piety in traditional terms, measured by conformity. Spinoza, in contrast, asserted that "to take away the liberty to philosophize is to take away piety." This protest against any form of thought-control is actually as much in the spirit of the ancient rabbinic literature as it is in the new tradition of liberalism. It was the idea of freedom of thought expressed in this aphorism that Spinoza developed into the brilliant statement of his *Theologico-Political Treatise* (*Tractatus Theologico-Politicus*), anonymously published in 1670. The *Treatise* was a merciless attack upon the churches' power in secular affairs. Having experienced the narrowness of religious exclusiveness, Spinoza hated it and offered as an alternative a way of life based upon mutual respect and toleration. He argued that freedom of religion is in the interest of a peaceful and secure community.

The closest approach of Spinoza's thought to his Jewish studies is to be found in his doctrine of God. Like Crescas, whom he had read, Spinoza rejected the view of the medieval Aristotelians that an infinite could not be asserted. Accordingly, he described God as infinite substance. He argued, then, that such an all-inclusive totality must have independent existence; "its essence necessarily involves existence" in a rational universe. If God is all-inclusive substance, then there can be no other substance. All the particular things to which we ascribe existence must be overflowings of the infinite creative richness of the Infinite being of God. There can be nothing to limit God's pure creativity; the outpouring and overflowing must, therefore, continue until every possible thing becomes actual, until there is a perfect and complete universe. Spinoza's doctrine of God is properly called pantheism, the doctrine that God is All there is, because He exists in two ways. He is the infinite creative activity, and He is the infinite creation. Although this doctrine of God goes beyond any that is found in the Jewish tradition, except possibly among the Kabbalists, it is an extension of the idea of the immanence of God which is repeatedly defended among Jewish writers.

God is manifested to the human mind through reason; therefore there is something in reality that corresponds to every "clear and distinct" idea in the human mind. God is manifested in nature as necessary law. It must be remembered that everything in nature is of one substance, and that substance is God. But "God acts from the laws of His own nature only, and is compelled by no one." The necessity that Spinoza finds in the universe is, then, the operation of God's own nature, not a mere mechanical determination. Spinoza is particularly insistent on denying the view that God determines nature to suit man's purposes. This view, so persistent in the history of religion, was to Spinoza an especially arrogant form of anthropomorphism. God does what He does because it is His nature to do so, not because of man's desires or man's needs. Man achieves freedom by using his reason to rise from imagination to science, and from science to a third kind of knowledge, which Spinoza calls "intuitive science," in which imagination and science are somehow brought into one. Imagination is concerned with particulars; science loses sight of particulars in its quest for universals; in "intuitive science" particulars are once more seen, but now in the light of their individual characteristics and their universal aspects simultaneously.

To develop this vision is to become one with God. "As each person therefore becomes stronger in this kind of knowledge, the more he is conscious of himself and of God, of himself, that is in God, and of God as in himself." In becoming one with God, man becomes most completely himself. Now man thinks as God thinks and loves as God loves. But God thinks because it is His nature to think. And God loves, because it is His nature to love. God's love is general, not particular. "God loves no one and hates no one." So, too, when man reaches the height of knowing himself as one with God, his love becomes general. He does not love particular persons as themselves, but as the outpourings of the Infinite. All love, then, is love of God. To reach this "intellectual love of God" is man's highest blessedness. The man who has achieved this pinnacle of identification with God needs no belief in the world-to-come, for he has already attained blissful eternity. He is one with the timeless and the infinite. His wisdom is "not a meditation upon death but upon life."

CHAPTER NINE

Enlightened Ideas and Jewish Emancipation

In URIEL DA COSTA and Spinoza we have seen the birth of a new rationalist spirit, akin to the enlightened Deism of Lord Herbert of Cherbury and other secular, non-Jewish philosophers of the seventeenth century. Unlike the earlier rational attitude of the Middle Ages, which sought to find a support in reason for the traditional beliefs and practices of the Jewish religion, this newer rationalism was universal and abstract. It strove to eliminate the provincial particulars of Judaism and to discover those elements of rational religion upon which all reasonable men could unite. Like the older rationalism, this new variety interpreted the moral life as a life led in accordance with reason. Maimonides and Spinoza were as one in agreeing that blind obedience to the precepts of the Law was a lower order of morality than a reflective intelligent re-creation of the necessity of the Law.

Just as there had developed, after the extreme of medieval Jewish rationalism, an attempt on the part of Crescas and Albo to turn the weapons of reason to the defense of traditional Judaism, so after Spinoza there came those who tried to base the argument for sustaining the tradition on a Spinozistic method. David Nieto (1654–1728), a leading rabbi in eighteenth-century England, maintained, for example, that Jewish theology could be justified by the mathematical methods of science that were so prominent in the intellectual life of that Newtonian age. He held, indeed, that science had been a part of the thought-world of the Jews from Biblical times. He even went so far as to claim that the sciences were originated among the Jews of antiquity, rather than among their neighbors. The wisdom of King Solomon, according to Nieto, included knowledge of the sciences. This wisdom and the books in which it was written down were lost in the course of the Exile from the Holy Land, and, as a result, proper credit for scientific originality has never been given to the Jews. Moreover, when the rabbis had prohibited the reading of philosophic and scientific books, this prohibition was not intended as an absolute denial of the value of such books. It was meant only to exclude the study of those books with heretical tendencies, and even this prohibition applied only to laymen. For all of his concern to show that the Jewish tradition had never been as opposed to the rational sciences as had been charged, Nieto was intent on justifying the doctrines of Judaism, not challenging them. In fact, Nieto did not even wish the license claimed by Maimonides to interpret the text of the Bible figuratively. He was satisfied to accept it in its literal sense.

The attempt of Nieto and others like him to rationalize the Jewish tradition may have been undertaken solely in the hope of lessening the influence of the extreme position to which Spinoza's thought led. But it is more likely that it was also in reaction against an extreme of irrationalism that had swept through the Jewish world as well as that of the non-Jews in the seventeenth century. For the Jews, this flood tide took the form of the messianic movement of Sabbatai Zevi, a false Messiah whose claims were taken seriously not only by the ignorant masses but also by such outstanding leaders of Jewish life as Menasseh ben Israel. Sabbatai Zevi's downfall led to apostasy and disheartenment. It may have caused a lowering of the estimation in which the Jews were held in western Europe. The attempt of rational traditionalism was to find a middle ground between unbridled irrational frenzy and the unchecked coldness of pure reason.

JEWISH EMANCIPATION

Meantime, however, in western Europe, for several centuries, the transition from a more or less unified Christian community to a number of independent and competing national states had been under way. In addition, the basis of social organization was changing from status to contract. The Jews could never have been an organic part of a unified Christian community. They would always have to be on the outside, as a group, although individual Jews might win position by unusual abilities. Moreover, to be a Jew was to be a member of a status group without status; it is one of the ironies of Jewish life in medieval times that, since society was organized in status groups, a special status had to be found for those who could not be part of the society. As contract organization replaced status organization, individuals, rather than the groups to which they belonged, became the basic units of life. An individual Jew could make contracts with other individuals, whether those others were Jewish or not. A Jew, like any other member of a society, could be rich or poor, intelligent or stupid, honest or dishonest, brave or cowardly. Theological distinctions among religious groups do not affect the qualities of individual men to any significant extent.

Further, especially since the new national states were founded on an economy that was largely commercial and capitalistic, and since the Jews had, for many centuries, been engaged chiefly in commerce, their enterprise was an important part of the economic life of the nations in which they were resident. For all these reasons, it became increasingly clear, as the seventeenth century waned and the eighteenth came over the horizon of time, that it was folly to exclude Jews from the life of the nation around them. Point by point the walls of exclusion fell before the onslaught of a new age, until, by the end of the eighteenth century, one wall only remained standing—the wall that separated the Jews from citizenship, from political participation in the countries in which they dwelt. The American Revolution and the national Constitution on which the union of the newly independent American states was grounded breached that final wall. Jews became full citizens of the United States of America from its first establishment. Once a gap had been made in this wall, other nations followed the example of the United States of America.

The philosophical views of the enlightenment of the eighteenth century contributed in some measure to the movement toward the emancipation of the Jews. We should certainly not claim that any philosophic movement, in any age, has direct social or political consequences. Philosophy reinforces other tendencies of its time. Enlightened philosophy was contractual in its political theory, individualistic in its moral theory. Its practitioners were advocates of humanitarianism and of toleration. Most importantly, they viewed religion as an individual rather than a corporate matter, something between a man and his God. Society had no right to meddle with an individual's religious convictions, nor to impose any restrictions upon the individual because of his unwillingness to conform to the beliefs of the majority. The question of common concern was whether a man was a good man, not whether he was a good Christian. The philosophers of the Enlightenment were spokesmen of a free secular society. In the society they envisioned, a Jew might be as good a citizen as any other man.

MOSES MENDELSSOHN

Even before the American and the French revolutions had brought political emancipation to the Jews, there were some Jewish thinkers who had entered into the spirit of those enlightened times. One of the earliest of these to win renown was Moses Mendelssohn (1729–86). In his younger days, Mendelssohn followed the usual program of Jewish studies in the rabbinic literature. In addition, he pursued secular learning, for which he had great native talent. After moving from his family home in Dessau to the metropolitan center of Berlin, Mendelssohn associated with a number of the leading figures of the intellectual and literary world of Germany. He became a good friend of the towering German writer Gotthold Lessing. Indeed, it is believed that Lessing modeled the central character of his drama *Nathan the Wise* on Mendelssohn.

Moses Mendelssohn, from his place near the center of the literary and intellectual coterie of Berlin, wrote philosophic and critical works that established his reputation for acumen and taste. He used his position to work without rest for the acceptance of his fellow Jews as men among men. At the same time, he tried to induce his Jewish brethren to meet enlightenment halfway by the study of secular subjects and a fuller participation in the culture of their German hosts. Just as his own pre-eminence in German cultural life had been achieved without sacrifice of Jewish learning, so, he was convinced, could be the attainments of other Jews. Mendelssohn, it might be said, undertook the difficult task of mediator between cultures; he strove to interpret German culture to the Jews and to exemplify Jewish culture to the Germans.

Mendelssohn's chief distinction as a philosopher was won by his writings on the theory of art and by his dialogues on general philosophic subjects. These works established his reputation as "the Jewish Socrates," but they are not central to the story of Jewish philosophy. The book by virtue of which he belongs in this story was called *Jerusalem* (1783). From the very first page of *Jerusalem*, Mendelssohn mounted a full-scale attack on the union of church and state. This union, wherever and whenever it had occurred, he charged, had been responsible for the loss of human freedom. The object of enlightened political action should be to keep church and state separate, so that men might not be ground down between them. Separation is reasonable, because the state is an organization of men dependent upon force, while the church is a voluntary organization. Compulsion, which is at the heart of all political life, is altogether foreign to the life of the spirit. Religion based upon coercion is meaningless. "The works of religion must come from the free will of the soul, or they amount to nothing."

Mendelssohn realized that his critics would be able to make a strong case against him from the historical record of force or other forms of coercion used by Jews against other Jews. He maintained that there was a mitigating explanation for what appeared, on the surface, to be spiritual compulsion. The Jewish community had a double aspect; seen from one perspective, it was, indeed, a religious communion, within which compulsion was wrong, but, from another angle, it was a social or political community, existing, as other communities do, by its capacity to support its enactments by force. Those historical instances in which coercion had taken place were to be understood as acts of the community, not of the communion. This explanation accounts for the record of post-Biblical times. Further, it leads to the suggestion that, as the necessity for an autonomous Jewish community is weakened by the advance of the new European idea of individual dignity, there will be no need for internal compulsion in Jewry.

The Biblical enactments also specify forms of punishment. Mendelssohn explains this in like fashion. There was, he suggests, for a limited time, a unique historical phenomenon, the "Mosaic society." The Biblical code of laws contained the regulations imposed upon this society. Like the proper laws of other civil societies, the laws of Mosaic society specify what people are to do or not to do; they do not tell what is to be believed. The Bible is free of any attempts to control beliefs. The Jewish revelation is of a mode of conduct satisfactory to God, not of a creed. Mendelssohn's humanism appears in his assertion that the Jewish law contains legislation designed specifically for the Jewish people. The Bible does not express those eternal and universal principles that are open to discovery by human reason. Because these principles can be discovered by all people, everywhere, they are not fit subjects for revelation. They are, however, the presuppositions, unexpressed, on which the Bible rests. The Bible is simply the special set of supplementary rules given by God to the Jews. God could not have meant observance of these special rules as the sole road to salvation, for He gave them to the Jews alone, not to all men. To have limited the revelation to Jews and yet to have required observance of this revelation by everyone would have been a prime form of injustice, and God cannot be called unjust. From this argument, Mendelssohn draws the conclusion that God must have intended many different avenues to lead to salvation.

This line of argument certainly might be thought to point to the possibility that the laws specifically revealed to the Jews as a code for governing their lives in the Mosaic society were no longer in force once that society had been destroyed. Mendelssohn goes so far as to acknowledge that some of the regulations, particularly those relating to group life, were annulled by the destruction of the Jewish state. Regulations having to do with the personal conduct of individuals, however, are still operative. Mendelssohn contends, too, that the ceremonial laws of Judaism are still valid. We may not see the reason for a particular ceremonial law, but we are not at liberty to repudiate it, for this would be arrogance and presumption, placing our judgment on a plane with God's. God gave the ceremonial law of Judaism; only God is entitled to repeal it. Beyond the law of the Bible, Mendelssohn defends also the authority of Talmudic law over the Jews as a proper extension of Divine revelation.

What Moses Mendelssohn proposed was by no means easy; he would have had the Jews of his time govern themselves by three laws, each valid in a particular sphere. The law of reason should govern their thoughts; the laws of the state should rule over their political and social life; and the Biblical and Talmudic codes should hold sway over their moral and religious life. He was not inclined to subordinate any one of these three laws to any other; each had its own domain. In *Jerusalem*, Mendelssohn stated an abstract principle to guide the life of his fellow Jews: "Comply with the customs and the civil constitutions of the countries in which ye are transplanted, but, at the same time, be constant to the faith of your forefathers." It might be said, without great exaggeration, that the entire story of Jewish thought since Mendelssohn has been a commentary on this sentence, an attempt to flesh out, in one way or another, its skeletal structure. This has been done with varying degrees of fidelity to the historical Jewish tradition.

THE TREND TOWARD REFORM

Mendelssohn was not a voice crying in the wilderness. His call to the Jews to participate in western European culture while remaining loyal to the Jewish religion awakened a group of active disciples of Enlightenment (*Maskilim*). They published a Hebrew magazine to bring literary culture to the Jews. In 1778, while Mendelssohn was still alive, the Jewish Free School of Berlin was established, and here secular subjects were taught as well as the traditional religious subjects. All instruction was carried on in the German language. At one time, toward the end of Mendelssohn's life, he was instrumental in gaining employment for the brilliant but roguish Solomon Maimon (1754–1800) as a translator of "scientific" works into Hebrew, in the hope of extending enlightenment to the Jews of Poland.

When, after the French Revolution and the Napoleonic conquests, emancipation had come to virtually all the Jews of western Europe, a further, and unintended, consequence of Mendelssohn's thought came to light. Many of the Jews saw no reason for continuing to maintain the distinction, on which Mendelssohn had insisted, between civil participation and religious separation. Admitted to full citizenship, despite religious difference, they proceeded to eliminate the last remaining difference by accepting the religion of the majority. Even among those who did not go the whole way to conversion and assimilation, there was a tendency to place reason at the center of Jewish life and tradition at the periphery. A demand was voiced by many for reform of belief, to make the "creed" of Judaism conform to the principles of reason, and for reform of ritual, to make the worship of the synagogue take on some of the dignity and decorum of the Christian churches. One of Mendelssohn's disciples, David Friedlaender (1756–1834), pioneered in the call for internal reform, though his urging was not immediately translated into action. Others followed and actually established reformed synagogues.

It remained for Abraham Geiger (1810–74) to provide a philosophical grounding for the practical activities of the early reform movement in Judaism. This Geiger did in his book called *Judaism and Its History* (1865). Geiger adopted from the Protestant movements in Germany an emphasis on the inwardness of religion. Religion, he said, is neither theology nor ritual, neither belief nor ceremonial. Nor can religion be reduced to mere ethics. It is a spiritual attitude that blends together a profound humility and an exalted pride. Men have cause to be humble when they consider the limitations of their finite reason; but men have cause, also, to be proud when they regard their worth, their free will, the outreach of their reason. True religion is the attitude generated by the simultaneous consciousness of man's "eminence and lowness; the aspiration to perfection, coupled with the conviction that we can not reach the highest plane." In this awareness of man's infinite reach and finite grasp, there comes to him an intimation of God. Man has a modicum of free will; this little suggests to him that there must exist a Being whose acts are entirely governed by His own freely acting will. Man has limited wisdom; its limits point him to the idea of a Being of unlimited Wisdom. Man's very achievements and abilities teach him that there is more, that there is a "Highest." Religion is a facing both ways; it is "the jubilation of the soul conscious of its eminence and, at the same time, its humble confession of finiteness and limitations."

In the eighteenth century, many writers had suggested, out of the cynicism of enlightenment, that religion was an invention of a dominant class for keeping men under control. Somehow, it was believed, a priestly caste had played on man's fears to impose an ingenious system of regimentation. To this view, Geiger, a true product of the turn to romanticism in the nineteenth century, opposed the belief that the tensions between humility and pride in the human spirit prove that religion is natural to man, not arbitrarily imposed upon him. "Religion is not an invention of idle priests," he protests. "It existed and exists in mankind, and every good and noble aspiration . . . is the work of religion." Since religion is natural, as long as there are men, there will be religion. Religion is not a despotism to be thrown off when man has become sufficiently enlightened; it is an expression of a perennial human need.

Although the origin of religion is to be sought, as we have seen, in the tension between the sense of dependence and the realization of worth, Geiger does not believe that an account of origins is an adequate explanation of the total place of religion in human life. The end of religion must still be seen: it is ethical progress, man's gradual learning to supplant his self-centered values by the higher values of the community. There is no aspect of life, no phase of human existence, which is specifically religious. All the actions of men, insofar as they are motivated by the striving to reach a higher moral plane, are "the work of religion and the results of religion." Life is shot through and through with religion. Even patriotism, which has seemed to many thinkers the rival to religion, is interpreted by Geiger as religious, "when man, putting aside his seclusive selfishness, lovingly and fervently attaches himself to his country and gives to it his own life and welfare and gladly labors for all and is filled with the desire to strive toward the Highest."

Thus religion is eternal in man and is expressed through all of man's activities when these activities are carried on in the perspective of "the Highest." Since religion is eternal, Geiger cannot claim that it is changing, for better or for worse. The essence of religion must always have been the same. It is man's understanding of religion that Geiger sees as changing; and as man's understanding becomes progressively better, his understanding of religion will improve. The more man develops, the more he will find in himself the need for religion, for he will increasingly realize the distance that separates his limited and finite power from "the Infinite and Eternal Wisdom." Man's longing and man's imperfection will always remain; but human enlightenment will stimulate his longing for higher things more than it will decrease his imperfections.

GEIGER'S PHILOSOPHY OF JUDAISM

Thus far, we have examined the outlines of Geiger's general philosophy of religion and noted its tendency to disparage patterns of belief and ceremonial and to find the wellspring of religion in a universally felt, inward sentiment. He was, however, a philosopher of Judaism who faced the problem of interpreting the history of the development of the Jewish religion so that it would fit his general theory. There were two lines of argument that Geiger followed in his interpretation of Judaism. First he introduced a new tension, one relating to group life, to supplement the tension in individual life that was central to his view of the nature of religion. The new tension was one between the sense of nationality, leading to special claims such as the "Chosen people" doctrine, and the sense of universality. Judaism, he claims, is unique in that it has worked its way, over the course of centuries, through this tension to the point at which the sense of nationality has yielded completely to the sense of universality. With this, however, Geiger pulls the rabbit of paradox out of the hat of history, for, he says, the very fact that Judaism has transcended its particularism constitutes its special virtue. "Judaism has proved itself a force outliving its peculiar nationality, and therefore may lay claim to special consideration."

The first reason, then, for regarding Judaism as a religion deserving of survival is that it has survived the nationality within which it was originally formulated. The second reason is that an extraordinarily pure idea of God, completely in consonance with the leadings of reason, and an unusually exalted system of moral concepts have been developed in the course of Jewish experience. For, Geiger points out, the God-idea in Judaism recognizes in God both Supreme Reason and Supreme Good. These two terms define God, but they also define the relation of man to God. Each of the terms of the Jewish conception of God fixes a direction for human striving. Man's reason, "being a ray from Divine Reason," is the ennobling feature of his make-up. Man's consciousness of the workings of his own reason, we have seen earlier, points him toward God; man's reason itself arouses in him a yearning to rise toward the Supreme Reason. Judaism, for Geiger, exemplifies best this general principle of religion. To an even greater extent, Jewish ethics illustrates how the moral life of man is an aspiration toward the Supreme Good. The most essential element in the human being, according to Geiger's interpretation of Judaism, is "the consciousness of his moral power, which is innate in him and is the foundation of his real nobility; and which, even because it awakens his aspiration to perfect purity, makes him feel his limitations along that line, and the bars to moral life so much the more."

In addition, Geiger writes, the mutual attachment of man to man in Judaism emerges out of this noble conception of the relation of man to God. The terms of human interrelationship are, so to speak, discovered in their purity in God. God's love, His justice, His sympathy, and His pity are the ideal forms of the relations that men should have with each other. Just as God's justice is universal, man must strive to be just not only in his relations with his fellow Jews but also in relation to all men. In this way Judaism can be seen to be "the religion of humanity," not merely the religion of Jewry. This is the sense in which Judaism has survived its original national particularity. "It is an exalting strain resounding from all prophets and poets in the idea that the acknowledgement of God will spread over all the world; it is not to be a narrow nationality but a complete humanism."

Geiger was, of course, enough of a historian to realize that the Hebrews of Bible times and the later Jewish formulators of Judaism were not nineteenth-century philosophers. He was faced, therefore, with the problem of explaining how, among a simple, non-philosophic people, so exalted and philosophic a religious view had arisen. In order to do so, Geiger asserts that the Jewish people have and have had from their beginnings a special genius for religion. Once again we are faced by paradox, for the assertion of a special genius for religion is the ascription to the Jews of a national talent, and, as we have already seen, Geiger believed that Judaism had transcended its nationality. The very force that Geiger claims as the distinctive and special virtue of the Jews and Judaism is their ability to rise above their own special ability. Is not a national talent for universal thought a self-limiting concept? Would it not be as reasonable to speak of a national genius for national suicide?

The answer to these questions may be suggested by a brief consideration of the non-Jewish philosophers who inspired Geiger's ideas. When we examined the Jewish philosophers of the Middle Ages, we found them responsive to ideas gained from the Muslim philosophers of their time, but ultimately reaching back to the chief philosophers of Greek antiquity, Plato and Aristotle. In the nineteenth century, Jewish philosophers like Geiger found inspiration not in these earlier thinkers, but in the great figures of a great age in German philosophy, Kant and Hegel, Fichte and

Schleiermacher. The philosophers to whom Geiger looked were Schleiermacher and Hegel. Schleiermacher had defined religion in terms of a sense of dependence; Geiger accepted this view, but modified and extended it by borrowing from Hegel the concept of polarity, that every thought generates its own negation. In line with this Hegelian position, as we have seen, Geiger supplemented man's sense of dependence by introducing into his theory of human nature an opposing element, man's justified pride in his own reason. Furthermore, Hegel had asserted that, in the pattern of thought and in the pattern of life, the polar opposites are brought together into a synthesis which includes both. Geiger follows Hegel here by making true, inward religion the synthesis of dependence and pride. Thus far, Geiger has not gone significantly beyond his sources; it is in his assertion of the dialectical polarity of nationality and universality in Judaism that he makes original application of what he has learned from Hegel; national genius for universal thought is not, as it seems at first, a paradox, but rather a synthesis, a bringing together of opposites into a unity that includes both poles.

Geiger was very deeply imbued with the spirit of his age; the extent of its influence upon him is shown by his denial of the historical character of the Bible as uniquely "revealed" truth. Any idea of reason was, for him, revealed and true. Where reason led to an idea that negated a Biblical statement, reason was to be followed. Furthermore, in his reading in non-Jewish writers, he came upon ideas that he regarded as more in accord with reason than those he read in the Bible. One such was the idea of original sin, which has never been a prominent element in Jewish belief. Geiger's view is, again, dominated by an emphasis on religious inwardness. Man, he says, "feels that sensuality accompanies him from his infancy, that it is a part of his nature, so that a conflict is started between his sensuality and his spiritual ideals." This is, however, as far as Geiger goes in merely adopting a Christian conception, for Christianity holds that the redemptive power of

Jesus and the grace of God alone can relieve man of the burden of original sin. Geiger makes the power of triumphing over original sin rest in the redemptive force of the human will. "At the entrance into the outer world, in our connection with it, sin is lurking; but thou art a man, endowed with the sublime power of the will, who is not bound to yield to sin, to whom sin is not an external, invincible power, but a desire within, which can be kept down by using thy better force." Thus Geiger first borrows a Christian doctrine, and then Judaizes it.

LESSER LIGHTS OF REFORM
JEWISH PHILOSOPHY

There were a number of other thinkers of the nineteenth century, in Europe and in the United States, who followed in the footsteps of Abraham Geiger in the attempt to ground a modified and modernized form of Judaism on latter-day philosophies. Some of these men were led to take positions more extreme than Geiger's while others showed more regard for traditional conceptions of Judaism. Solomon Ludwig Steinheim (1790–1866), for example, based his thought upon his reading of the philosophy of Immanuel Kant, the founder of German Critical philosophy. Steinheim's large work on *Revelation according to the System of the Synagogue* (1835) was an examination of the boundaries that mark off the limits of the competence of human reason from the area reserved for revelation. In tracing the limits of reason, Steinheim followed closely the argument of Kant's *Critique of Pure Reason*. Where Kant looks to intuition as a guide in the areas beyond the scope of reason, however, Steinheim substitutes the idea of revelation, of supernatural knowledge bestowed upon men by Divine grace.

Steinheim departs from his master on another very important question. Kant's ethical writings had argued that man's moral actions are guided by the absolute demand of reason for universality. Steinheim thinks that this is too constricted and inflexible a view to explain the way in which man's ethical awareness actually arises. He substitutes for Kant's formal principle the idea, so frequent in occurrence in Jewish thought, that the ethical life is the voluntary service a free man gives to his God. In this way he is able to sketch another route back to Judaism. This additional way is necessary because his conception of revelation is not summed up in the truth of the Bible. Revelation is the Divine Word given to man, but it was not all given to men at one time and one place. There is genuine revelation in the Bible, but it is mixed with much other material that is not genuine. Which part is genuine and which is not cannot be discovered by reason alone, but must be discovered by an act of faith. The evidence of this basic act of faith is the living of an ethical life.

Samuel Hirsch (1815–89) was another of the German Jews who tried to elaborate a new philosophical justification for Judaism. His book, *The Religious Philosophy of Judaism* (1842), goes even further than Geiger in building on the philosophy of Hegel. Like Steinheim, Hirsch, too, accepts the ethical emphasis as the dominant note of Judaism. As a result, he seems to have the words of Hegel, but not the music. This is particularly evident in a comparison of the views of Hirsch and Hegel on freedom. For Hegel, as, indeed, for Spinoza, God's freedom consists in His following the laws of His own nature; for Hirsch, God's freedom consists in His ability, as demonstrated in the miracles recorded in the Bible, to set aside the laws of nature. For Hegel, again, human freedom is gained by reaching such an understanding of God's will that man performs voluntarily the actions that he would necessarily have to do in any case; for Hirsch, man's freedom is his capacity to choose among options, all of which are equally possible for him. In 1866, Samuel Hirsch emigrated to the United States to join the growing group of Reform rabbis there.

The chief architect of the Reform Movement in the United

States was Isaac M. Wise (1819-1900). Wise was not so much attracted to philosophic speculation as he was to organizational practice. He was, however, the guiding spirit behind the Platform accepted by the Central Conference of American Rabbis, meeting in November 1885. The Platform was built of eight planks, each of which is recognizably influenced by German-Jewish thinking in Abraham Geiger and others. In the first place, while recognizing that every religion represents "an attempt to grasp the Infinite One," and that every sacred revelation gives evidence of a belief in God's "indwelling" in man, the Platform asserts that Judaism has taught, throughout the ages, the very highest conception of God. This idea of God was not achieved at one stroke; as man progressed, his God-idea was "developed and spiritualized by the Jewish teachers in accordance with the moral and philosophical progress of their respective ages." The second plank asserts that the Bible is not a perfect and unique revelation, but rather "the record of the consecration of the Jewish people to its mission as priest of the One God." This view of the Bible makes it unnecessary to reject or to struggle against scientific theories and discoveries, for the Bible reflects "the primitive ideas of its own age," and sometimes cloaks an advanced conception of theology and ethics in a mantle of "miraculous narratives."

Third, the American Reform rabbis of 1885 argued that the moral laws of the Bible are still binding, but that those ceremonial laws that are "not adapted to the views and habits of modern civilization" may be dispensed with. Ceremonies of a traditional nature are to be maintained only if they "elevate and sanctify" the lives of these moderns. Fourth, all dietary laws, enactments regarding dress, and priestly regulations are to be rejected. "Their observance in our day is apt rather to obstruct than to further modern spiritual elevation." In the fifth place, the Platform declares the nineteenth century "the modern era of universal culture of heart and intellect," to herald the gradual approach of a messianic era. Those elements traditionally incorporated in the

Jewish messianic hope are abandoned in this Reform Platform: "We consider ourselves no longer a nation but a religious community, and therefore expect neither a return to Palestine, nor a sacrificial worship under the administration of the sons of Aaron, nor the restoration of any of the laws concerning the Jewish state." Thus the Reformers indicate their dissent from the philosophies of Jewish nationalism that were beginning to emerge in the nineteenth century.

Sixth, the drafters of the Platform declare that Judaism is "a progressive religion, ever striving to be in accord with the postulates of reason." They have a sense of historic continuity, of identity with the past; that is to say, they would not be willing to abandon Judaism and submerge it into some new faith. They are willing, however, to let bygones be bygones, in relation to Christianity and Islam. These "daughter-religions of Judaism" share the mission of spreading the truths of monotheism and high ethical ideals. Seventh, the Platform reasserts the doctrine of the immortality of the soul, but denies both resurrection of the body and the eternity of rewards and punishments. Finally, the Platform concludes with a demand for social justice, "in full accord with the spirit of Mosaic legislation." Thus the philosophic structure of Reform Judaism was embodied concretely in the "constitution" of the Central Conference of American Rabbis.

THE TRADITIONAL RESPONSE
TO REFORM

Even among the earliest of the adherents of the Reform Movement there were some who felt that its principles were too extreme. So, for example, Zechariah Frankel (1801–75) left the Reform group and became the spokesman for what he called "positive-historical" Judaism, which allowed full freedom for scholarly and scientific investigation, of religion as well as of other subjects, but required conformity to the traditional practices and laws. Although the later emergence of a Conservative Movement in Judaism owes much to the influence of Frankel's separation of belief and practice, he should not be regarded, in a strict sense, as a representative of traditional Judaism, nor can his compromise position be accepted as philosophically sound.

Much of the response of traditionalists, properly so-called, to reform was, in fact, not philosophical. It was shaped in the heat of controversy; it was bitter and violent. Much use was made of the weapon of excommunication, which is, of course, not an argument but a way of putting a stop to argument. Excommunication, however, had lost its force in the nineteenth century, after emancipation. For only when the community is solid, whether because of pressure from outside or because of devotion from within, can the banning of an individual from the community be effective. As soon as the individual Jew had alternative ways of life, outside the Jewish community, open to him, excommunication became merely a vehement gesture.

In one case, however, in Germany in the nineteenth century, an attempt was made to reply to Reform by reworking the theology of traditional Judaism. Samson Raphael Hirsch (1808–88), rabbi of a congregation with traditionalist leanings in Frankfurt-am-Main, counterattacked vigorously to stem the advances that the Reform Movement had been making. He declared that it was the obligation of those Jews who believed that the traditional observances ought to be maintained to secede from congregations in which Reform had made headway and to set up separate congregations. Quite early in Hirsch's career as scholar and rabbi, he published the book for which he is best known, *The Nineteen Letters of Ben Uziel* (1836), which became the guide to a somewhat modernized traditional Judaism often called Neo-Orthodox.

Hirsch's position is not, in a strict sense, new. It might, in fact, be regarded as a return to the medieval attempt to support traditional Judaism by means of rational argumentation. His goal was the statement of an enlightened orthodoxy. Thus he hoped to appeal to both modern intellect and traditional feelings. Hirsch's view of Judaism was, like that of the Reform Movement, doctrinaire. He shaped his conception of enlightened orthodoxy around a definite set of beliefs as well as observances. Perhaps the outstanding instance of Hirsch's responsiveness to the spirit of emancipation is his readiness to abandon the idea that there is a Jewish nationality. He is willing to agree to a non-political interpretation of the Jewish state and Jewish territory of olden times as the means by which the Hebrew people could fulfill its "spiritual calling." Hirsch is not responsive to the idea, which is so prominent in later Jewish thought, that the historical career of the Jewish people is marked by the polarity of Exile (*Galuth*) and Homeland (*Eretz*). "Land and soil," he writes, "were never Israel's bond of union." The bond was spiritual from the very beginning. Therefore, he maintains, "It is our duty to join ourselves as closely as possible to the state which receives us into its midst, to promote its welfare and not to consider our wellbeing as in any way separate from that of the state to which we belong."

Judaism, for Hirsch, is to be understood as a historical phenomenon. It cannot be judged, therefore, nor can its success be measured, by criteria that are imposed from outside its own tradition. Judaism must be conceived in accordance with its own sources, the Bible and the rabbinic tradition, and must be judged by its internal point of view. As Hirsch analyzes this internal point of view in the Bible, he finds that the world is seen as centered in the idea of service to God. "Everything serves God, each in its place, in its time, with the quantity of forces and means given it." When we examine the world, this analysis is confirmed. "Thus water, having penetrated the earth, is collected in cloud, and sea; light, having pierced the earth and brought forth plants, . . . is concentrated again into sun, moon, and stars . . . —thus one glorious chain of love, of giving and receiving, unites all creatures." Man is the highest being in the world. He receives more service than any other being and has the obligation to give more service to the world, to his fellow humans and especially to God. Man is emancipated from slavery to his passions by his duty to give service to God; this duty is, therefore, man's highest freedom.

Each people has a Divine mission to perform in the world. The mission of the Jewish people is to bear testimony in its history and in its daily life to the sacred duty of man to serve God. The revelation at Mount Sinai commanded the people to center their lives on the Divine will and to proclaim without cease the cardinal truth that God is One, and is the Creator, Lawgiver, and Father of all beings. The Biblical law does not announce those truths that are common to all mankind—the Unity of God, His Providence, and human immortality. Doctrines such as these are assumed by the law; belief in them is not commanded. Bible law, so to speak, is a training program for the special mission of the Jewish people; the emphasis is placed upon the discipline of observance of every detail, however minute it may be. The Jews were chosen for their special mission because of the character of Abraham, who displayed the three ideals of love, faith, and fear. The law is designed to develop these three qualities in all Jews.

Israel's special mission requires spiritual separation from the rest of the world. To the extent that emancipation allows the maintenance of this isolation, while encouraging certain types of worldly participation, emancipation is a good thing. Emancipation, however, if it leads to Jewish materialism, "would show that Israel had not comprehended the spirit of its own Law." The model for the separation of the Jews is to be found in the intricate network of regulations laid down in the Bible and the work of the rabbis. Observation of all these laws effectively prevents the Jewish people from falling to the level of materialism. The separation of Israel must be maintained until the great day when, purified, exalted, and refined by the example of the Jews, all men will turn to God and acknowledge him. Only then will the mission of Israel be fulfilled. Israel accepts the necessity of being different, not for its own sake, but for the sake of all men. We see here how Hirsch resolved the problem of keeping the particularistic doctrine of the Chosen people, while reinterpreting it in ethical and universal terms.

JEWISH NATIONALISM

Reform Judaism, as we have seen, completely rejected the idea of a Jewish nationality, and Hirsch, reacting against some of the views of the Reformers, was sufficiently under the spell of emancipation to translate the concept of Jewish nationality from a political to a spiritual context. Yet the flame of nationalism which had burned steadily in the Jewish heart for so many centuries could not so easily be extinguished. Messianic movements like those of David Reubeni in the sixteenth century and Sabbatai Zevi in the seventeenth were, at least in part, expressions of the longing of the Jews for a return to the Holy Land. The nineteenth century marked the true beginning of practical schemes for achieving this goal by secular and non-messianic means. It may be that the impetus to the development of these plans derived originally from Napoleon Bonaparte's official proclamation of April 20, 1799, urging "all the Jews of Asia and Africa to rally under his banners, in order to re-establish ancient Jerusalem." Whether it was, in fact, Napoleon who supplied the original impulse or not, the earlier years of the nineteenth century were marked by the appearance of plan after plan for restoration.

Somewhat more theoretical justifications of Jewish national re-establishment are to be found in the work of Zevi Hirsch Kalischer (1795–1874), who published, in 1861, a book entitled *The Correct Faith (Emunah Yesharah)*. Kalischer argues, in this work, that there is justification in the Bible and Talmud for a return to the Holy Land without supernatural intervention. This was a singular concession for an orthodox rabbi, and Kalischer could not have gone this far from the traditional doctrine of a supernatural

Messiah had he not been able to use his skill in the interpretation of texts to vindicate his theory. Another writer whose work shows some theoretical concern is Moses Hess (1812–75), whose *Rome and Jerusalem* (1862) argues that it would be inconsistent on the part of those other nations which, in his time, were striving to establish themselves among the family of nations to deny to the Jewish people the very same right. Hess's views were strongly influenced by the social-democratic movements of the mid-century. His advocacy of national independence for the Jews had, as an ulterior end, the betterment of relations between capital and labor! "A common native soil is a primary condition if better and more progressive relations between capital and labor are to be created among Jews." Such a common native soil for the Jews could be found only in Palestine.

More substantial contributions to a philosophy of Jewish nationalism were made by Nahman Krochmal (1785–1840), whose thought represents a high point in the enlightenment movement (*Haskalah*) in eastern European Jewry. Krochmal's *Guide for the Perplexed of Our Age* (*Moreh Nebuche ha-Zeman*) appeared only after the author's death, in 1851. Like other representatives of eastern European enlightenment, Krochmal was more traditional in his approach to Judaism than were the western European writers. His chief problem in his *Guide* was to reconcile the traditional view of Judaism as eternally revealed truth with the newer insights that had been brought to bear on the history of Judaism by men trained in scientific methods. It was the conflict between the scientific study of religion and the traditional approach through faith that seemed to Krochmal the source of perplexity for the Jews of his time. His resolution of this conflict borrowed from Hegel the thought that each nation had its own "idea" or spirit; this national idea blossoms out in all the achievements of the people as a whole and of creative individuals within the group. Krochmal goes so far as to refer to the national idea of each nation as its "god."

These varying national ideas, inspiring the creative genius of

283

each of the nations of the past and present, are aspects or phases of an Absolute Spirit. Each is, so to speak, a partial view of this Absolute Spirit. A people fulfills its national destiny by exploring its own national idea to the fullest possible extent. But the treasure does not remain the sole possession of the nation that created it. It becomes part of the universal culture of humanity. When any people has exhausted the creative possibilities of its idea, that people loses its specific national identity; the people becomes absorbed in humanity along with its fulfilled idea. The Absolute Spirit toward which all nations have moved in partial and limited ways has been, from the very beginning, the focal point, the national idea of the Jewish people, the God of Israel.

Since this is the case, the Jewish national idea cannot disappear or be merged into universal culture; it is the end, the final goal, toward which mankind has always striven. Because the Jewish people has always served the inclusive idea, the eternal and lasting idea, the Jewish people itself cannot perish or be absorbed. There are stages along the road of history in which it seems that humanity is approaching the Absolute Spirit; at such times, the Jew feels at home in the world. At other times, men seem farther away from the Absolute Spirit, and then the Jew feels himself alienated. The Jewish national spirit is expressed by the persistent dedication to the Eternal Spirit; Judaism is, therefore, not one culture among others, but an all-embracing harmony of the goals of all cultures. It is clear that Krochmal changes the stress of the Jewish tradition; the religion of the people is replaced by the people themselves as the center of attention. Observance of the ceremonies of the Jewish religion is not justified for its own sake, but to maintain connection with the historical "ideal" of the Jewish people.

Here, too, should be mentioned the great German philosopher, follower of Kant, Hermann Cohen (1842–1918). After a period in his youth, in which he inclined to abandonment of Judaism and assimilation, he returned to the Jewish fold under the spur of emergent anti-semitism. It was much later, however, before he became any more than nominally an observant Jew. His development of the religious implications of his Kantian philosophy was the major preoccupation of his professional life. It was only incidentally that he concerned himself with the philosophic understanding of Judaism. Indeed, he identified the spirit of Judaism with the spirit of "Germanism," since he saw in both two central conceptions, on which they agreed: the ethical independence of the individual (Kant's "autonomy") and the unity of God. Only toward the very end of his life did Cohen enter significantly into the area of Jewish thought with a book called *The Religion of Reason, on the Basis of Jewish Sources (Die Religion der Vernunft aus den Quellen des Judentums)*. In this book Cohen makes it appear that Judaism, as he understands it, is the actual form of the ideal "religion of reason" of which Kant had written.

Cohen's contribution to the discussion of Jewish nationalism is his distinction between "nationality" and "nationhood." Nationality is a historical and biological fact, whereas nationhood is a matter of political organization. The Jews, as the proponents of monotheism, have a historical mission, and thus a nationality. There is, however, no necessity for nationality being supplemented by nationhood. Nationality may be the foundation of a religion instead of the foundation of a state. The world has suffered enough already from the urge of nations to self-government. For the Jewish people to yield to the temptation to follow others into the quicksand of nationhood would be for them to give up their historic religious destiny, which Cohen calls the messianic ideal. Thus Cohen, in the beginning of the twentieth century, which was to see the establishment of the State of Israel, tried to hold back the tide of national aspiration by a philosophic distinction harking back to the spirit of the early days of enlightenment and emancipation.

CHAPTER TEN

Philosophies of Judaism in a Secular Age

PHILOSOPHERS of Judaism in the nineteenth century carried on their thinking in a life situation in which the effects of the emancipation of the Jews were barely beginning to emerge into clear view. Not until the end of the century (in the Dreyfus affair in France) and the beginning of the twentieth century (especially in the Germanic countries) did it become evident that the emancipation of the Jews had not put a period after anti-Jewish agitations and persecutions. Even in the United States, where discrimination against the Jews had never been a matter of public policy, and where the freedom of the Jew to practice his religion had never been abridged in the slightest degree, it became apparent in the twentieth century that there were powerful forces of social discrimination and of professional restriction actively fermenting below the placid surface of emancipated life. Anti-Jewish ideas became a strong working-force in Germany under the spur of the intense nationalism of the First World War; the fruits of this resurgence of Jew-hate became a world scandal in the decade and a half of Nazi domination and the attempt of Hitler and his aides to accomplish the destruction that thousands of years of Jewish existence had avoided.

Under the circumstances thus briefly summarized, it is not at all surprising that many of the philosophies of Judaism developed in the twentieth century have looked with a somewhat jaundiced eye upon emancipation, though their authors differ in the degree to which they reject emancipation and in the type of Jewish nationalism that they substitute for it. Not many go as far as the recent English book by E. Berkovits, *Toward Historic Judaism* (1943), in asserting that even the Neo-Orthodoxy of Samson R. Hirsch represented too great a concession to emancipation. Berkovits sees Judaism from the perspective of the Hitler era; in essence he accepts the Nazi idea of the inescapable difference of the Jewish people, but the interpretation he places upon this difference is religious, not "racial." He finds the central theme and meaning of Judaism in the Exile (*Galut*). Exile is perpetual strangerhood, alienation, to which the Jews are destined. But Exile is not a break in the historical destiny of the Jews and their religion; it is an intrinsic element in that history. "We went into Galut to bide our time there, to wait; to wait, however long it might be, until the time when the establishment of the State of God on earth might be attempted once more."

Emancipation, from this standpoint, was not a blessing but a curse, for its delusive promise led the Jews to yield their special status as strangers. The historic role of the Jews was "to be steadfast, to remain 'the strangers' and continually to point to the intrinsic hypocrisy that ruled relations between men and nations." Exile, enabling the Jews to fill this special role, had an additional advantage. It precluded the Jews from national existence, and therefore prevented the Jewish people from falling into "the guilt of national existence in a world in which national existence meant guilt." By accepting emancipation, Jews became partners in national guilt, "accomplices in all the hypocrisy and mutilations of justice of which this kind of emancipation was one symptom." By accepting emancipation, the Jews betrayed the central meaning of Judaism and thereby betrayed humanity. There is a certain objectionable smugness in Berkovits' view of pre-emancipation Jewish life: "We have often been trampled upon, but let us thank God that it was not we who trampled upon justice, decency, free-

dom, human dignity, whenever it suited our selfish purposes."
Needless to say, from his extreme position, Berkovits is not en-
thusiastic about secular political Zionism, because its object is
nationalism rather than religion.

In addition to the growing doubts of Jewish thinkers as to the
wisdom of the emancipation, a second important feature of
twentieth-century life should be noted. We have seen earlier, indeed until the beginning of the modern era, that no sharp gulf
existed between the sacred and the profane in Jewish thought.
Judaism could, in fact, be described as the sanctification of the
everyday. In the modern period, and almost universally in the
twentieth century, the increasing dominance of secular activities,
heightened by the impact of a world view dominated by physical
science and its technological consequences, has moved the area
of specifically religious concern from the center of life to its sub-
urbs. The life of every individual has become increasingly specialized, broken down into compartments, each of which has its own
set of rules. Religious life, a concern with ultimate sacred aspects
of existence, has become a small sector of the total life economy,
limited to particular times and places and concentrated in special
activities. This reduction of religion to a minor activity in the
life of man is the real meaning of the secularization of modern
times. Every philosophy of Judaism in the twentieth century is a
response to secularization.

THE PRIORITY OF LIFE TO THOUGHT

The attitude of specialization which is responsible for the secular character of the modern world can also be described in terms
of its rationality. It assumes that each aspect of life has its own
rationale, in complete independence of the total life pattern. It
holds that man's behavior, in his business life, for instance, should
be regulated entirely by the objective conditions of the market

place, and that personal or emotional factors should not be permitted to intrude into the calculations of economic activity. In opposition to this rationalization, one branch of twentieth-century philosophy (often called "Existentialism") puts stress on subjectivity rather than objectivity, the whole man rather than than specialized activities, and the priority of life to any possible thought about life. Historically, this emphasis comes into philosophy as a protest against the submergence of individuality in the rational universe of Hegel. But since Hegel carried to an extreme a tendency in modern thought to understand the religious process of salvation as God working through history, the protest, too, has its religious form in its insistence that God's redemptive force must be exerted through individual human beings.

Franz Rosenzweig (1886–1929) is in some ways the best example of the anti-rational emphasis in modern philosophy of Judaism. Fully trained, in his student days, in the academic philosophies of Germany and in the history of philosophy, he moved further and further away from his Jewish heritage until he was on the verge of conversion to Christianity. But he was also moving, under the influence of E. Rosenstock, whose example led him to consider conversion, toward an existentialist standpoint in philosophy. He became convinced that to become a Christian properly, he should repeat the life experience of the founders of Christianity; that is to say, he felt that he should try to find himself religiously in the Jewish atmosphere of the synagogue, and thence to break through into Christianity. With this intention, Rosenzweig attended services on the Day of Atonement in 1913. Instead of this experience leading him to Christianity, however, it led him to discover *in his own life* the meaning of Judaism. From this time to the end of his life, he devoted himself to Jewish scholarship and produced, among other works, a remarkably suggestive philosophic book entitled *The Star of Redemption* (*Der Stern der Erlösung,* 1921).

Behind this work lies the new attitude in philosophy. Rosenzweig wrote that "a philosophy, to be adequate, must rise out of thinking that is done from the personal standpoint of the thinker." The demand for objectivity is justifiable, but it is only a demand "that we survey the entire horizon; but we are not obliged to make this survey from any position other than the one in which we are, nor are we obliged to make it from no position at all. Our eyes are, indeed, only our own eyes; yet it would be folly to imagine we must pluck them out in order to see straight." Philosophy had claimed for itself a standpoint that went beyond the personal standpoint, but the criticism of Kierkegaard, Schopenhauer, and Nietzsche led back to the realization that philosophy was not about abstract problems, but about life, and that life was the individual human being, the one who thought. "Hitherto, philosophical interest had centered exclusively on the knowable Whole; man could only become a subject of philosophy through his relation to that Whole. Now this knowable world was confronted autonomously by something else, by the living human being, and the Whole by that one which makes light of everything general." With this realization, the philosopher "gained ascendancy over . . . his own philosophy."

What has happened? The traditional concern of philosophy with essences has been confronted with the irreducible fact of existence. Thinking revolving in a narrow circle about thought has come face to face with that which is not thought, that which is prior to thought, with life itself. There are three primary subjects of all philosophy: God, man, and the world. Philosophy in the modern world has made man as the experiencing self—thinking man—fundamental; the Middle Ages made God fundamental; Greek antiquity made the world fundamental. Each period, however, tried to reduce the three primary subjects to one. Rosenzweig insists on the differences among the three; he "prefers to trace his experience of the world back to the *world*, and his experience of God to God," rather than "basing the experience of the world and of God on the experiencing self." Three primary realities confront each other, not timelessly, as philosophy had boasted, but at specific moments, past, present, or future.

In his supplementary notes to *The Star of Redemption*, Rosenzweig wrote brilliantly of the ways in which time enters "the new thinking": "What God has done, what he does, what he will do; what has happened to the world and what will happen to it; what has happened to man and what he will do—all this cannot be disengaged from its connection with time. One cannot, for instance, perceive the coming kingdom of God as one perceives the created world, and one must not look upon creation as one looks upon the kingdom of the future; no more than one should allow the flash of present experience to char a past, or wait for the future to bring it; for this lightning flash is always only in the present and to wait for it is the surest way to prevent it from striking. . . . Thus the tenses of reality cannot be interchanged. Just like every single happening, so reality as a whole has its present, its past, and its future, without which it . . . cannot be properly known. . . . To have cognition of God, the world, and man, is to know what they do to one another or what is done to them by one another. And here we presuppose that these three have separate existence, for if they were not separate, they could not act upon one another. . . . Within reality, and that is all we can experience, the separation is spanned, and what we experience is the experience of the spanning. God veils himself when we try to grasp him; man, our self, withdraws, and the world becomes a visible enigma. God, man, and the world reveal themselves only in their relations to one another, that is, in creation, revelation, and redemption."

In the new thinking for which Rosenzweig pleads, speech, or better, dialogue—talking things through—takes the place of the solitary monologue of traditional philosophy. Dialogue is a process that involves at least two participants and that takes place in time, and these advantages are, it seems to Rosenzweig, summed up in the recognition that dialogue means speaking to some definite and specific other person, and thinking with him. He contrasts this with thinking for no one else and speaking to no one else, and notes that for "no one" we might substitute "everyone" or "all the world" without changing the meaning of the statement. The specific other person with whom a dialogue is carried on "has not merely ears, like 'all the world,' but also a mouth"!

BETWEEN PHILOSOPHY AND RELIGION

Surely no major book was ever written in so unusual a way as Rosenzweig's *Star of Redemption*. The philosopher was serving, during World War I, as a non-commissioned officer in the German Army. During his service on the Macedonian front, while he was in the hospital, and along the march of the retreating force, always fearing that he would not survive the war and yet feeling that what he had to say must be said, he wrote the book in small sections, on postcards which he mailed home to his mother, who then copied his writing for later publication. Unfortunately a large part of the time that remained to him after the war was spent in the grip of a creeping paralysis, so that the full program of which *The Star of Redemption* was but the opening exercise could never be brought to fulfillment. But even under this most desperate of handicaps, Rosenzweig read and he wrote, in the attempt to complete his personal account of what Judaism, the religion he had discovered, meant in terms of his subjective and existentialist philosophy.

Rosenzweig had been reared in an atmosphere dominated by the emancipation; his family had long deserted the tribal customs of ghetto Jewry. Yet when he came to examine the Jewish life of his own time to see what was left as a foundation on which to rebuild a "living Jewishness," he found that emancipation had been a disaster. "Emancipated Jewry lacks a platform of Jewish life upon which the bookless present can come into its own," he wrote. Before emancipation, there was a unity of Jewish life in the home and the synagogue under the law. The three elements of Jewish existence were whole and unseparated. Emancipation broke down the unity, so that its three elements became parts, broken away from each other. Law, home, and synagogue have become three, instead of one. Here Rosenzweig is proclaiming that the effect of emancipation has been the specialization that leads to secularism. "Slowly but surely the home has lost its dominating position in Jewish existence. Life comes from outside and makes its own demands. The Jewish home can and probably will try to assert itself against the outside world, but the most it can still do is maintain itself. . . . The home has become at best but 'one thing' in life, with 'another thing' by the side of it, and *outside* it." The synagogue, too, has fallen victim to a specialization of functions. It has become "quite in keeping with the spirit of the culture-obsessed, pigeonholing nineteenth century, a 'place of religious edification.' . . . 'Religion,' to which life has denied a real place—and rightly, for life rightly rejects such lifeless, partial demands—seeks a safe and quiet little corner." And the Jewish Law has become less a way of distinguishing between Jew and non-Jew than a way of distinguishing between observant Jew and non-observant Jew.

It was Rosenzweig's conviction that the way to restore the unity that emancipation and secularization had destroyed was by taking "the Jewish individual seriously, here and now, as he is in his wholeness." Primarily it is the individual that each one is that he aims at. That is to say, he is not suggesting that each Jew say "Brother" to every other Jew, but that each Jew must say to himself "I am *wholly* Jewish." Any form of partial Jewishness is, he says, a caricature. This involves the readiness to do without formulas and without touchstones of any sort. "All recipes, whether Zionist, orthodox, or liberal, produce caricatures of men, that become more ridiculous the more closely the recipes are followed. . . . There is one recipe alone that can make a person Jewish and hence—because he is a Jew and destined to a Jewish life—a full human being: that recipe is to have no recipe." The Jew is to be saved by a subjective turning to Jewishness, without renunciation of the non-Jewish world in which he lives. The alienation of the Jew from his own tradition has been subjective; such too must be his return. The need is not to give up anything, but to "lead everything back to Judaism."

The form of learning and of teaching—the two are inseparable—is to be discussion, dialogue. The distinction between teacher and student cannot be maintained if true dialogue, thinking together, is to take place. "The teachers will be discovered in the same discussion room and the same discussion period as the students. And in the same discussion hour the same person may be heard as both master and student." The discussions that go on must be a kind of public forum, a generalized conversation in which anyone who happens to be present can join in. Rosenzweig set these requirements forth in talking of an envisaged school of Jewish studies, but they express very well his general theory of thinking as dialogue and there is no need to limit them to a school situation. Rosenzweig was convinced that Jewish men and women in the twentieth century could find themselves, but only if they sought and found themselves as Jews. This, he knew, would not come about by listening to speeches; he thought it could happen by participating in conversations. He had small respect for the "lions of the lecture-platform," especially in the role of teachers. "There has been enough of speechmaking," he declared. "The speaker's platform has been perverted into a false pulpit long enough among us—just punishment for a rabbinate that, for the most part, has been able at best to convert the pulpit into a speaker's platform."

These samples show how Rosenzweig's philosophic existentialism, rooted in the alienation of an emancipated Jew in twentieth-century Germany, led him in the direction of a revivified Jewish religion. To this religious rebirth, all the distinctions and mutual exclusions that had grown up between Jew and Jew seemed alien. For Rosenzweig's philosophy and his religion were centered in the person, not in the concept. Concepts can become formulas; formulas easily transform into dogmas; dogmas are readily available as shibboleths. But the meeting and the conversation of persons is a flowing back and forth of living speech; it feeds on questions and doubts and desires. It has no room for proclamations and programs and manifestoes. The experience of conversation can be noted but not defined; in this it is like the experience of man's meeting with God. One can say "I have experienced God," but having said this, there is no more to be said, no answer to anyone who asks "What was He like?"

REALIZATION THROUGH DIALOGUE

Far better known than Rosenzweig as a spokesman for the life of dialogue is his friend and co-worker Martin Buber (born 1878). Like Rosenzweig, Buber was brought up in the world of West European scholarship and learning. Unlike Rosenzweig, Buber had access, even in childhood, to that other intensely pious world of the East European Jew, the world of his grandfather, Solomon Buber. By the meeting and fusion of the best of these two worlds in the mind and thought of Martin Buber, the contemporary understanding of the living possibilities of personal religion has been much enriched. Yet the fusion of worlds did not develop instantly. For a part of his life, Martin Buber had, one might almost say, two parallel careers: one as a scholar, the other as a Jew. As a scholar, he edited and translated early literary and religious classics of the Chinese, Welsh, and Finnish peoples, but shied away from similar works in the Hebrew language. He published a volume of *Ecstatic Confessions* (1909), drawn from the autobiographical accounts of ancient and modern mystics, but did not discuss Jewish mysticism. As a Jew, he was, temporarily, in revolt against the very spirit of personal religion which so interested him in other cultures and which had at first impressed him deeply in the group to which his grandfather belonged. From the earliest years of the twentieth century, Buber's Jewishness expressed itself in active participation in the movement of cultural Zionism; he followed the lead of Asher Ginzberg (1886–1927), who wrote under the name of Ahad Ha-am—"one of the people"—in seeking in Jewish nationalism not merely the establishment of a Jewish state but also the re-creation of a Jewish culture.

During these earlier years of the twentieth century, Buber had become a student of mysticism and had joined with other young men in thinking through what amounted to a rather mystical sociology. The group was attempting to discover the inner bond of ideal community; they thought it to be the sense of each individual that he was in organic unity with all of mankind. Buber translated this general principle of communal cohesion in terms of his interpretation of Jewish character. Although the emphasis of rabbinic Judaism for many centuries had been on a legalistic morality, Buber felt that this was not truly representative of Jewish character. On the other hand, he saw that ascetic retreat from contact with the world in order to maintain purity was equally untrue to the age-long character of the Jewish people. He replaced both of these conceptions with his own view that the distinctive note of Jewish thought is the realization that the spirit of God is present in all life; that, therefore, all life is holy; and that nothing is alien to Judaism in which the spirit of life can be found. When he had reached this point in his thinking, Buber recognized that the mystical piety of his grandfather's circle in eastern Europe embodied the essence of this sort of spiritual community and was a prime example of the sanctification of all life. Thus he was led to the study of the Hasidic movement, to which he devoted many years of concern. He was convinced that "Nowhere has the spiritual power of Judaism so manifested itself in recent centuries as it has in Hasidism."

Buber valued particularly the fact that Hasidic piety involved a ready acceptance of the ever-presence of God in day-to-day life. It was little concerned with dogma or ritual, but attempted to establish a community of human beings on the foundation of Divine truth. Buber explained that the teachings of Hasidism can be compressed into one sentence: God can be seen in every-thing and can be reached by means of every innocent act. Another feature of Hasidism that attracted Buber was that it was a great popular movement among the Jews of eastern Europe. Never, he claimed, had such a vast popular movement of piety been seen in Europe. It was neither a separatist brotherhood nor a monastic order, but "a folk community in all its spiritual and social multi-plicity, in all its mixture." Again, years later, Buber remarked that "the decisive factor for the nature and greatness of Hasidism is not found in a teaching, but in a mode of life; and, indeed, in a mode of life which shapes a community, and regulates a com-munity in accordance with its own nature."

Although Buber does not seem to be aware that this is the case, it is most probable that the concern for community, the emphasis upon discovery of the inner springs of social life, that is a pervasive theme of his philosophy, is a search for what is missing in the life of the Jews of western Europe since emancipation. When men are living in organic unity, they do not produce theories of organic community; only when community has been lost do theories arise as a means of seeking return to the sense of completeness, of fulfill-ment. Although in general Buber's thought is akin to the existen-tialist trend of the twentieth century, his stress upon the social character of the self differentiates him from most thinkers of this school. Buber's sharpest comments on Kierkegaard come in a critical essay directed against Kierkegaard's conception of the Single One. Buber says that the great Danish theologian's con-ception is "as sharply opposed as possible to politics." This is its weakness, for it is only the individual who takes up the life of the crowd into his own life who "changes the crowd into Single Ones."

An individual who remains aloof from the masses cannot aid mankind in the great work of this age, which is to restore community where now there is merely collectivity. "True community and true commonwealth will be realized only to the extent to which the Single Ones become real out of whose responsible life the body politic is renewed." Life in community is a perpetual life of dialogue.

I AND THOU

Martin Buber's earliest attempt to state his philosophy of religion is to be found in a series of "five dialogues on realization" published under the title *Daniel* (1913). At this time of his life, Buber's way of thought was closer to mysticism than his later and more developed expression. Partly for this reason, and partly because of the difficulty of the ideas he is trying to express, *Daniel* is a very obscure and difficult book. One of the important conceptions that Buber presents in *Daniel* is that there are two attitudes with which men face the world they experience. One, the attitude of ordinary experience, he calls "orientation." This is an attempt to get things in their proper perspectives in space and time; with respect to other people, orientation is the realization of their otherness, and, therefore, the attitude of orientation is a self-assertive attitude. We recognize the otherness of other things and people by an awareness of our own selves as different from them. The second general attitude Buber calls "actualization," and this is the going-out with one's entire being to meet all things. When this concept of actualization is applied to other people, there is a denial of selfhood in living toward the others. Men must first become conscious, through orientation, of the distinction of the self from others, and then, by actualization, must overcome the distinction by living in unity.

The best-known work by Buber, and the book in which he was

most successful in expressing the heart of his religious philosophy, is *I and Thou* (*Ich und Du*, 1923). This is a prose poem, not a treatise, and its total effect depends upon the direct appeal of the author to the reader. Buber's main theme is that there is a fundamental difference between a man's attitude toward other men and his attitude toward things. The first is a *relation between* persons; the second is a *connection with* things. In the personal relation (*I-Thou*), one subject confronts another subject. In the impersonal connection (*I-It*), a subject experiences and uses an object. These are the two basic situations of human life, the world of *Thou* and the world of *It*.

In the world of *Thou* there are two centers of consciousness that meet. Neither one can absorb or appropriate the other. Neither can become an object to the other. The meeting of the two is the core of the relation between them. When we speak of knowing another person, we do not mean that he has become part of our experience, but that we have come into relation with him. By contrast, in the world of *It* there is only one center of consciousness, the one who experiences an object, appropriates the object to his own uses. We regard objects either as tools capable of being employed to further our interests or as obstacles to be removed from our path. To speak of knowing an object means that it has become part of our experience, that we have learned (by common sense or by science) how to use it for our own benefit. The world of *It* seems to have the qualities of what Buber earlier called the attitude of orientation, whereas the world of *Thou* is what he had called the attitude of actualization. If we try to transform our relation with other men into an understood connection, we make the other, the *Thou*, into an object of experience; we convert the *Thou* into an *It* and thus fail in our loyalty to the truth of the meeting with the *Thou*, which is the relation of dialogue.

There is one *Thou* which can never become an *It*. This is "the eternal *Thou*," or God. In the relation between God and man lies the perfection of the life of dialogue. God, Buber says, may be "addressed, not expressed." The lines of all other relationships, extended, meet in God. "Every particular *Thou* is a glimpse through to the eternal *Thou*; by means of every particular *Thou* the primary word addresses the eternal *Thou*. Through this mediation of the *Thou* of all being, fulfilment, and non-fulfilment, of relations comes to them: the inborn *Thou* is realized in each and consummated in none. It is consummated only in the direct relation with the *Thou* that by its nature cannot become *It*." Even the difficulties of expression, the struggling to say what cannot be said but must be felt, reveal that Buber has a mystical tone; but his denial that he is a mystic should be respected, for what he means is that he is not concerned with what has been the characteristic quest of the mystic, for the absorption of the self in God. If the self could be absorbed in God, then Buber's claim for the dialogic relation of *I-Thou*, that it is a meeting of two subjects, neither of whom can absorb the other, would be invalidated. Buber's mystical tendencies are there, but they do not lead him into mysticism but rather into a receptive attitude toward the universe.

To achieve total receptivity requires a conscious abandonment of the self-centered attitude, and a readiness to devote our energies to a creative task. The nature of the task must remain unknown to us until we have lived in the *I-Thou* relationship. Every situation in which we find ourselves may be the starting point of creative activity; if it is, the nature of our task will be made clear to us in the situation itself. It is these creative acts that make us real; in our creativity, we help God to create the world. God, of course, does not need man's help; but God "wills to have need of man." Specifically, God's will is that man should be of assistance in completing the work of creation, and since God wills this aid, "the use of man for this work becomes an effective reality."

Man cannot actively seek out God, either by renunciation of the world or by exclusive devotion to the world. "To step into pure relation is not to disregard everything but to see everything in the *Thou*. . . . Men do not find God if they stay in the world.

They do not find Him if they leave the world. He who goes out with his whole being to meet his *Thou* and carries to it all being that is in the world, finds Him who cannot be sought." The discovery of the Eternal *Thou* is "a finding without seeking." The self-consciously "religious" life is as inadequate as the self-consciously "secular" life. The determined materialist tries to reduce everything to the world of *It;* the determined mystic also tries to make God an object to the self. Both are false to the world of *Thou* in their common denial of the essential twoness of the relation of dialogue.

There is a distinctively social and ethical character in Buber's idea of "confronting" the Eternal *Thou.* The purpose of the meeting is to provide a foundation on which there can be a living relationship between man and his fellow man. "Meeting with God does not come to man in order that he may concern himself with God, but in order that he may confirm that there is meaning in the world." The living word of revelation appears in history in those times in which "the solidarity of connexion between *I* and the world is renewed." This renewal tends to create community, genuine community, and to replace mechanical forms of public life and mechanical institutions. Such re-creation cannot be achieved simply by the direct approach of people to people in a warm common humanity of feeling. For Buber, community without God is unthinkable. Each person must first take his stand "in living mutual relation with a living Center," and then, derivatively and secondarily, he will be in "living mutual relation" with his fellow men.

COMMUNITY AND COLLECTIVITY

In a shorter essay, called "Dialogue," written in 1929, Buber supplements this discussion by a brilliant statement of the distinction between community and collectivity or mere numerical aggregation. This distinction is formulated here in a new and striking fashion, but it is not completely new to Buber's thought. It is, rather, a reaffirmation of the concern that marked his very earliest work, the search for the roots of social solidarity in the individual spirit. Buber concedes that, in a revolutionary association or conspiratorial group, "the comradeship which fills it is of value," but only because it increases the effective power of the band for gaining its end. Concentration upon the cohesiveness of the group as a way of strengthening its "reliable assault power" is, however, not the way to achieve the values of community. "The feeling of community does not reign where the desired change of institutions is wrested in common, but without community, from a resisting world." One might say, again using Buber's own terms, but from a different period, that such collective activity takes place with an attitude of orientation, while community demands an attitude of actualization. Collectivity is grouping in the world of *It*, while community is grouping in the world of *Thou*. Only where there is a "community struggling for its own reality as a community" is collectivity overwhelmed. The collectivities of both the Right and the Left are marching into a common abyss in which both dialogue and monologue are forever silenced.

Most men do not even know what community is. "Who in all these massed, mingled, marching collectivities still perceives what that is for which he supposes he is striving—what community is? They have all surrendered to its counterpart." The difference between collectivity and community is to be measured by the type and the amount of life together. "Collectivity is not a binding but a bundling together: individuals packed together, armed and equipped in common, with only as much life from man to man as will inflame the marching step. But community, growing community . . . is the being no longer side by side but *with* one another of a multitude of persons." Community requires communication, dialogue, "a flowing from *I* to *Thou*." Again, "Collectivity is based on an organized atrophy of personal existence, community on its increase and confirmation in life toward one another." So we may conclude that, just as God is not found by deliberate seeking, so community cannot occur by deliberate planning. A real estate development corporation can found a collective colony, but its use of the word "community" in its advertising does not create a community. Whether a community develops out of the collective depends upon the personal relations that emerge in the situation. "Community is where community happens."

Buber's social philosophy is of one piece with his religious thought, as this discussion of community makes evident. The dialogue of religion has both its starting point and its climax in the dialogical society, the community. This is, in Buber's terms, necessarily so, for it is the very nature of dialogue to be not merely talking with another, not even merely thinking with another, but a living toward the concrete reality of another's life. Dialogue is more than an intellectual activity; it is a vital relation. It is a turning-toward another with intense concentration of intention. There is a great drain on us in the dialogical relation, as there is not in the collective connection. But the great drain is compensated for by a great renewal of our forces. Person-to-person calls in our spiritual life enable us to realize ourselves, to become real.

It should not surprise us to learn, in the light of this emphasis on spiritual community, that at one stage in his career Buber believed that the only true Judaism was what he called "underground Judaism," that is, those groups, like the Essenes, that attempted to achieve the perfection of human society. Buber outgrew this limitation of view and came to see that there is a fusion of ethical and religious elements in Judaism about the two centers of a God who is remote and yet in immediate relations with man, and a redeeming power everywhere and at all times active in the world "and that yet nowhere and at no time is there a state of redemption." Again we find in Buber, as we have so often in our survey, that the essence of religion is found in the tension between God remote yet related to men, and God near at hand. The unique spirit of Judaism is attuned to the essential message of religion that human life is to be dominated by the consciousness of the presence of God. This domination is to be achieved, not by a turning away from the world, but by the sanctification of the world. The aim of religion is to bring the light of God into the actual world.

Although the Jewish spirit is in tune with this aim, the Jew himself is torn between the ideal and the real, between the spirit and the flesh. The urge to attain an inner unity in place of this inner disunity finds its chief expression in the practice of the religious life. It is not a passive inner unity that is sought. There is an active striving to actualize the ideal in the real world, to bring about a unity between thought and action. The doctrine of the Chosen People means to Buber that the Jewish people are committed to begin immediately the redemption of the world by the actualization of the ideal. The Jews must not wait until other peoples are ready to join them in this work. They must begin at once, because "the Jew, as part of the world, experiences perhaps more intensely than any other part, the world's lack of redemption. . . . The burden of the unredeemed world rests on him." The program of Jewish nationalism to which Buber ultimately came was centered upon the idea that the work of redemption could best be begun by building, in Palestine, an ideal co-operative community in which men would live in constant awareness of their duty to God, and where their every act would be true service to Him.

Without losing sight, at any point, of man's need for God, Buber's philosophy of religion and his philosophy of Judaism emerge into a social philosophy of redemption because of God's need for man. The "word of dialogue," the "sacramental word," is the speech of God; but it is also the binding force of human community. Buber's philosophy, however ethereal its expression

304

may seem at times, is never remote from the everyday concerns of men. Community without God is unthinkable; so, too, is God without community. The meeting of the *I* and the Eternal *Thou* takes place not in the Heaven of Heavens, or in the Holy of Holies, or yet in the Heart of Hearts. Man and God meet in the dialogical relation of community.

RELIGION AS A GROUP AFFAIR

Both Franz Rosenzweig and Martin Buber responded, out of a youth spent largely in non-Jewish studies, to elements they found in Judaism that countered the force of a secularized and rationalized world. Mordecai M. Kaplan was born in 1881 into the Jewry of eastern Europe and lived under its strictest regulation. Even as a child he was extremely observant. He recalls that when he was no more than six he found himself alone "on a street far from home. It was a summer day and a thunderstorm with heavy lightning broke out. I overcame my fears by reciting the appropriate benediction. When I got home, I described my adventure, taking care to mention the fact that I had looked around to see that the four ells in which I stood were free of dung before I recited the benediction. I do not recall the circumstances under which that law had been imparted to me." An experience of this sort would have been totally foreign to the background of either Rosenzweig or Buber. They came to the Jewish tradition in mature life after a youth of secular learning; Kaplan's early training was almost exclusively traditional, and he came upon the world of scientific learning only during his college years.

Perhaps this difference in background can help to account for the fact that Buber and Rosenzweig, each in his own way, reacted against ritualism in Judaism and secularization in the world of the Jew by a restatement of a theory of revelation, whereas Kaplan

305

reacted against the traditional doctrine of revelation, but sought, by a principle of reconstruction, to adapt traditional Jewish ritual to the celebration of the *sancta* (holy things) of a secularized Jewish people living in a secular world. Kaplan is, on principle, a conservative in the Jewish ranks and, by affiliation, a participant in the Conservative Movement in American Judaism. But his message is the unusual one that what is to be conserved is the practices of the past, not the meanings associated with these practices. Wherever the ancient meaning is no longer vital, a new meaning is to be supplied, after conscious study, so that the old practice may be continued, unfossilized. For Kaplan, reinterpretation becomes a conscious process, carried out with the aid of all the modern tools of historical, sociological, and psychological research, rather than an unconscious process of adaptation.

Quite early in his career as a rabbi, attempting to discover for himself and his congregants some way in which living as a Jew could be made compatible with living in a modern environment —that is to say, in trying to face the major problem arising out of the emancipation of the Jews into the secular world—Kaplan realized that the great stumbling block was the acceptance of the belief in supernatural revelation. "As long as Jews adhere to the traditional conception of Torah as supernaturally revealed, they would not be amenable to any constructive adjustment of Judaism that was needed to render it viable in a non-Jewish environment." Kaplan, we might say, became a semi-naturalist; he rejected revelation as the central core and sanction of a Jewish way of life. He went so far as to abandon the traditional God-idea. In a striking passage, he indicates the extent to which his thought about God was presented in the context of an evolutionary understanding. "The traditional conception of God," he said, "is challenged by history, anthropology, and psychology; these prove that beliefs similar to those found in the Bible about God arise among all peoples at a certain stage of mental and social development, and pass through a process of evolution which is entirely conditioned by the developments of other elements in their civilization."

This stress on Kaplan's negations is, however, unfair save as a point of departure. Kaplan is not, and never intended to be, a destructive thinker. He has never advocated the rejection of any traditional position except when he has had an alternative to offer. Kaplan did not try to destroy faith, but to replace untenable faith with tenable faith. "We must have implicit faith in the difference between reality and illusion, good and evil, right and wrong, truth and falsehood, the beautiful and the ugly," if we are to live intelligently in the world. This kind of faith does not require "faith in a specific tradition concerning miracles in contravention of laws of nature." The purpose of religion is to make life a more meaningful adventure; Jewish religion has to make life as Jews more meaningful. The dogma of revelation seemed to Kaplan to fail in that regard. He came, however, through his studies to a deeper appreciation of the intrinsic worth of the Bible. He searched for a theory that would take full account of this supreme worth and value without grounding it on unthinking acceptance of a supernatural origin.

In the reading of Matthew Arnold, Kaplan tells us, he found an answer that satisfied him, to discover a way of appreciating the Bible for its "expression of human nature at its best, the most articulate striving of man to achieve his salvation or self-fulfilment, and an expression of his most conscious recognition that only through righteousness can he achieve it." Corresponding to this "humanistic" understanding of the Bible was the new "naturalistic" understanding of God that Kaplan developed, also as a result of his reading of Matthew Arnold. For both the traditional "God of miracles" and the theological "God of metaphysics," Arnold taught Kaplan to substitute the "God of experience." Human experience teaches us that there is so much evil in the world that we need, in order to account for the good in the world, to assume that there is a Power, not ourselves, that makes for righteousness.

The three poles of Jewish thought had traditionally been God, the Bible, and the Jewish people. Kaplan's maturing philosophy now had a basically functional, or pragmatic, interpretation of God and the Bible. The third pillar of his thought, his understanding of the nature of the Jewish people, he worked out after a careful study of the cultural Zionism of Asher Ginzberg (Ahad Ha-am). Here he came to the view that "throughout Judaism's universe of discourse, the people of Israel was the central reality, and that the meaning of God and of Torah can be properly understood only in relation to that central reality." Pragmatism insists that the meaning of any idea is to be found in the differences it makes in human conduct. Kaplan's pragmatic Judaism asserts that this religion "uses the belief in God to make Jews aware of the natural conditions that have to be maintained for the Jewish people, if it is to achieve salvation collectively and individually."

Religion, in Kaplan's view, is a group affair to a far greater extent than it is an individual triumph. In this point, his antithesis to Rosenzweig and Buber is clear. "The feeling of togetherness," Kaplan once wrote, "is indispensable to the realization of God, for without it we cannot experience God at all." This emphasis on the group did not mean that Kaplan lost sight of or denied all value to the individual. In agreement with such expounders of the pragmatic philosophy in the American tradition as John Dewey and George Herbert Mead, Kaplan dismissed from his thought the traditional sharp antagonism between the individual and the social. Instead he saw that the isolated self, a staple of traditional philosophy, is a meaningless concept. To be an individual is to be the product of a social environment. Interaction with one's fellow members in a social group is the source and origin of the human qualities that we call mind and personality. But it is also the case that to be an individual is to be responsible in one's role as a member of the social group; because of the factor of individual responsibility, the social group is dependent on individuals. Thus neither group nor individual can be conceived as existing in independence of the other.

JUDAISM AS A CIVILIZATION

Kaplan expressed his novel understanding of the mutual dependency of the individual and the group in Jewish life by what he calls "a modification in our Jewish semantics." No longer did he use the word "Judaism" to mean the religion of the Jewish people; on the analogy of such terms as Americanism he used Judaism as a term to denote "the entire civilization of the Jewish people." Within the civilization that is Judaism, the Jewish religion is essentially the heightened consciousness of the interests and values of the group. "Judaism is more than the Jewish religion. It is the sum of *everything* about the Jewish people, past, present and future, that makes of the Jews a distinct and identifiable society. . . . Judaism embraces the entire cultural heritage of the Jews." If, as has been suggested, God is not discoverable by solitary man, but only by man as a participant in the life of a group, then the God of the Jewish people must be found in the life of the Jewish people.

To speak of "the God of the Jewish people" does not imply that He is merely a tribal deity, inferior to the universal God of other high religions. "Human experience," Kaplan declares, "teaches that God is a correlative term. . . . As 'father' implies 'child' and 'king' implies 'subjects,' so God implies a 'human society.'" However universal the conception of God may be, His expression is through a particular social unit. Men come to know God through the particular society of which they are members. Holy objects are always objects that are hallowed by their connection with the life of a particular society. "If we consider all the various objects, institutions and persons that have been declared holy, not only by the Jewish religion but by any of the other religions, . . . we find that they are the objects, institutions and persons that particular groups felt to be of supreme importance to them." From this it follows that religion has its meaning, its significance, in terms of the vital interplay of group life. The social function of a religion is its preservation of the hallowed objects deemed vital to the continuity of a particular group. Jewish religion is no different in this respect from other religions. It "cannot function in a vacuum."

The civilization of the Jewish people, Judaism itself, in Kaplan's idiom, is the matrix that must be maintained if the Jewish religion is to continue to live and to be relevant to human life. It is as the "folk religion" of the Jewish people that the Jewish religion can maintain its vitality. Kaplan's objections to the Reform Movement in Jewish religion center in its "formal demobilization of the Jewish people as an organic entity." Reform Judaism, he charges, did not take the Jewish civilization seriously as a necessary foundation for Jewish religion. He demands a recovery of cultural nationalism, including the Land of Israel as the place "where Jews could in freedom live their own civilization to the full." If the survival of Judaism demands a Jewish people aware of its own civilization, its own cultural heritage, then we come to the inevitable conclusion that it is in the best interest of Jewish religion to stress Jewish secular culture! The more exclusively the spiritual leaders of the Jews emphasize Jewish religion, the less are the chances of that religion for survival. "The spiritual regeneration of the Jewish people demands that religion cease to be its sole preoccupation." The spirit of Jewish worship will be renewed when Jewish communal life is re-established.

Kaplan's specific proposals for the restoration of Jewish communal life would be out of place here. These have their place in a discussion of his life as a practical leader in the rabbinate and in the Jewish Center movement. What is germane to the story of philosophy in the Jewish religion is Kaplan's insistence that the civilization of the Jewish people can be shown to have changed and developed over the course of its long history. Since this is so, and since the Jewish religion is a functional aspect of Jewish civilization, these changes in the civilization must have produced corresponding changes in the religion. As the civilization of the Jews has changed, some of its older *sancta* have lost their meaning and new meanings have become hallowed. Superficially, this would seem to lead to change and discontinuity. But Kaplan became convinced that in "the dynamics of religion" the *sancta* remain constant and thus provide the element of continuity, while "the power or holiness of these *sancta* is accounted for differently, in keeping with the changes in general outlook and conception of God." The continuity of the sacred objects creates the sense of group identity through the generations; the change in meaning preserves the vitality of the religion under new environmental conditions. This is both the conservative and the reconstructive principle in Kaplan's philosophy of Judaism. As long as the Jewish people maintain the *sancta* of the forefathers, the Jewish religion remains the same; within this framework there can be a conscious and deliberate introduction of new meanings that are in keeping with the new age in which twentieth-century Jews must live.

Mordecai Kaplan is true to the Jewish heritage in that the deepest wellsprings of his philosophy are ethical. To a considerable extent, however, his ethical discussions are couched in a social context. Most particularly, Kaplan is one of the deepest students of democracy, considered not solely as a form of political organization, but as a moral and religious way of life. The ethical principle underlying democracy Kaplan finds to be "the will to live abundantly." This he calls the only universal frame of reference; he also refers to it as "the will to salvation." This is a bold revision of the religious ideal of salvation, for in equating the will to live democratically and abundantly with the will to salvation, Kaplan is transferring salvation from an other-worldly and supernatural context to a natural, this-worldly frame. Salvation of this sort is defined as the "maximum good or optimum which man expects to achieve with the aid of the culture in which he lives and has his being." Every culture, democratic or non-democratic, breeds such expectations and is, therefore, a vehicle of salvation for its members. The search for "a common universe of discourse for the various cultures which divide mankind into nations" is called by Kaplan Soterics, or the theory of salvation.

CONCLUSION

If this were a story of the philosophers who happen, by birth or by affiliation, to be Jews, there would be many more names to be mentioned, many more philosophic themes to be discussed. One of the consequences of the emancipation of the Jews is that Western intellectual life has been enriched by the thought of a vast number of men and women who take part as equals in the advancing of intellectual frontiers in all fields. There have been, especially in the twentieth century, a very large number of philosophers in this group. But to the very degree that they are emancipated, these philosophers and men of wisdom have given their best thought to the discussion of the problems that arise out of the common life of all mankind, rather than to the specific problems of Jewish life and Jewish religion. The gain to the world must be weighed against the loss to the life of the Jewish people of a vast reservoir of talent and ability.

But this has been the story of philosophic reflection on the Jewish religion. It has been intended to open out to the modern reader an aspect of the Jewish heritage that is not as well known as many others. Not every Jewish philosopher has been mentioned, nor has every theme been discussed. Enough has been said to make it clear that Judaism has been not only a religion of practice and of faith, but also a stimulant to intellectual reflection. In those periods of history when the Jews lived a life that was largely enclosed, shut away from the currents of thought in the surrounding world, the philosophic reflection of the Jews was carried on as a kind of interior monologue. In those periods when the Jews lived in close contact with their neighbors in the world, and were subject to the influences of their intellectual environment, Jewish philosophy became more of a dialogue, an exchange of thought that enriched all the participants. The level of technical philosophic skill and awareness has varied, too, from age to age. We have moved back and forth, in our story, between naïve and unsophisticated questioning and highly sophisticated probing. There is room, at any time and any place, for both types of quest and query. There is room, too, for simple and unquestioning faith.

FOR FURTHER READING

THIS supplement includes only works in English. It is designed as a first guide for those who wish to read beyond the limits of this book. In general, listings here follow the order of presentation in the book.

There is no general history of Jewish philosophy written in English. Jacob Agus has written a most useful and stimulating book, *The Evolution of Jewish Thought* (London and New York: Abelard-Schuman; 1959), which carries the story from Biblical times to the end of the eighteenth century in greater detail than this book. It is to be hoped that the continuation Dr. Agus promises will be completed soon. Until it appears, an earlier and less well-presented book by the same author, *Modern Philosophies of Judaism* (New York: Behrman's Jewish Book House; 1941), contains supplementary information about some nineteenth- and twentieth-century Jewish philosophers.

Most of the books dealing with the philosophy of the Bible are by Christian scholars and take for granted the interpretation of the Bible as given by Christian theology. An exception should be made for Yehezqel Kaufmann, whose exciting but rather eccentric philosophy of Jewish history is incorporated in his *Religion of Israel* (Chicago: University of Chicago Press; 1960). On the Book of Job, it is still worthwhile to consult Horace M. Kallen, *The Book of Job as a Greek Tragedy* (New York: Moffat, Yard and Company; 1918). Robert Gordis has discussed Ecclesiastes significantly in *Koheleth, the Man and His World* (New York: Bloch Publishing Company; 1955) and Irwin Edman's introductory essay in his *Ecclesiastes* (New York: Odyssey Press; 1946) is a philosophic gem comparable to the work it introduces. A special work, most unusual in its subject, which the reader should not overlook is Joshua Bloch, *On the Apocalyptic in Judaism* (Philadelphia: The Dropsie College; 1952). There are selections representing the more philosophical aspects of apocryphal literature in Salo W. Baron and Joseph L. Blau, *Judaism: Postbiblical and Talmudic Periods* (New York: Liberal Arts Press; 1954).

The works of Philo are now completely available in English translation in the Loeb Classical Library. The most comprehensive and detailed study of the philosophy of Philo is Harry Austryn Wolfson,

Philo: Foundations of Religious Philosophy in Judaism, Christianity and Islam (Cambridge, Mass.: Harvard University Press; 1947). An earlier work by Erwin Goodenough, *By Light, Light: The Mystic Gospel of Hellenistic Judaism* (New Haven: Yale University Press; 1935), presents a radically different view of Philo which ought not to be neglected by the careful reader.

Excellent translations of the Talmud and of Midrash Rabbah are now available under the imprint of England's Soncino Press. Herbert Danby has made a very competent translation of *The Mishnah* (London: G. Cumberlege; 1954). Jacob Z. Lauterbach has translated *Mekhilta* (Philadelphia, Pa.: The Jewish Publication Society of America; 1933–35). Thus a considerable body of rabbinic literature is now available to the reader of English. Of the many interpretive works, Max Kadushin's *The Rabbinic Mind* (New York: The Jewish Theological Seminary of America; 1952) and his earlier *Organic Thinking* (New York: Behrman's Jewish Book House; 1938) best suggest the philosophic aspects of the thought of the rabbis. George Foot Moore's masterpiece, *Judaism in the First Centuries of the Christian Era: The Age of the Tannaim* (Cambridge, Mass.: Harvard University Press; 1927) is unrivaled as a systematic presentation of the rabbinic ideas of the early period.

Gershom Scholem's *Major Trends in Jewish Mysticism* (New York: Schocken Books; 1946) is a masterly account of all forms of mystical and occult thought in Judaism; Scholem's book is particularly valuable for its treatment of the practical aspects of the Kabbala, otherwise rarely discussed in English. An interesting sidelight on the Kabbala may be found in Joseph L. Blau, *The Christian Cabala* (New York: Columbia University Press; 1944). Most of the *Zohar* may now be read in English translation in the Soncino Press edition. Very little else in the literature of Kabbala has been translated.

There is a good *Karaite Anthology*, edited and translated by Leon Nemoy (New Haven: Yale University Press; 1952). Besides this, there is very little available in English on the Karaite movement. Isaac Husik, *A History of Medieval Jewish Philosophy* (Philadelphia: The Jewish Publication Society of America; 1916), contains very thorough, careful summaries of all major and many minor medieval philosophers, both Rabbanite and Karaite. Saadia's *Book of Beliefs and Opinions* has been accurately and readably translated by S. Rosenblatt in the Yale Judaica Series (New Haven: Yale University Press; 1948). Hartwig Hirschfeld's translation of Jehudah Halevi's *Book of Kuzari* (New

York: Pardes Publishing House, Inc.; 1946) is complete, but reads most awkwardly. A more readable translation is to be found in the abridged version by Isaak Heinemann (Oxford, England: East and West Library; 1947). The standard English translation of Maimonides' *Guide for the Perplexed*, by M. Friedlander (London: George Routledge & Sons, Ltd.; 1928) lacks completely the graces of English style. Abridged translations with far more grace are available. Bahya's *Duties of the Heart* has been adequately translated by Moses Hyamson (New York: Bloch Publishing Company; 1925–1947). Isaac Husik has made an excellent translation of Joseph Albo's *Book of Principles* (Philadelphia: The Jewish Publication Society of America; 1946). Competent studies and translations of Gersonides and Crescas are much to be desired, although Harry Austryn Wolfson did a superb but very highly specialized study of *Crescas' Critique of Aristotle* (Cambridge, Mass.: Harvard University Press; 1929), and Abraham L. Lassen has translated the philosophically interesting *Commentary of Levi ben Gerson (Gersonides) on the Book of Job* (New York: Bloch Publishing Company; 1946).

There have been very few accessible English studies of Jewish thought in the Renaissance. A valuable exception is Ellis Rivkin's fine *Leon da Modena and the Kol Sakhal* (Cincinnati, Ohio: Hebrew Union College Press; 1952). Cecil Roth's *The Jews in the Renaissance* (Philadelphia: The Jewish Publication Society of America; 1959) helps to fill in some of the gaps, but much work remains to be done. There is, of course, an oversupply of books about Spinoza and of English-language editions of Spinoza's chief works, but there is nothing on Uriel da Costa.

Jakob J. Petuchowski has written a workmanlike monograph on *The Theology of Haham David Nieto: An Eighteenth Century Defense of the Jewish Tradition* (New York: The Bloch Publishing Company; 1954) to rescue its subject from oblivion. There is no adequate English translation of Mendelssohn's *Jerusalem* and no significant study of his philosophical position. Abraham Geiger's *Judaism and Its History* (New York: The Bloch Publishing Company; 1911) and Samson Raphael Hirsch's *Nineteen Letters of Ben Uziel* (New York: The Bloch Publishing Company; 1942) are available to suggest cross currents of nineteenth-century Jewish thought.

Nahum Glatzer has presented *Franz Rosenzweig: His Life and Thought* (New York: Farrar, Straus and Young, for Schocken Books; 1953) for the English reader with devotion and care. Most of the writings of Martin Buber are readily available, as are those of Mordecai M. Kaplan. Of books about Buber, those by Maurice Friedman and Malcolm Diamond have particular value. Ira Eisenstein and Eugene Kohn edited *Mordecai M. Kaplan: An Evaluation* (New York: Jewish Reconstructionist Foundation, Inc.; 1952); the articles by Samuel Dinin, Eugene Kohn, Harold C. Weisberg, Henry N. Wieman, Harold Schulweis, and Joseph L. Blau will be of particular interest to the reader who wishes to know more of Kaplan's philosophic outlook.

NOTES

P. 40, l. 7. John Dewey: *Reconstruction in Philosophy* (New York: Henry Holt and Company; 1920), p. 196.

P. 45, l. 26. Max Laserson: "Power and Justice: Hobbes Versus Job," *Judaism*, II (1953), 52–60.

P. 54, l. 17. Philo: *Allegory of the Laws*, III, 32, 98, as quoted by Harry Austryn Wolfson: *Philo: Foundations of Religious Philosophy in Judaism, Christianity and Islam* (Cambridge, Mass.: Harvard University Press; 1947), II, 77. The rabbinic passage, cited by Wolfson in a footnote on the same page, is from Genesis Rabbah, 39, 1.

P. 70, l. 12. Max Kadushin: *The Rabbinic Mind* (New York: The Jewish Theological Seminary of America; 1952), Chap. VI.

P. 71, l. 17. George Foot Moore: *Judaism in the First Centuries of the Christian Era: The Age of the Tannaim* (Cambridge, Mass.: Harvard University Press; 1927), I, 364.

P. 89, l. 2. Gilbert Murray: *Five Stages of Greek Religion* (New York: Columbia University Press; 1925), especially Chap. IV, "The Failure of Nerve." For the quotation, see p. 155.

P. 91, l. 27. Robert M. Grant: *Gnosticism and Early Christianity* (New York: Columbia University Press; 1959), p. 17.

P. 93, l. 30. Gershom Scholem: *Major Trends in Jewish Mysticism*, revised edition (New York: Schocken Books; 1946), p. 50.

P. 94, l. 4. Rudolf Otto: *The Idea of the Holy* (London: Oxford University Press; 1923), especially Chap. V, "The Wholly Other."

P. 105, l. 29. Scholem: *Major Trends in Jewish Mysticism*, p. 120.

P. 107, l. 26. From an unpublished manuscript by Abulafia, translated by Scholem: *Major Trends in Jewish Mysticism*, p. 134.

P. 114, l. 3. S. Karppe: *Etude sur les origines et la nature du Zohar, précédée d'une étude sur l'histoire de la Kabbale.* (Paris: Alcan; 1901), p. 236.

P. 162, l. 4. As translated by Isaac Husik: *A History of Medieval Jewish Philosophy* (Philadelphia: The Jewish Publication Society of America; 1916), pp. 69–70.

P. 163, l. 28. Stephen S. Wise: *The Improvement of the Moral Qual-*

ities, an ethical treatise of the eleventh century by Solomon ibn Gabirol. . . . (New York: Columbia University Press; 1902), p. 5.

P. 212, l. 1. The most fertile of the Jewish translators of Arabic philosophic literature into Hebrew were members of one family, ibn Tibbon, who lived in Spain and Southern France in the twelfth and thirteenth centuries. Judah ibn Tibbon (1120–ca. 1195) was born in Granada but later moved to France. Among his many translations were the Hebrew versions of the work of Bahya and Saadia. His son, Samuel (ca. 1150–ca. 1230), was the translator of Maimonides' *Guide for the Perplexed.* Samuel's son Moses was the translator of Maimonides' *Treatise on Logical Terms.* Other members of the family also took part in this important work of translation.

P. 253, l. 7. Cecil Roth: *The Jews in the Renaissance* (Philadelphia; The Jewish Publication Society of America; 1959), p. 133.

P. 255, l. 24. See Ellis Rivkin: *Leon da Modena and the Kol Sakhal* (Cincinnati, Ohio: Hebrew Union College Press; 1952).

INDEX

Abba Saul, 88
Abrabanel, Don Isaac, 252
Abrabanel, Judah, 252, 253
Abraham, 10, 60
Abraham bar Hiyya, 183-185
Abraham ben David of Posquieres, 103
Abu Hanifa, 124, 125
Abulafia, Abraham ben Samuel, 105-109, 111, 113
Academic school, 50
Ahad Ha-am (Asher Ginzberg), 296
Ahriman, 29
Ahura Mazda (Ormuzd), 29
Akiba (Rabbi), 88
Albo, Joseph, 242-246, 247-250, 261
Alfasi, Isaac, 198
Alkabez, Solomon, 118, 119
al-Kumisi, Daniel, see Daniel al-Kumisi
Amos, 18-22, 24, 27, 28, 80
Anan ben David, 123-128, 139, 153
Antigonos of Socho, 79, 82
Arnold, Matthew, 307
Aristobulus, 58
Aristotle, 53, 59, 130, 133, 138, 180, 187, 202, 215, 217, 223, 224, 226, 231, 273
Augustine, 43
Averroes (Ibn Roshd), 231
Azriel, 103

Bacon, Sir Francis, 6
Bahya ben Joseph ibn Pakuda, 167-169, 170-180, 183, 211, 249
bar Hiyya, Abraham, see Abraham bar Hiyya
Baruch, 25
Benedict XIII (Antipope), (Peter de Luna), 243
ben Gerson, Levi, see Gersonides
ben Gurion, David, 257
ben Kolonymus, Samuel, see Samuel ben Kalonymus

ben Merwan al-Mukammas, David, see David ben Merwan al-Mukammas
ben Nahman, Moses, see Nahmanides
Benjamin of Nahawend, 127-129, 153
ben Yohai, Simeon, see Simeon ben Yohai
Berkovits, E., 287, 288
Bonaparte, Napoleon, 282
Brothers of Purity, 180
Buber, Martin, 295-305, 308
Buber, Solomon, 295

Clement VI (Pope), 232
Cohen, Hermann, 284, 285
Cordovero, Moses, 118-121
Crescas, Hasdai ben Abraham, 236-239, 240-243, 249, 258, 261

da Costa, Uriel, 255-257, 261
da Modena, Leon, 254-256
Daniel, 30
Daniel al-Kumisi, 129
Dante Alighieri, 245
Darmesteter, James, 62
David (King), 10, 13, 22, 80
David ben Merwan al-Mukammas, 130-135, 139
de Leon, Moses, 109, 111, 112, 114, 118
del Medigo, Elijah, 251, 252
de' Rossi, Azariah, 253
de' Rossi, Salomone, 251
Dewey, John, 40, 308
Donnoto, Sabbatai, 99

Eleazar ben Arach, 81
Eleazar ben Azariah, 73
Eleazar of Worms, 100
Eliezer ben Jose Ha-gelili, 69
Epicurus, 39
Ezekiel, 25, 30, 91
Ezra, 103
Ezra, 63, 64

ABOUT THE AUTHOR

JOSEPH LEON BLAU was born in Brooklyn in 1909. He received his bachelor's, master's, and doctor's degrees from Columbia University, and has also done most of his teaching there. Professor Blau has taught at the University of Minnesota, University of Arkansas, New School for Social Research, and California Institute of Technology as well. His special subjects are the history of American philosophy (*Men and Movements in American Philosophy, Cornerstones of Religious Freedom in America*), the philosophy of religion (*The Christian Interpretation of the Cabala*), and the history of Judaism. He has been a fellow of the American Council of Learned Societies (1944–45), and of the American Jewish Tercentenary Committee (1954–55), and has held a research grant from the Columbia Council for Research in the Social Sciences. Professor Blau is married and has two children.